DENIS SEGALLER

Post Books

Published in Thailand by Post Books
The Post Publishing Public Company Limited,
136 Na Ranong Road, off Sunthorn Kosa Road,
Klongtoey, Bangkok 10110, Thailand.

First published 1982
Reprinted with corrections 1989
Second edition 1995

ISBN 974-202-034-5

Cover Design: Watchara Ritmahan
Photograph: Boonlong Phan-Udom

Set in New York

Printed in Thailand by Allied Printers, Bangkok.

CONTENTS

INTRODUCTION TO THE FIRST EDITION

Many Thai traditions and customs are very different from those of other countries, especially of the West, a fact which makes them of great interest to non-Thais, and to Westerners in particular. Yet if one digs a bit deeper, often enough one finds that the differences are not as great as they appear on the surface; all of us, non-Thais and Thais alike, are very much the same human beings under the skin.

This book forms a sequel to "**Thai Ways**" and like the first book it is a collection of articles which originally appeared as part of a regular weekly column in the **Bangkok World.** It aims to give the non-Thai reader some insight into the delightful people of Thailand, how they live, and how they react to life's varied situations — as seen through the eyes of an Englishman.

This book is dedicated to my wife Laddawan, without whom a great deal of the material in it would never have been written; to the late delightful and highly knowledgeable expert and friend, Mom Rachawongse Ayumongol Sonakul, who was always ready to give helpful and correct answers to my questions, who also carefully checked those sections of the book where accuracy is important and I might have slipped up; and to the many other Thai friends who have told me things about Thailand which I did not know before, and have helped with translating from Thai.

My sincere thanks also go to the **Bangkok World**, for printing the articles in the first place; to the Post Publishing Public Company Limited for publishing this book, and especially to Michael Gorman, David Thomas and Kalayanee Kanchanadul for their initiative, encouragement and help; to Miss Vimolphan Peetathawatchai for kindly allowing me to adapt the section on cloth weaving in Northeast Thailand from her book **Esarn Cloth Design**; and finally, to members of the foreign community in Bangkok and elsewhere in Thailand — and especially the American Women's Club of Thailand — for their continuing support and appreciation of the original "Thai Ways," which gives perhaps rather more basic information than this book.

My thanks are also due to Thai Airways International for permission to adapt certain sections in this book which originally appeared in their inflight magazine, **Sawasdee**.

The weekly "**Thai Ways**" column had been running continuously in the **Bangkok World** since August 1975. And as with the first book, when going through the printed articles to compile this book, I found it difficult to be selective, objective and logical about its presentation in book form. The divisions between ceremonies, customs and beliefs are bound to be blurred, and details in different sections of the book sometimes overlap. Many of these repetitions have been deliberately retained from the original articles. Not only do they help to make each section more or less complete in itself; they also help to convey a feeling of the intricate network of customs and ideas that make up the life and culture of Thailand.

A note about the spelling of Thai words in this book

The Thai language has its own beautiful, decorative and historically rich script which carries overtones of the ancient Sanskrit, Pali, Mon and Khmer languages. The spelling of Thai words in **Thai script** is precise and logical. However, when "transliterated" or "Romanised" into the Western "ABC" alphabet, there are no hard and fast rules (although Thailand's Royal Institute has laid down an official system showing which Thai letters correspond to which Western ones). This imprecision can be illustrated by a little anecdote.

Soon after I first arrived in Thailand, I was talking on the phone with a Thai friend, who said "You must contact Mr. X" (telling me a Thai name). "How do you spell that?" I asked. "Well," he answered, "let's see; **how would you like to spell it?"**

In fact the same Thai name is often spelt in a variety of ways in the Western alphabet, as is mentioned elsewhere in this book. It is all rather arbitrary and a matter of personal choice. In this book I have followed my own system of spelling Thai words, which approximates most closely to the sounds I think I hear, with a few universally recognised exceptions. I have indicated this system (which I freely admit to not using entirely consistently) in a table in Chapter Four.

Denis Segaller
Bangkok, April 1982

In this Second Edition, a lot of material which is now seriously out of date has been removed.

The weekly "**Thai Ways**" column stopped in 1985.

Denis Segaller
Pathum Thani, 1995.

CHAPTER ONE
ROYALTY AND NOBILITY

Founder of a dynasty

The Founder of Thailand's present Chakri Dynasty was a great and truly remarkable man, and his story makes interesting reading.

An English historian once wrote: "We see the Siamese humbled to the dust again and again by a more powerful neighbour, yet always rising up and regaining their freedom ... Those who believe in the survival of the fittest will admit that they must possess some special qualities...."

And an old Thai saying holds that "Ayutthaya (that is, the Thai nation) never lacks good men."

Three such brilliant leaders rose up and together rallied the nation after the fall of Ayutthaya in 1767. The fortunes of all three were to be inextricably linked by fate in the years that followed.

The eldest of the three, Sin, was to rise to the highest ranks of the nobility and as an army general was to gather the scattered Thai forces together to repel the Burmese and so become king of Thailand less than a year after the sacking of Ayutthaya.

The other two were brothers named Thong Duang and Boonma, sons of a high-ranking official in the reign of one of Ayutthaya's last kings.

As General Chakri, Thong Duang was also eventually to become king of Thailand and founder of its present Chakri Dynasty; his younger brother Boonma was to become his "second-in-command" or Deputy King.

When only six years old, Thong Duang was sent to the Royal Court at Ayutthaya, where he became a page.

Sin, two years older than Thong Duang, was also a page at this time, and the two boys became close friends. They were both ordained as young novices at the same temple in Ayutthaya at the ages of 11 and 13, and later, after reaching manhood, Thong Duang was ordained again, this time as a full monk.

After leaving the monkhood during the reign of Ayutthaya's last king, Thong Duang was assigned to serve under the Governor of Ratchaburi. Here he married a lady named Nak from a wealthy family. Thong Duang's duties, like those of all government servants in those days, were both military and civil combined.

Serving in Ratchaburi, Thong Duang was not in Ayutthaya at the time of its fall. Neither was his younger brother Boonma, who by now had also risen in rank.

Sin had meanwhile become Phya Tak, the Governor of Tak Province in the North, and was now known as General Taksin. He was mustering an army in the thriving seaport town of Chanthaburi.

Boonma and Thong Duang sailed to join him, as all three men shared a deep love for their country and a fierce desire to free it from the invading Burmese. General Taksin elevated both brothers in rank, with appointments roughly equivalent to those of senior police officials today.

Over the next 15 years, Thong Duang took part in 11 major campaigns which were ultimately decisive in liberating Thailand from the Burmese threat.

Within a year of Ayutthaya's fall, King Taksin, as he had now become, had recaptured it, although it was then little more than an empty shell of the magnificent city it had once been. Taksin established his new capital at Thon Buri, on the west bank of the Chao Phraya River.

Three years later he again elevated Thong Duang to the rank of Chao Phya Chakri (the whole title, including "Chakri", had long held the meaning of "commander-in-chief"). Boonma was also given a high-ranking title, Chao Phya Surasih.

During the first seven years of his reign King Taksin himself led all the campaigns against the Burmese, invariably accompanied by his two trusted and brilliantly capable generals, Chakri and Surasih. Later Taksin remained in his capital to govern the country, while General Chakri had independent command of all the fighting, with his brother as second-in-command.

In the remaining years of Taksin's reign, General Chakri succeeded in subduing not only the Burmese, but also the then principalities of Chiang Mai, Luang Prabang and Vientiane, which became King Taksin's vassals.

At one stage in this period the Thai and Burmese armies met on horseback during a temporary truce. The aging Burmese general, Maha Thihathura, praised the 40-year-old Chakri's generalship and prophesied — correctly — that Chakri would one day become King.

Later, General Chakri brought the priceless Emerald Buddha image from Vientiane to Thon Buri. This carved nephrite image is believed to have taken over a thousand years to travel from northern India via Sri Lanka to Laos and Thailand. It now resides permanently in Wat Phra Kaeo, the Temple of the Emerald Buddha.

While he was on a campaign in Cambodia in 1781, news reached General Chakri that there had been a revolt in Thon Buri and King Taksin had been deposed. The General and his brother immediately hurried back to Thon Buri as fast as their elephants and men could march. On his return to the capital the entire Thai army and all the officers of state offered him the throne.

General Chakri accepted, thus founding the present House of Chakri as King Rama I. The date was 6 April 1782 and he was then 45. This date is celebrated every year as Chakri Day and is a public holiday.

The official proclamation of the new king and his first coronation took place in June the same year. It was followed by a more official coronation in much grander style some three years later.

The new king immediately set about building a brand new capital.

Aware that Thon Buri on the west bank of the Chao Phraya River was always potentially threatened by further Burmese attacks — and he felt certain there would be more — he chose the site of the flourishing little trading centre of Bangkok on the east side. (Its original name had been "Bang Makok" — village of wild olives.)

King Rama I saw that the mighty Chao Phraya River would act as the best possible defence against attacks from Burma. Moreover, at this point there was a wide bend in the river, enclosing a large area of land easily defended by digging canals on the east, north and south and thus ideally suited for the new capital.

A rich Chinese merchant occupied the area chosen for the Royal Palace, which would become the administrative centre of the city, and he was asked to move to an uninhabited area beyond the new city's confines, which grew into a flourishing Chinese community. Today, over 200 years later, this area is known as Sampeng and is the centre of Bangkok's Chinatown.

Before the construction of the Royal Palace and its accompanying structures began, an important and historic ceremony took place. This was the fixing in the ground of the Lak Muang or City Pillar, a huge 15-foot laburnum log representing something like the foundation stone of the new city. This is believed to house the guardian spirit of the city, who takes care of all its inhabitants.

The construction of all the new palace buildings, including the Throne Hall and the Temple of the Emerald Buddha, went ahead with all speed. King Rama I designed the layout of all the great halls, places of worship and other rooms to correspond as closely as possible to the old Royal Palace in Ayutthaya, as he was determined to preserve Thailand's ancient heritage to the utmost. Bricks were brought from Ayutthaya and even dismantled from Thon Buri for further building, especially of fortifications.

King Rama I then gave the capital its new name: "City of Angels, great city of immortals, magnificent jewelled city of the God Indra, seat of the King of Ayutthaya, city of gleaming temples, city of the King's most excellent Palace and dominions, home of Vishnu and all the gods."

In Thai this title is all one word, beginning with " Krungthepmahanakornamornratanakosin..." Its 152 letters in romanised spelling, not surprisingly, have earned it a place in the Guinness Book of Records as the world's longest place-name.

While he was creating the new capital, King Rama I as founder of a new line elevated all his children and relatives to royal rank. He appointed his brother, Boonma or Chao Phya Surasih, as Maha Uparaja or Deputy King, and had a special palace built for him known as "the Palace of the Front" or "Wang Na", which is now Bangkok's National Museum.

Many new temples were also built, including Wat Chetuphon or Wat Po (the Temple of the Reclining Buddha) and Wat Suthat, which was filled with ancient art treasures including a famous

Buddha statue from the old capital of Sukhothai.

The Grand Palace, a full square mile in area, was the centre not only of the capital but of the whole country — a fortress city within a city. Within its walls the king lived and worked with the Royal Secretariat, the Court of Justice, the Ministries and the Treasury, the Artillery and Guards Regiments, the Art Studios and School, and the stables for the royal horses and elephants. Further walls enclosed the "Inside" where the King had his private residence, his gardens and the residences of his queens and other wives.

But the Burmese continued to harass Thailand during King Rama I's reign, as he had foreseen. Determined to foster the country's ancient cultural values, he was equally steadfast in his purpose of freeing Thailand once and for all from the ever-present threat of Burmese invasion.

Renewed attacks by Burma began while Bangkok was being built, and the wars dragged on more or less continuously over the next 17 years. According to another Thai saying, Thailand is shaped like an axe with the sharp end pointing eastward towards Cambodia and Laos: so these countries have never posed a serious threat to Thailand's sovereignty. But Burma to the west is confronted only by the axe's blunt rear end, which is why Burmese attacks have had such a lasting effect on Thailand's history.

Among the legends of stirring deeds at this period, none is more famous in Thailand than the true story of two sisters who saved the southern province of Phuket.

The province's governor had just died when the Burmese marched in, and his widow and her sister rallied the populace. With typical feminine guile they rounded up all the island's womenfolk and disguised them as male soldiers. Coconut-palm leaves were roasted over fires until they became blackened and curled, looking for all the world like the barrels of guns from a distance. The women "soldiers" brandishing their palm-leaf "guns" were scattered among the real soldiers to give the invading Burmese the impression that Phuket's army was very much larger than it really was and positively bristling with armaments.

Finally the two sisters adopted a scorched-earth policy and gathered all the island's population within the town walls in a state of siege. The Burmese had the choice of retreating or starving to death, and wisely chose the former course. The grateful King Rama I ennobled the two sisters, and their statue graces the island of Phuket today.

In all the major wars against the Burmese, the King himself led his troops into battle, with his brother the Deputy King in full support. When Thailand in its turn launched an attack on Tavoy in Burma, this involved crossing a high and unexpectedly steep mountain range. The transport and pack elephants had to haul themselves up the mountainside by coiling their trunks round trees, and the King, then nearly 50, pulled himself up by ropes tied to trees like the rest of his men.

After more battles ranging from the South to Chiang Mai in the North, the Burmese were finally driven off for good in 1802, and friendly relations developed between the two nations in the years that followed.

While personally waging the long and arduous wars against the Burmese, King Rama I displayed the true mark of a brilliant king.

He was able at the same time to govern his people well and justly, codify the old laws dating back to Ayutthaya, revise the Buddhist religious canon, maintain the rich cultural traditions of Thailand's past, and inspire the literature of the Court, which reached one of its highest peaks during his reign.

At his second coronation, in the words of Prince Chula Chakrabongse in his book Lords of Life, "...The high officers of state presented him with the royal possessions, such as the great gold coaches, palanquins... the royal palace buildings, the weapons and arms... and finally the rice fields and forests of Siam.

"King Rama I said to them: 'All of these things will you take good care of. Together we will govern the State, together we will defend and prosper the Buddhist religion, and together we will defend the kingdom'."

As Prince Chula pointed out, King Rama I's monarchy was a paternal one based on the ten virtues of a king according to the ancient law: charity, moral living, support for religion, honesty, compassion, freedom from wrongful ambition and from thoughts of revenge, loving the people as their father, moderation in punishment, and constant care for the people's welfare and happiness.

To achieve these aims meant a threefold revival — moral, legal and cultural.

King Rama I was a devout believer in the Buddhist doctrine, always intent on promoting the purity of Buddhism and the monkhood. One of his main concerns was the installation of famous and historic Buddha statues in the new temples built in his reign. He also restored the Shrine of the Buddha's Footprint in Saraburi Province, one of Thailand's most revered places of worship.

After revision of the Buddhist texts by the council which he set up in the seventh year of his reign, a new edition of the Tripitaka, or Scriptures, was produced, which was later printed in the form of 45 large volumes.

King Rama I reorganised the old Ayutthaya laws. His attention was drawn to a particular case, an inconsistency in the divorce law. A plaintiff from Nakhon Si Thammarat in the South claimed he should be entitled to his wife's property as she was the guilty party, but the law indicated otherwise. Rama I agreed that the old law was unjust (and perhaps unclear too) and this led him to set up a committee to revise and codify all the laws of the land. In doing so, his aim was to develop a high moral standard among his people, and especially among his courtiers and officials.

He was also a strong and capable legislator in his own right, and enacted 45 entirely new laws and decrees.

Many traditional and splendid ceremonies were organised during his reign, including the tonsure ceremonies for his young children. He commissioned beautiful and ornate royal golden barges. Several white elephants from the provinces were presented to him amid all the ancient royal pomp necessary on these occasions.

King Rama I was an accomplished poet, and himself converted the Indian epic poem, the Ramayana, into Thai verses known to every schoolchild in the land today as the Ramakien. He had artists paint huge murals of many scenes from this story inside the Temple of the Emerald Buddha. His Court became a centre where literature and the arts flourished — especially classical music and dance. Among the poets at the Court the most famous was Sunthorn Phu, who produced literature which has been compared with that of Shakespeare in its shrewd observation of ordinary people.

The King also commissioned a large and elaborately designed furneral urn of gold, with an inner urn of silver in which his own body would be placed after his death. He was so delighted with it that he kept it in his bedroom, which greatly upset one of his wives. The King is said to have retorted that if he did not see it from the outside while he was still alive, how would he ever be able to see it?

The country's economy prospered under King Rama I's firm guiding hand. There were taxes on gambling, alcohol and fishing, duties on goods taken to the market, and a field tax payable in rice. But by far the biggest source of the nation's revenue was its sea trade with China.

King Rama I had the strength of character and the skill necessary to make quick decisions and to choose good advisers — qualities essential to give his country the impetus to rise again as a sovereign nation from the chaos after the fall of Ayutthaya. His physical strength was every bit as great; he had a sound and healthy constitution right to the end of his life. He rose early every day and offered food to the monks on their morning almsround. At about 10.30 a.m. a group of invited monks would eat their main meal in his presence in the council chamber, after which the King received reports from the Treasury. He then gave his daily audience from the throne to various groups of people. After meeting his family at lunch he took his afternoon rest. Another audience was given in the evening, always opened by a sermon preached by a monk. Generally the audience ended at 9 or 10 p.m., but sometimes it continued far into the night.

King Rama I had 42 children from 29 wives. After a short illness, he died in 1809 at the age of 72. He was one of Thailand's most outstanding rulers, and his ability to weld his people together gave birth to the modern Thai nation.

Eight of his descendants have been Chakri kings after him, including His Majesty King Bhumibol Adulyadej, the present King. His memory is honoured by a bronze statue at the foot of the Chakri Memorial Bridge in present-day Bangkok; and in April 1982 His Majesty King Bhumibol officiated at a ceremony to proclaim King Rama I "The Great".

* * *

Much of the material in this section was obtained from Prince Chula Chakrabongse's book **Lords of Life**, *published by Alvin Redman, London, 1976, and from* **The Restoration of Thailand Under Rama I, 1782-1809**, *by Klaus Wenk, published by the Association for Asian Studies, University of Arizona Press, Tucson, Arizona, USA, 1968.*

Chulalongkorn: The Beloved and Great King

Dusk was falling over the plains of Central Siam one evening about 100 years ago. A farmer living beside a canal saw a small group of men who had moored their boat nearby, and were preparing to cook their evening meal on the bank.

One of the men seemed quite ordinary, neither particularly rich nor poor, and the two or three others appeared to be his servants.

With true Thai hospitality, the farmer invited them into his house to share his own meal and spend the night there. The men accepted.

While they were eating, they chatted about the affairs of the local village, in which the stranger seemed unusually interested. The farmer hinted at corruption and oppression from some government officials in the area.

"Really?" said the stranger. "Does the King know about this?"

"Oh, no," replied the farmer, "the King knows nothing of it — he never visits these parts. He stays in his palace in Bangkok."

During the conversation the farmer's young son kept on darting quick glances at the stranger, comparing him with a portrait hanging on the wall.

After muttering a few times "Meuan jing jing!" ("He really does look the same!"), the boy suddenly prostrated himself at the stranger's feet. When he saw this, realisation dawned on the farmer. "Your Majesty!" he whispered, and he too crouched on the floor....

The stranger was indeed none other than King Chulalongkorn himself. It was as much for his deep concern for his people's welfare as for all his other great works, that posterity has called him "The Beloved and Great King".

"So you see," said His Majesty to the farmer, smiling but with more than a little concern in his voice, "the King does visit these parts — but he does so in order to find out about the very kind of injustices you have mentioned. Please keep quiet about my visit and let me remain incognito; I am just a stranger passing through. I want to find out how well or poorly the people are being treated."

This is one version of a well-known story, of which there are several others. It is certainly based on fact, for King Chulalongkorn often travelled incognito in the countryside to mingle freely among the people and learn about their grievances and problems.

The scarcity of newspapers and photographs during his reign (from A.D. 1868 to 1910) made this easier. The King usually went unrecognised — except, as in the anecdote above, by an occasional sharp-eyed youngster.

These intimate journeys among his people, and the very obvious compassion for them which caused him to make so many historic changes in the destiny of his nation, enabled them to get to know their King well — to love and revere him as a father.

October 23 is enshrined in the Thai people's hearts, because it was on this date that their beloved King passed away in 1910. As already mentioned, Thais refer to King Chulalongkorn as "Phra Piya Maharaj" — "the Beloved and Great King" — and October 23 is called "Wan Piya Maharaj" or "the Beloved and Great King's Day." Foreigners know it as Chulalongkorn Day, and it is a national holiday.

Two things were the driving forces behind all the work this great King accomplished during his 42-year reign: his deep concern for his people's well-being, and for the very survival of his country in a time of swift and uncertain world change.

Not only did he succeed in preserving Siam's independence and put the country squarely on the world map; he completely reorganised its administrative and legal systems, finance and tax collection, education, public health services, communications — he founded Siam's railway system, and had many major new canals dug....

The King also founded 12 new ministries, established postal and telegraph services, built new temples such as the magnificent Marble Temple, new roads, bridges...

And he abolished slavery forever...

In short, he brought Siam into the 20th Century, continuing the work begun by his illustrious father King Mongkut (Rama IV).

King Chulalongkorn was born in September 1853, the eldest son of King Mongkut and Queen Debsirin. He learned to read and write from the "ladies of the Inside," who also taught him Siam's royal traditions and court etiquette.

His father was determined that he should have an early and thorough grounding in English, for which British and American tutors were hired. As for such sports as horsemanship, his father taught them himself.

Following royal custom Prince Chulalongkorn underwent his tonsure ceremony when he was 13, presided over by King Mongkut who himself cut off the first three tufts of hair with golden shears.

During the same year the Prince was ordained for a short period as a Buddhist novice.

When King Mongkut died in 1868, Prince Chulalongkorn succeeded him on the throne. But the new King was only 15, so the Chief Minister, Chao Phya Srisuriyawongs, became Regent and governed the country.

During his five-year minority, the young King travelled to Singapore, Java and India to study colonial government and administration. From these visits he gained enormously in knowledge and understanding, and even at that young age he foresaw that many drastic changes were needed for Siam. But he was equally well aware that his country's ancient and deep-rooted traditions could not be changed or swept away all at once.

In 1873, when he was 20 and therefore of age, King Chulalongkorn had his second coronation and assumed the full task of governing the country.

He immediately set about preparing the groundwork for his reforms, some of which were to take more than 30 years to complete. "I wish to see whatever is beneficial to the people accomplished gradually according to circumstances, and unjust customs abolished," he said. "But as it is impossible to change everything overnight, steady pruning is necessary...."

He repeatedly stressed that reform must be a gradual process, with first things being tackled first.

"We will administer the country well if we develop opportunities for the people to earn their living so that they are benefited by the government, for then they will pay the taxes which are the economic foundation of the government. Therefore an efficient administration and fostering ways of providing for the people's livelihood are the most important and final purpose of the kingdom."

In 1874, when he was still not yet 22, he took those first steps in reforming the administration and the judiciary — and towards abolishing slavery: he established a Council of State, Siam's first real Cabinet, and a privy council.

In his proclamation speech, King Chulalongkorn characteristically explained that the council's purpose was to bring greater well-being to the people. At the same time, he unexpectedly announced one of his earliest reforms, a highly dramatic and moving one: "His Majesty wished to remove oppression and lower his status so as to allow officials to sit on chairs, instead on prostrating themselves in his presence."

The King saw that his own government must have Western methods and ideas as its guidelines. Partly with this in mind he sent four of his sons aged about 10 or 11 to England for their education so that later they could help him carry out his many reforms. He also sent other sons and relatives to Europe later on, for the same purpose.

In his letters to his young sons in England, he wrote: "In sending you abroad to study, my sole purpose is for you to acquire knowledge: therefore, do not boast that you are a prince, but apply all your efforts to your studies, so that you may have a chance to give useful service to your country; for if you think that just because you were born a prince you need do nothing all your life, such an existence would be no different from that of an animal."

As he had foreseen, administrative reform turned out to be a very slow process.

But in due course, his purpose of revising all Siam's laws in order to bring about the people's maximum well-being and happiness was largely achieved.

The whole country was systematically divided into "circles" or "monthon", provinces ("changwad"), districts ("amphoe") and sub-districts ("tambon"). In this way the power of the King was extended downward towards the people, for at the village level the headman or "puyaiban" would be elected by popular vote, while each "tambon" would be headed by a "kamnan", an official to be elected by all the "puyaiban" and answerable to the provincial and ultimately the central government.

In the country's legal and tax-collecting sysems, it was a similar story of gradual but steady and determined progress. King Chulalongkorn inherited an antiquated and unworkable judicial system. For instance, the ancient Law of the Three Seals, which dated back to the 13th-century Sukhothai period, involved trial by ordeal. The truth of the plaintiff's or defendant's claims was decided by seeing which of the two could stay longer under water.

Tax collection, too, had become hopelessly confused and corrupt, with the right to become a "tax farmer" or collector going to the highest bidder. The King was determined to change all this into a fair and just system equal for everyone on the land, and which would protect the individual and his property.

This aim was also the cornerstone of his foreign policy: Siam must transform its legal system into a pattern accepted by the world's great powers, for only then would the country become safe from the threat of foreign annexation.

By 1892 King Chulalongkorn was able to proclaim his new Ministry of Justice with a steamlined organisation for Bangkok's law courts. And by 1908 a firm and centralised judicial structure covering the whole country was achieved — the culmination of 34 years of patient, painstaking legal reform.

Similarly, the tax system was reorganised by establishing a central Revenue Department, which in 1892 became the Ministry of Finance. (Later in King Chulalongkorn's reign, one of those same four young sons whom he had sent to be educated in England, Prince Kitiyakara — grandfather of Her Majesty Queen Sirikit, the present queen — was to become Minister of Finance.)

Through all these reforms, the rights of every private citizen were guaranteed by law to an extent never before achieved in Siam. The people were protected against the whims of corrupt officials such as those hinted at in the anecdote at the beginning of this section.

And in making the reforms, the King had the benefit of advice from skilled European experts — for he spoke English fluently.

Together with his administrative and legal reforms, there came a gradual improvement in Siam's economy through increased trade and more efficent tax collection. So much so, that the national revenue grew from eight million baht at the beginning of the reign to 61 million at the end. Over the same period, the country's rice exports multiplied 15-fold.

"All children, from my own to the poorest, should have an equal chance of education." With these words in 1881, the King opened Suan Kularb School, today one of Thailand's biggest and best boys' secondary schools.

By 1982, the King's reform of Siam's education had made it possible to set up the first full Ministry of Education, with a comprehensive and nationwide programme from primary school to top secondary level. The programme, largely adapted from the British system of the time, included the education of women, teacher training, the production of textbooks and many other important features.

In 1897, the King founded a scholarship scheme to enable commoners to study abroad, as his own sons had done.

In 1902 he founded the Royal Pages' School for future government employees, and in the following reign this developed into Thailand's first (and still most distinguished) university, named in the great King's memory as Chulalongkorn University. Its emblem is the "Phra Keao", a tiered crown resting on a silk tasselled cushion, the crown being a replica of the six-inch headpiece worn by King Chulalongkorn as a boy to keep his hair tidy.

King Chulalongkorn also instituted a Public Health Department including Siam's first hospital, now Siriraj Hospital, and medical and nursing schools. When the hospital was first opened in 1888, it was difficult to find any patients; everyone believed that to go to hospital was to die. So it was suggested that some of the city's beggars with skin diseases be taken to the hosptal for treatment — but this idea met with an unsuspected snag: the beggars protested indignantly that curing their condition would deprive them of their means of livelihood!

However, it was not long before the public's fears evaporated and the hospital became so sought-after that there were not enough beds to go round.

From the very beginning of his reign, King Chulalongkorn was determined to do away with slavery — but as with all his other reforms, he realised that this could only be done gradually. He began his measures in this direction as early as 1874, by decreeing that henceforth any child born into slavery would automatically become freed at the age of 21.

A step-by-step approach to the problem of slavery was essential in order to avoid causing suffering either to the nobles and rich men who had long been used to employing slaves, or to the slaves themselves, who were utterly dependent on their masters for food and shelter. "To emancipate them straight away," said the King, "would be to put them in danger of being neglected and left to die by themselves."

More than 30 years later, in 1905 gradual reform had made it possible for a Royal Edict to decree that all children of slaves be immediately freed; and complete abolition was finally achieved in the following reign, less than two years after King Chulalongkorn's death.

All these great and sweeping reforms at home helped to give the King a free hand in his foreign policy and allowed him successfully to walk the tightrope between the colonial aspirations of France and Britain. Although he could not avoid giving up 90,000 square miles of territory to those two imperial powers, he succeeded brillantly through revised treaties in preserving his country's independence, and so proved himself a statesman of the highest order. Morever, this skilful diplomacy vastly enhanced Siam's prestige among the great powers.

Among King Chulalongkorn's most important achievements in the international field were his two visits to Europe, in 1897 and 1907 — the first time any Siamese king had even been outside Asia. On both trips, he had the gratification of seeing how high his prestige was in the world.

The tours were a huge success, for he was also the first Asian ruler who had ever been able to converse freely and informally in English with British and European royalty. This was because since his earliest childhood English lessons, he had always loved to speak English, and often mixed it with Thai when talking.

These two visits to Europe, and the warmth and cordiality of the King's relations with European heads of state, led to an invaluable understanding between Siam and the West. In France, he was gratified to find he was well received, both officially and spontaneously by the French people.

During his second European visit in 1907, he spent an enjoyable weekend at Windsor Castle as the guest of King Edward VII and Queen Alexandra, at which he met Prince and Princess Andrew of Greece, parents of Britain's present Duke of Edinburgh.

But during both his visit to Europe, his thoughts often flew back home to his own people. In a telegram to Queen Saovabha he said, "I have taken pains to spend my time in a manner which will benefit our beloved land..."

A charming description of his weekend at Windsor Castle was given in his letters to a favourite daughter, Princess Nipha, sent on three consectutive days in June 1907. These were later published in Thai under the title "Klai Ban" ("Far from Home") — but not, unfortunately, translated into English. "Apart from a garden party for 8,500 people and a formal dinner party, it was a friendly weekend..." he wrote.

He very much enjoyed Western food, and in these letters to his daughter he described with relish some of the dishes he had tasted — an omelette, sandwiches, and an enormous and juicy pear. In touching words he described how, while eating the pear, his thoughts suddenly turned to her and his eyes filled with tears, for he longed to share the delicious fruit with her.

King Chulalongkorn was in fact a connoisseur of good food, whether Thai, Chinese, Malay or European, and he was himself an excellent cook. He even wrote a cookery book containing nearly 200 European recipes including soups, meat, lobster, fish, sandwiches and salads. He particularly enjoyed dining out in Paris, and always made a point of first visiting the kitchen and talking to the chef. Best of all, he loved to cook and eat at picnics.

Besides cooking, he had a great many other hobbies, of which keeping Leghorn hens and photography were his favourites in his later years.

King Chulalongkorn had 77 children from 37 wives. Altogether he had 92 wives, but only four were created "Phra Nang" or Queens — the Princesses Sunanda, Sawang, Saovabha and Sukhumala. Queen Sunanda was created "Somdech Phra Nang" — "Her Majesty" — but drowned tragically in a boating accident before she was 21. The "Somdech" title was also bestowed on Queens Sawang and Saovabha, the latter being later made "Somdech Phra Barom Rachinee Nart" or Supreme Queen.

This great and many-sided King had a wide knowledge of the world — geographically, historically and constitutionally; he was indeed one of Asia's greatest statesmen.

A French historian, writing about King Chulalongkorn's achievements, said "One stands confounded before the grandeur of such work accomplished." And indeed the King was tireless in his efforts for his country, often working far into the night and seldom retiring before three a.m.

His reforms and other achievements in preserving the independence of his nation and ensuring a better life for all of his people were so many and so sweeping that it is doubtful whether even half of them have been covered.

But it should also be mentioned that in 1904 he created the National Library — just one more of his ceaseless efforts to bring Siam into the modern world.

In 1908 he celebrated 40 years' rule amid wild rejoicing and an unprecedented display of loyalty and love. The public subscribed a large sum of money to erect a memorial to him — something never before attempted for any Thai, alive or dead. The King agreed to have a modest equestrian statue put up outside his Dusit Palace — the statue where every year, thousands pay homage to his memory. If you want to see a demonstration, straight from the heart, of the Thai people's love and reverence for one of their greatest rulers, go early on October 23, Chulalongkorn Day and a national holiday, to the Royal Plaza.

Here you will see thousands of university students and others prostrating themselves in homage before the equestrian statue of King Chulalongkorn the Great. You will witness one of Thailand's greatest spontaneous public displays of reverence and affection for a past ruler.

* * *

*Much of the material for this section was obtained from five books available in the Siam Society and AUA libraries, to the authors of which the present writer would like to express his thanks: "**Lords of Life**" by HRH the late Prince Chula Chakrabongse; "**Chulalongkorn the Great**" by Prachoom*

Chomchai; "**Law and Kingship in Thailand in the Reign of King Chulalongkorn**" *by David M. Engel;* "**A History of Thailand**" *by Rong Syamananda; and* "**Popular History of Thailand**" *by M.L. Manich Jumsai.*

When a Royal baby "comes of age"

Many Thai ceremonies are partly Buddhist and partly Brahmin. An example, rich in tradition, was the ancient Royal ceremony held in the Amphorn Hall at Dusit Palace early in 1979. Dating back to the Ayutthaya period, the ceremony solemnises the occasion when a Royal baby reaches the age of one month (sometimes three months) and is officially installed in its cradle.

On this particular occasion the ceremony was held for the Royal grandchild, the baby daughter of His Royal Highness Crown Prince Vajiralongkorn and His Royal consort Princess Soamsawali.

His Majesty the King had expressed the wish that this ceremony should be held in identical fashion to that which took place when the Crown Prince himself was one month old.

The team of Royal Astrologers had previously calculated the auspicious day and time — between 9.49 and 10.09 a.m. on Thursday, January 11. They also examined the baby princess' horoscope so that His Majesty could bestow a suitable name for her.

According to Royal custom, the day before the ceremony the holy water to be used was prepared and blessed by 10 monks led by His Holiness the Supreme Patriarch.

Early in the morning on the day of the ceremony, the same 10 monks were offered food at Dusit Palace.

Their Majesties and their two daughters arrived from Chitrlada Palace at 9.15 a.m. and were welcomed by the Crown Prince and Princess Soamsawali and also by the King's sister, Her Royal Highness Princes Galayani Vadhana, and other members of the Royal Family, government officials and His Holiness the Supreme Patriarch together with other monks.

Everyone proceeded to the ceremonial hall, where His Majesty lit candles and joss-sticks and paid homage before the Chaiyawat Buddha statue.

The Supreme Patriarch and the monks chanted a blessing, and at half-past nine His Majesty poured the holy water into a large bowl. Another high-ranking monk completed the intial part of the ceremony by placing in the bowl fish and prawn cages and coconuts wrapped in gold and silver paper, after which some of the holy water was put into a gourd.

The main ceremony consisted of three basic procedures: Cutting the Royal baby's hair, bestowing her name and placing her in the cradle.

At the auspicious time, the baby Princess was brought to the King by her nurse, Miss Raka Nakachart. His Majesty poured holy water from the conch shell onto his grandchild's forehead and gave her a "bai matoom" or leaf from the Indian bael tree. He then took the Royal Thai Scissors and cut off a few locks of the baby girl's hair. After pouring more holy water from the gourd, His Majesty tied sacred threads round the baby's wrists and anointed her forehead with "peng krajae" or fragrant white paste. She was then taken away to rest for a while.

The monks started chanting; a Brahmin blew on a conch shell: lords-in-waiting sounded the drums, and the entire orchestration of gongs, conch shells and trumpets began in characteristic Thai Royal tradition.

At the end of the chanting, the nine monks left the hall; the Supreme Patriarch remained behind.

His Holiness now poured holy water to anoint the frame from which the cradle would be suspended, after which the cradle itself was attached.

A sign was hung on the frame, and the mattress was put in the cradle along with various ceremonial objects — a grindstone of the type used in traditional medicine, a winter melon coated with a special kind of chalk, and bags containing grains, beans and sesame seeds. The cradle was then anointed with holy water.

Then the second procedure started in which His Majesty gave the baby Princess her name. The King placed various traditional Royal regalia symbolically inside the cradle and immediately took them out again: A gold box containing the baby girl's horoscope, silver bullion, a bag of coins, a gold water-bowl overlaid with enamel, a pedestal and gold water-pot together with gold padlock and key, a sewing box, and the gold name-plate with the Royal Grandchild's name engraved on it — Phra-ong Chao (Her Royal Highness) Bhajara Kitiyabha, which means "Bright with Honour and Virtue that are as Precious as Diamonds." The baby girl was briefly dipped in water in the bowl.

The King then requested the Supreme Patriarch to pour water over the baby Princess' hands, after which came the third main procedure: The Princess was officially placed in the cradle attended by Tao (Lady) Sophanives and the nurse. The Chief Brahmin now rocked the cradle while two Brahmin attendants sang a lullaby. Other Brahmins struck up the traditional Thai music again on the conch shells, trumpets and drums.

A red cloth was laid down round the ceremonial area and the Brahmin officials formed a circle to perform a "wian-tien" in celebration, in which candles were passed from hand to hand, each official wafting the smoke towards the Royal baby in the cradle to bring her good fortune. The "bai-sri", auspicious cooked rice ornately wrapped in banana leaves, was placed near the cradle, and after a further anointing, threads of nine different colours were placed across the Royal Grandchild's feet. Her Royal Highness Princess Galayani Vadhana also anointed the baby Princess' hands and presented gifts.

The Prime Minister presented the Crown Prince with the Princess' birth certificate, after which other members of the Royal family and high-ranking officials presented Princess Soamsawali with gifts for the Royal Baby.

His Majesty paid final homage in front of the Buddha statue. And so the rich, ancient and colourful Royal occasion came to an end.

The "Chula" graduation ceremony: a ballet without music

Every year His Majesty the King presides over Chulalongkorn University's annual graduation ceremony. Reading about it brings back memories of this beautiful, moving and impressive ceremony full of pageantry and dignity, which I once attended in 1966.

On that occasion I was working at "Chula", and a physics lecturer invited me to witness the ceremony. He warned me that once we were in our seats in the auditorium we would have to remain there for three hours. And it was an experience I'll never forget.

In 1981 His Majesty conferred degrees on more than 3,800 people and the ceremony was, as is usual these days, spread over three separate days. I'll try to describe it.

During the two weeks before the ceremony every new graduate-to-be is drilled in rigorous rehearsals until everyone knows his or her routine perfectly, on stage as well as off. Two days before the ceremony begins there's a series of mass rehearsals in the auditorium.

On each of the three graduation days, the students put on the shimmering translucent white-and-gold robes, each one trimmed with the colour of the respective Faculty. Beneath their gowns the men wear white shirt and trousers of the "rachapataen" or "Royal Pattern" uniform.

The mornings are taken up with much lightearted photograph-taking. Evey new graduate-to-be gathers with his or her family for group photos in "Chula's" large grounds.

Shortly after one p.m. a dozen or so Royal Household Guards in spiked helmets line up in front of the auditorium entrance. The 3,000-seat auditorium fills up as members of the academic staff and thousands of new graduates take their places. No student's parents are allowed inside. Chairs are set up outside under awnings facing a battery of closed-circuit television receivers which relay the proceedings to perhaps another 2,000 people. Many of these are poor; some have made long, tiring journeys from every corner of the Kingdom to capture, on television, that magic moment when the child for whose education they have scraped and sacrificed for years becomes a graduate of the country's oldest and most respected university.

Towards the appointed time, a hush falls on the crowd outside. Then suddenly a murmur ripples through them — "He's coming."

His Majesty steps out of the Royal car. After a brief moment's pause he ascends the auditorium steps, protected by a huge blue umbrella and preceded by Palace retainers in traditional headgear.

At the top of the steps His Majesty walks along a carpet strewn with rose petals by kneeling girl students. He is welcomed by the University authorities and goes inside and onto the stage.

Immediately and dramatically, the Royal Anthem strikes up. Some 5,000 loyal subjects, inside and out, stand to attention. His Majesty lights candles at the altar near which are seated a row of monks beside the Buddha statue. It is a moment charged with emotion. The air is alive with the people's deep love and respect for His Majesty.

The King then takes his seat on the stage where he will remain for the next three hours.

After a brief speech of welcome by the Rector, the Dean of the first Faculty of the day takes his place at the rostrum on the left of the stage. He starts calling out the graduates' names in alphabetical order. The first 30 or so of these are already standing lined up at the left-hand side, ready to go on stage.

From now on, the ceremony is like a ballet without music. There are eight students on stage at any one time, including the two standing on the steps of the left and right-hand sides. The students form a line stretching across the stage from left to right; the one in the centre walks towards His Majesty as his name is called out. He bows, and all the other students on stage bow in unison: the girls curtsy. The King hands the student his or her blue-bound certificate. Then everyone moves one place forward. The three who have passed His Majesty walk backwards so as to remain facing him, and bow or curtsy again; the last student turns and walks off stage while those who have passed His Majesty again bow or curtsy in unison. A new student has meanwhile come on stage from the left.

The continuous procedure follows a measured rhythm. It's almost as if the "ballet" is "conducted" by the Dean's regular announcement of each student's name — as indeed it is. The pattern formed by the students on the stage never varies: bow or curtsy — move on one place — bow or curtsy again. It makes a wonderful sight, with the students' glittering robes picked out by spotlights.

Fresh batches of students rise from their seats, a whole row at a time, as their turn draws near. They too bow or curtsy in unison with those on the stage, then make their way to the left-hand side of the hall in readiness for the great moment.

Students who have left the stage and are returning to their seats bow or curtsy singly, but still in rhythm with the rest, before entering their row of seats.

And so the great ceremony goes on, hour after hour. The steady, regular beat never changes, pausing only for brief bursts of clapping and for one Faculty and Dean to give place to the next.

A never-to-be-forgotten event for students, parents and onlookers alike — including this writer.

The House at the End of the Slope

April 28 is the anniversary of the birthday of His Royal Highness Prince Narisranuwativongse. Prince Naris, as he is usually known, was the half-brother of King Chulalongkorn, and the son of King Mongkut (King Rama IV, who reigned from 1851 to 1868) and Princess Bannarai. The Prince was born on April 28, 1863 and died at the age of 83 on March 10, 1946, the last surviving son of King Mongkut.

The Prince's descendants organise a "Naris Day" ceremony every year on April 28 at "Baan Plai Nern", his summer residence at No. 1160, Rama IV Road, Klong Toey, Bangkok.

The entrance to the grounds is a short distance down a driveway on the south side of Rama IV Road. Travelling in the direction away from the city centre, this driveway is on the right-hand side of the street, barely 50 yards past the railway crossing and the overpass bridge carrying the Din Daeng-Tha Rua Expressway.

The name "Baan Plai Nern" — "the house at the end of the slope" — dates from the days when Prince Naris and his family used to travel to and from his summer residence in a horse-drawn carriage which could not negotiate the then steep slope leading up to the railway tracks (Rama IV Road was quite a bit lower than it is today) and down again to the house, unless the driver got out and pushed! Even then, the horses had to recover their breath before proceeding over the bridge across the canal to the Prince's house.

The group of three beautiful old Thai-style houses, some of which date from the reign of King Rama III, are in a most charmingly rural setting in a large and very lovely private garden surrounded by beautiful trees.

Prince Naris was a great patron and discerning connoisseur of the arts, and was at one time in charge of the Department of Performing Arts. He designed the Marble Temple and murals in the main chapel of Wat Rachathiwat. He also saved many art treasures that had been neglected and preserved them at Wang Tha Phra, his former official residence (now the Faculty of Interior Design of Silpakorn University).

The works of art that he protected so lovingly were later transferred to Baan Plai Nern, and are on display to visitors every year on Naris Day.

The Prince was also a composer of music and drama, and several of his literary works are considered masterpieces of Thai literature, such as his rewritten version of the very ancient (pre-Buddhist-era) story from Sanskrit literature called "Anirudh" or "Unaruth" in Thai. The Baan Plai Nern amateur traditional ballet group performed this play on Naris Day in 1981. Here is a brief synopsis of Prince Naris' version of "Unaruth".

Unaruth, whose royal grandfather was a reincarnation of Phra Narai (the Hindu god Vishnu), went hunting one day with his courtiers and had to stay overnight in the jungle. Before going to sleep, the courtiers paid homage to Phra Sai, the spirit of the banyan tree. The spirit was so pleased that he took the sleeping Unaruth to the bedchamber of Princess Usa, daughter of the king of Krung Phan.

Foreseeing that there would be trouble due to the enmity existing between the two royal families, the banyan tree spirit cast a spell over Unaruth and Usa so that they were both struck dumb. But even though they could not speak, it was love at first sight between them.

Before dawn, the spirit carried Unaruth, still asleep, back to the banyan tree and his courtiers.

When each of them woke up in the morning and failed to see the other, they were in despair. However, Usa had a very talented governess named Supalak, who volunteered to sketch the portrait of any young god, prince or king likely to have been the nocturnal visitor. (This episode gives the Thai choreographers the chance to devise the most intricate movements as Supalak travels in search of her mistress' "Prince Charming." She sees devas (angels) dancing, and mingles with them to observe closely any male likely to be the cause of her mistress' despair.)

The 1981 performance ended with Supalak presenting her sketches to Princess Usa. But in the original story, there was no sketch of Unaruth, so Usa wept bitterly. Supalak therefore took Usa's "sabai" or shoulder-scarf to Unaruth, who recognised Usa's scent on it and immediately went back with Supalak to his beloved, to the great joy of both the lovers.

But this is still not the end of the story, for Princess Usa's father, learning of the unauthorised union, became angry. Unaruth was tied with a "naga" or magical snake, and suffered shame and torture until his royal grandfather came to his rescue. Battles followed, and Unaruth became conqueror of both realms — and several other ladies' hearts.

A granddaughter of Prince Naris kindly took me to see part of a semi-dress rehearsal in the beautiful Baan Plai Nern grounds. To the tinkling taped music of a "ranad" or classical Thai xylophone (a full-scale Thai piphat band provided music on the day) some 30 young girls of school age in bright red "panungs" with the ends rolled together and tucked between the legs in classical Thai fashion danced on the lawn to the hand-clapping rhythm of their teachers and choreographers.

And now, some more details about the house itself. Although I said Baan Plai Nern is three houses, it is really only one house—but it looks like two houses! This is because the old, steep-roofed Thai-style wooden houses were built so that they could be completely dismantled, panel by panel and wall by wall. They could then be transported in their "completely knocked-down" state (to borrow an expression from modern technology in the furniture and other trades) and re-erected in a different village, town or city. This was possible because no nails were used in their construction — only wooden pegs which could be hammered out and later hammered back in again.

In the case of Baan Plai Nern, His Royal Highness bought several such houses. They could be acquired quite cheaply in the early 1900s, because they were considered old-fashioned; people preferred the new-fangled bungalows with corrugated-iron roofs.

Today these old-style houses are quite rare and seem to have come back into favour again; they can fetch high prices — if you are lucky enough to find one in good condition in a country town or village! Baan Plai Nern is actually made of the very rare "golden teak."

The Prince arranged the houses so that they were interconnected by raised balconies at first-floor level (second-floor, in American parlance) as was usually done with these old-style Thai houses.

He lived there for 30 years, making modifications to the complex by roofing the connecting balconies over and walling them in. Thus the three houses became in effect one house. But as seen from Rama IV Road, there are still two separate gabled roofs, so the impression from outside is of two houses!

I have chosen some excerpts from the book "Baan Plai Nern" by the Prince's daughter, Mom Chao Duangchitr Chitrabongse, which a friend has kindly translated into English and which provide interesting insights into the Princess' life there as a child.

Although originally Prince Naris lived at Wang Tha Phra, a palace opposite the northwest gate of the Royal (Grand) Palace, he suffered from bronchitis and found that the fresh breezy atmosphere in the Klong Toey area was much better for his health. ("Klong Toey" means Screwpine Canal, and was originally so called because of the many screwpine trees along the canal's banks). So after buying 7,200 square metres of paddy field and re-erecting the group of Thai houses on that land, he took up residence there in 1912.

At that time Klong Toey was an open, mainly uninhabited area of paddy fields and market gardens. The local people traded by boat along canals running parallel with Rama IV Road.

At the Sala Daeng area (so called on account of a small red-painted hut belonging to the Paknam Railway Company opposite Chulalongkorn Hospital), Rama IV Road consisted of two rows of bricks just wide enough for wheels of vehicles which were mostly horse-drawn carts or carriages. Sugar palms lined the whole length of the road.

There was also the railway owned by the Paknam Railway Company, which ran between Hua Lampong (Paknam Railway) Station opposite the present Hua Lampong Station, and Paknam (Samut Prakan).

"People living in our area would get on the train at Klong Toey Station and get off at Hua Lampong," writes Mom Chao Duangchitr. "Most convenient of all was to take the electric tram which was occasionally allowed to run on the railway line between Hua Lampong and Klong Toey when no train was in the offing...

"Whenever a train approached, there would be a warning hum all along the line, and the tram had to take refuge by shunting onto the nearest siding...

"The tram service had triangular red-painted metal plates nailed on posts to indicate the tram stops. When His Royal Highness had settled down permanently at Baan Plai Nern, one of these plates was fixed on the electricity pole in front of his residence.

"Moreover, the drivers and inspectors obliged us by fetching or taking things between Hua Lampong and the residence, and even volunteered to do some shopping for us...

"People from Wang Tha Phra would send a wooden dispatch-box with documents to His Royal Highness through the courtesy of the tram stationmaster, and the tram staff would take them back again after His Royal Highness had dealt with them. This kind gesture saved us a lot of time.

"In those days household electric supply was available, but there was as yet no public tap-water at Klong Toey. So we had to keep rows of "klong jars" to store water for our use.

"When we ran out of water, we had to send people in boats to fetch it from the public utility supply at Sala Daeng. But in those days the water in the canal was quite clean; if it became cloudy, we could make it clear by adding aluminium sulphate...

"In order not to indulge in great expense, His Royal Highness only had the land on which the houses were built filled in. The rest was left as paddy fields, though some was elevated for a kitchen-garden in which we grew our own chillies, vegetables, bananas and so on.

"Gradually, the plot was filled in to make a lawn and grow flowers. There were no hedges, just trees to mark the boundaries.

" The person who had sold the first plot to His Royal Highness proposed selling the adjoining field at 2.50 baht a square wah (four square metres), and some other land at only one baht. His Royal Highness eventually owned 10 rai of paddy field, which he rented to farmers. We went to help in the fields at planting and harvesting time, and thoroughly enjoyed it.

"At first the houses were roofed with thatch. Some, like the main pavilion, had wooden frame walls which could be tilted out. Once all the panels were tilted, it really was open and there were only balustrades around. But during the rainy season, this arrangement proved inconvenient; the panels were difficult to close in stormy weather. Sometimes if they were not closed quickly enough, the wind would catch them and blow them away onto the lawn — in one case carrying off the servant who was closing them as well. Finally His Royal Highness had to install fixed wooden walls with wide, new-style windows.

"The roofing thatch had to be changed every two or three years. This was something which the children loved, because it involved the astrological casting of an auspicious day when there would be no rain. The change had to be done quickly; removing the old thatch took a whole day, and the re-thatching was done the following day. So the house was open to the sky for a whole night, and the children could gaze at the moon and stars.

"But if the horoscope had been miscast and it rained, then we just had to sit in the rain, which was most uncomfortable. The children, always after adventure and fun, used to sing the rain-begging song: "Nang maeo euy, khor chang, khor fon, khor nammon rot hua nang maeo" ("Lady cat, they tell us to ask for rain, to ask the sacred water to shower on the lady cat's head.")

"The grown-ups, afraid of being rained on, would scold the children and forbid them to sing such songs. But in fact the re-roofing always took place in the dry season and it hardly ever rained at all.

"Later the roof thatch was replaced with teak tiles."

M.C. Duangchitr describes the various buildings which made up Baan Plai Nern. "The main pavilion, which was like the sala in a temple, now consists of three rooms on the upper floor, with a balcony running all the way round.

"This pavilion originally belonged to a dignitary at the court of King Rama III and stood in front of Wat Rakang in Thon Buri. Prince Naris bought it to use as a parlour, with the front room for receiving guests and holding ceremonies such as offering food to monks.

"The second room is partitioned by three bookcases, with crayon sketches by the Prince above each. The drawings on the left and right show one of the Buddha's disciples and a theveda (angel) flying to meet the Buddha, who is shown in the centre descending from the Tawatimsa Heaven and performing the so-called 'Double Miracle'.

"The third room in the pavilion contains the Prince's dining-table and also a Chinese-style tribute table.

"To the west of the dining-room there was originally an open balcony, but later a wood-and-glass partition was added and the Prince used it as his study where he spent most of his time. The Prince's bedroom and other personal quarters and those of his servants also formed part of the main pavilion."

An open balcony led to three other buildings. Traditional Thai-style houses were normally grouped facing one another with a surrounding and connecting balcony. "But this arrangement did not allow the breeze to circulate freely, and made the house stuffy and uncomfortable," writes M.C. Duangchitr. "So His Royal Highness changed the layout to conform with the sun's path, each house overlapping the next to allow the southerly breeze to flow freely through."

Prince Naris died at the age of nearly 84, having collected a great many damaged and neglected but historic examples of Thai art. Nothing is in perfect condition.

After his death his family had to do a lot of repair work on the house and make structural alterations, so that the two-roofed Baan Plai Nern one sees today as one drives past along Rama IV Road is not quite the same as when Prince Naris lived there. (In fact the house was physically moved back from the road some years ago when the traffic started getting heavy. This can, of course, be done with Thai "pre-fabs"!) But it still vividly retains the charm and atmosphere of the early 1900s.

Although 75 per cent of the items in the art collection are half-ruined, they are still worth seeing on the two days each year when Baan Plai Nern is open to the public. They give a fine overview of all that is best in Thai art.

The proceeds from Naris Day go to the Naris Fund, which grants seven or eight prizes each year to the best students of Thai art from all over the country.

CHAPTER TWO
CEREMONIES

Dhevo-Rohana — a Northern alms giving ceremony

Some years ago I received details and pictures of a Thai Buddhist ceremony rather less well known than most others. It is called the Dhevo-Rohana alms-giving ceremony, and as far as I know it is associated mainly with northern Thailand. It takes place every year at the end of the three-month Buddhist Lent in October.

The Dhevo-Rohana ceremony is held every year in Chiang Mai under the auspices of the university at Wat Fai Hin, a temple under the patronage of the university's students and staff. Chiang Mai University is, I believe, the only Thai university with its own temple.

Wat Fai Hin, the "stone dyke temple", is said to be several hundred years old. It is said that a much revered northern monk, Phra Kru Ba Mara Sri Wichai, whose name means "glorious conqueror of evil", was once its abbot. More recently, from 1855 to 1914 A.D., Phra Apai Sarata, the first Chao Khana Changwat of Chiang Mai, was abbot there. ("Chao Khana Changwat" means the head monk among all the monks in a province, and the term "Apai Sarata" was bestowed on this particular monk by King Chulalongkorn or Rama V.)

Later, this once famous temple at the foot of the mountain slipped into obscurity. The lay folk who lived nearby moved elsewhere, and the temple fell into disuse.

But all things change in the course of time. Having fallen from its original fame and prominence, Wat Fai Hin's fortunes again took a turn for the better. Chiang Mai University was established nearby, and in 1969 the temple was officially adopted by the university. Students and staff members now go there to gain calmness and peace of mind. And, of course, also in order to preserve Thai Buddhist traditions, among the most important of which is the Dhevo-Rohana ceremony.

During the 25 centuries since the Buddha's lifetime, a vast traditional literature of legends has evolved, and one of these forms the basis of the Dhevo-Rohana ceremony. It is said that the Buddha made a journey to heaven to preach the Doctrine as an act of filial piety to his mother.

The day he returned to earth was named Dhevo-Rohana Day — the 15th day of the waxing moon in the 11th lunar month. The following day, the legend says, a great gathering of devotees celebrated the Buddha's return. This great event has been commemorated every year for many hundreds of years on the first night of the waning moon of the 11th lunar month, which coincides with Wan Ork Phansa, the end of the Buddhist Lent. The site of the temple, in its beautiful mountain setting, 367 metres (1,200 feet) above sea level, makes it an ideal spot for this magnificent ceremony.

All Buddhist ceremonies, from laying the foundation-stone for a new office or hotel to cutting a child's topknot, are opportunities for lay people to give alms to monks, and in the case of the Dhevo-Rohana ceremony this is its main purpose. The ceremony is organised by the university's academic staff students as well as the local people of Chiang Mai, who thus help to preserve Thailand's Buddhist tradition. Some 400 monks take part and 10,000 lay people attend.

The Buddha image leading the long procession of orange-clad monks slowly down the steps from the temple makes a unique sight every year, evoking the idea of the Buddha's decent from heaven, and bringing a feeling of peace and serenity to the onlookers, Thais and foreigners alike.

The Buddha image, Phra Buddha Dhevo Rohana Sri Sakya Muni, is carved out of teak and covered with gold leaf. Together with the lotus pedestal on which it stands, it is over two metres high.

When Jiap became a monk

In 1976, soon after I became a Buddhist, I entered the monkhood for four weeks. My stepson Jiap (Laddawan's son) was my "look-sit" or temple attendant; he swept my "guti" or monk's cell every day, washed my saffron robes, and generally looked after my material well-being.

Almost exactly six years later, in March 1982, it was Jiap's turn to enter the monkhood for a brief period. The roles weren't exactly reversed, except for one very important feature: when I was a monk, Jiap (and all lay people) wai'd to me and I did not return the wai; when Jiap was a monk, I wai'd to him — and of course he didn't wai back either. This is not a personal thing; one wai's to the saffron robes and what they represent — the temporary (or sometimes permanent) mode of life with its renunciation of the material things of this world, in accordance with the Dhamma or Teaching of the Lord Buddha.

In the book "Thai Ways", the forerunner of the present book, I described briefly the preordination ceremony of a "nahk" or monk-to-be, and even more briefly the ordination ceremony itself. The preordination ceremony, as distinct from the actual Buddhist ordination ceremony itself, is entirely Brahmin, and may be omitted in whole or in part. In my own case, I chose to omit it entirely; in Jiap's case, only the final part of it was performed. However, the whole occasion was once again somehow very Thai.

The ordination took place on a very hot Sunday in March, but preparations involving many members of Laddawan's vast family seemed to have been going on for weeks beforehand. Little golden pedestals or "pahn" with trays or "kan" appeared around the house, together with a pair of beautiful little golden flowering trees, a gift to the temple from our landlady.

One Sunday about two weeks before the big day, Laddawan said Jiap must pay his respects to me as one of his elders. "Just sit down in that chair," she said. I did so, and Jiap knelt in front of me, wai'd and presented me with one of the golden "pahns" on which was resting, as far as I remember, a packet of wax candles. Jeep then said to me in Thai, "If I have done you any wrong, please forgive me."

"Wait a minute!" my wife called out to me, "you're supposed to put 100 baht on the 'pahn' and give it back to Jiap so he can give it to the temple." Unfortunately I did not have a 100-baht note — only a 500-baht one. So Laddawan opened a cupboard, took a 100-baht note from the housekeeping money and gave it to me. I put it on the "pahn" which I then gave back Jiap, and that was the end of the little ceremony...

But not quite the end of the story; after Jiap had stood up again, Laddawan said, "Hey, let's have that 100-baht note back!" And back it went into the housekeeping money in the cupboard...

In case this gives a false impression, let me add that the expenses of the whole ordination ceremony ran well into five figures, although in typical Thai fashion a good deal came back in the form of donations from family and friends — all in order to "tam boon" or make merit.

The day before the ceremony, by chance I met an earnest and very likable young German writer who had only been in Thailand a few days. "I want to see the real Thai culture and customs as much as possible," he told me, so I invited him to Jiap's ordination the following day. "Come to my house 2.30 p.m.," I said, and he eagerly accepted.

However, since I was officially Jiap's "father" for the occasion, I had to go earlier to the temple with Jiap and Laddawan for the hair-cutting ceremony. So I left a note for my young German friend to wait for me at the house because he probably could not find his way to the small and little-known temple. Then off we went at one p.m.

At the temple there was a good deal of hanging around in front of the bot or main chapel; the ordination was not due to start until 3.30 p.m. I spent some time learning a new skill: how to fold the petals of green lotuses into attractive shapes. (Well, they should have looked attractive, but somehow mine looked more like a child's unsuccessful paper aeroplane!)

Eventually someone produced a packet of shampoo, and Jiap washed his hair at the standpipe tap, then he sat down in a chair (in the open) and there was a sudden hunt for scissors, which we realised we had forgotten to bring from the house. In the end we borrowed a pair from the temple. Laddawan cut off a few locks of Jiap's hair, then I did the same (with consummate skill I managed to avoid cutting off his ear) while a camera clicked away.

Meanwhile, the "glong yao" or long-drum troupe who had been hired for the procession arrived — about eight boys dressed in vivid yellow costumes from a school, arranged by a friend of Jiap's. (Persistent enquiries since then have failed to elicit any definite information about either the drums themselves — except that they are of Burmese or maybe Mon origin — or the significance, if any, of the yellow costumes.) They started playing, in a deafening but otherwise pleasant rhythm.

By now it was 2.25 and high time for me to go back to the house and pick up my young German friend.

As soon as the pair of us arrived back at the temple, things began to get moving. The drums began their deafening tattoo again, and although it was only 2.45 p.m., everyone started lining up for the procession. Evidently the ceremony had been put forward half-an-hour, though no one seemed to know why. As Jiap's "father", I had to carry his "talabat" or long-handled fan and his "batr" or alms-bowl in the procession. Laddawan, carrying his new set of monk's robes, was immediately in front of me, and Jiap, now shaven-headed, wearing a gold-embroidered, translucent white gown over a white shirt and white sarong and carrying three of those elaborately folded green lotuses in a wai, was immediately behind me. One of his friends shielded his newly-shaven head with a large crimson umbrella. The "glong yao", banging away for dear life, headed the procession.

It was at that moment that I suddenly became aware of a pressing problem.

It really was urgent. I knew that once the procession started, it would be followed immediately by the ordination itself inside the chapel, and there would be no let-up for well over an hour.

Back in England, I would have buttonholed the nearest man and whispered discreetly "Er — excuse me, can you tell me where the, er, the 'gents' is?" But this was Thailand, and whispering would have been useless with the din from the drums going on. At the top of my voice I bellowed "Khor bpai hong nam noy !" ("Please let me go to the toilet a moment!")

The effect was electrifying. The drums stopped instantly. No one batted an eyelid, though I received one or two very sympathetic smiles — and one of my young nephews-in-law helpfully escorted me to the nearest comfort station, which proved to be a 200-yard walk in the grilling sunshine...

As soon as I returned, the drums struck up again (and when I say "struck", I really mean it) and off we went, in procession, marching in time to the rhythm — three times clockwise round the chapel. (I hope it wasn't unorthodox of me, but not wishing to get sunstroke I shifted the "talabat" from time to time so as to shield my head from the sun.)

After the third circuit, the drums stopped and we went into the chapel where the abbot and chapter of monks were waiting for us. As Jiap went in, he flung out handfuls of coins from a bowl, symbolising his temporary relinquishment of worldly possessions; these were gleefully pounced on by the crowd of relations and friends outside, as they are supposed to bring good luck.

We then knelt and handed all sorts of elaborate gifts ceremonially to the monks. After that we sat in the "pap piap" position with legs tucked to one side and feet not pointing at anyone, as far as possible. (This is quite tiring for Westerners like me, but I can manage.) We stayed in that position throughout the 45-minute ordination ceremony, apart from occasional breaks when we knelt to hand over the robes and bowl.

Jiap had memorised — as I had done six years earlier — the 40 or so lines in the ancient Pali language which he had to recite. These included the 10 Precepts for novices — refraining from taking life, stealing, unchaste conduct, lying, drinking intoxicants, eating at the wrong time (from midday until after sunrise the following day), dancing, singing or watching entertainments, wearing garlands or any other adornment (even wristwatches are forbidden), lying on a bed or mattress, and accepting money.

There is one rather tricky passage of Pali when the "nahk" or monk-to-be is requesting admission into the order of monks, in which he is asked in rapid succession whether he has leprosy, ulcers, ringworm, TB or epilepsy (all these diseases were known in the Buddha's time). To each question in turn he must reply "Natthi Bhante" ("No, Sir"). Immediately, without any pause, the next question follows: "Are you a human being?" The "nahk" must be on his guard to answer "Yes, Sir" ("Ama Bhante") to this one, and to the next seven questions — Are you male? Are you free from debt? Have you your parents' permission to become a monk? And so on.

All these questions are asked and must be answered *twice* during the ceremony. Jiap managed the first time, but when answering the sixth question for the second time, "Are you a human being"? he accidentally answered "No, Sir." The Preceptor said nothing, but just looked at him quizzically until he corrected himself. "Yes, Sir."

In the middle of the ceremony, Jiap was hustled out of the chapel's rear door to change into his monk's saffron robes. And then — a touch of drama, missing at my own ordination — just before and as Jiap re-emerged in the monk's robes, the "glong yao," waiting outside the chapel, struck up another thunderous roll.

Meantime, a "farang" friend of mine, keen to get good colour photographs of the procession, had turned up at the time I had told him — 3.30 p.m. — only to find the ordination service already half completed.

Finally it came to an end. As we came out of the chapel, I could feel my photographer friend's accusing eyes on me. Before he could say anything, I retorted, "You've been in this country long enough to know that things often don't start on time. We started half-an-hour early!"

I haven't dealt with many of the smaller details and symbolism of the ceremony in this story; but I hope you have some idea of what a Thai Buddhist ordination ceremony is like.

In the days that followed, Laddawan and I rose early to put rice and other food into Phra Jiap's bowl and wai'd him as he came to the house on his alms round.

Lo Ching Cha — the Giant Swing ceremony

Even before I first came to Thailand, I gathered from tourist brochures that one of the major sights of Bangkok was the Giant Swing. And since I arrived in this country I've passed the impressive, towering structure from time to time whenever I happened to be passing along that end of Bamrungmuang Road near Wat Suthat.

But I was always disappointed that unlike the garden swings of my childhood, there was no seat! Also, although I'd heard and read a lot about the famous Giant Swing Ceremony (called "Lo Ching Cha" in Thai — the Swing itself is called "Sao Ching Cha") I somehow never actually got to see this ceremony.

And no wonder. I've just discovered that it hasn't been performed since 1935!

In 1972 they started dismantling the Giant Swing in order to replace the old teak posts. Huge teak logs were brought down specially from Lampang in the North to make the new posts. There was a ceremony to bless the new posts at which the then Chief Brahmin of Thailand officiated. Everything concerned with the Giant Swing is Brahmin.

There were plans to revive the Swinging Ceremony itself in 1979, but nothing came of them, and it's very doubtful if it will ever be held again.

A document in Thai about the Swing Ceremony came into my hands. It gives something of the interesting history and background of this colourful ceremony. What follows is a rough translation and rearrangement of it.

Referring to the ceremony carried out near the Giant Swing in 1978, the document says this was the traditional Brahmin New Year. Historically, this Royal ceremony dates from the Ayutthaya period, and is for the purpose of inviting the gods Phra Isuan

(Siva) and Phra Narai (Vishnu) to visit the earth. The ceremony therefore consists of two parts - "treeyampawai," a reception ceremony for Phra Isuan, and "treepawai" for receiving Phra Narai. (These ceremonies are distinct from the Giant Swing Ceremony and are still performed every year at the Brahmin Temple.) As part of the gods' retinue come the Sun, Moon, Phra Toranee and Phra Kong Kha (the spirits of earth and water), and the Nagas or mythical serpents also come to pay respect to the two gods. The Nagas then perform the Swing Ceremony, after which they throw water just as humans do during Songkran.

A procession carrying "u-loop" or flowers and rice on the shoulders is supposed to visit the King at night to bring him good wishes for the Brahmin New Year. As this is an agricultural ceremony to beg the Brahmin gods for good crops, in olden days the King asked his Minister of Agriculture to represent Phra Isuan and be Lord of the Swing Ceremony.

On the seventh day of the waxing moon in the second lunar month (actually some time in January) the ceremony starts early in the morning. The Lord of the Swing dressed in full uniform, is carried on a Brahmin-style wooden board in a palanquin — a replica of the board used as a seat on the Swing. When the stage near the Swing is reached, the Lord of the Swing seats himself on a piece of bamboo, keeping his right foot on his left knee throughout the ceremony. Should he fail to do this (well, you try doing it for two or three hours!) he forfeits his fee of one "chang" or 80 baht for performing the ceremony.

Now comes a description of the actual swinging, which sounds quite fascinating, if rather terrifying, to watch.

The Giant Swing has three teams of performers. Unlike the garden swing of our childhood days, the wooden board which serves as a seat is set lengthwise, along the same direction in which it swings to and fro. It's rather like the swing-boats at a fair.

Each team consists of three men. The two men in the middle make the board move faster or slower by rocking and heaving, thus controlling the height reached at the end of each to-and-fro Swing.

The man in the "bow" has the hardest job of all. In front of the Swing is fixed a bamboo pole something like a fishing rod, from the end of which dangles a bag of money. The job of the man in the "bow" is to seize the bag with his teeth.

There are three different heights at which the bamboo pole is fixed — one for each of the three teams. Surprisingly, the document says the money from the lowest position is the most difficult to get. After this, the second, medium-height pole is put in position, and lastly the highest one, from which it is said to be the easiest to seize the bag of money.

And how much money is in the bags? Not very much: 12 baht, 10 baht and eight baht respectively.

There are two complete rounds of swinging, on the seventh and ninth days of the waxing moon of the second lunar month. The "Lo Ching Cha" is performed twice each day — in the morning, and again in the afternoon. When the Lord of the Swing has seen the contest, he moves to another stage to see the "nariwan" or Nagas and the god Phra Isuan dancing and playing at "throwing water." In 1978, only one of the Original Giant Swing Ceremony performers was left since the time of the last ceremony in 1935.

CHAPTER THREE
CUSTOMS

Ratana-tri — the Triple Gem

One never stops learning new facts, especially about a country and culture that are not one's own. In my book "Thai Ways", I have probably done little more than reveal the tip of the iceberg, because that is all I know. And every once in a while I learn interesting new facts about something or other which it has never occurred to me to question before.

The reason behind all this preamble is that one day I learnt something quite new about that most familiar of religious offerings in Thailand — the "dorkmai-toob-tian," or a flower, a candle, and three joss-sticks. Many years ago when I was a Buddhist monk for a month and used to go out every day on the early-morning alms round with my fellow monks, I was occasionally given this set of offerings in addition to the normal ones of rice and other food.

The food was, of course, put into my alms bowl, but the slender group in which the flower was usually a green lotus bud, plus the candle and the three joss-sticks, all held together by a small rubber band, had to be held separately outside the bowl. This was not easy, as the bowl was hot (from the steaming rice inside it) and often quite heavy; besides which, there was always the need to concentrate on keeping one's robe properly arranged, and to try and avoid treading on sharp stones with one's bare feet.

I had always imagined — without giving it deep thought or asking anyone about it — that the flower, candle and joss-sticks were symbols of the "Ratana-tri" or Triple Gem — that is, the Buddha, the Dhamma or Teaching, and the Sangha or Order of Monks.

But then I found myself talking about this with a Thai friend, a knowledgeable man who had spent nine years of his youth as a "dek wat" or temple-boy. "Oh, no," he said. "It's not that at all. This is a Brahmin custom. You must remember that Brahminism is an older religion than Buddhism, and the Lord Buddha himself came from a Brahmin family.

"The flower represents all living or growing things, the unending continuation of life. And the candle and joss-sticks represent fire, which was worshipped by the Brahmins because it symbolises purification.

"Do you realise," he went on, "that this Brahmin idea of purging by fire or flame came from the same origin as the flame on Mount Olympus in Greece, or the Olympic runner's torch, if you like? And not only that — the Statue of Liberty in New York Harbour is also holding a torch aloft, and that is all part of the same original belief in purification by fire."

"That's certainly very interesting indeed," I said. "But why are there always three joss-sticks? Surely that represents the Triple Gem, doesn't it?" "Ah, yes," he answered. "You're quite correct about that."

So at least my idea was partly right. And in that slim group of objects held together by a rubber band lies yet another glimpse of the combination of Buddhism and Brahminism which is so often met in this country.

The Ratana-tri or Triple Gem are held in the deepest possible reverence by all Buddhists in whatever country (which in Thailand's case means something like 94 per cent of the total population). They lie at the very root of the Buddhist religion, because in paying homage to them, one is remembering the Buddha himself and his Enlightenment, the Dhamma or his Teaching of the Doctrine, and the Sangha or wise monks who listened and followed along the Path he showed them — and all other wise monks who have done so since.

One sees the Ratana-tri every time a monk or layman prostrates himself three times before the Buddha statue in a temple, or a householder does so before the statue in his own "hong phra" or Buddha-room at home.

One also sees it in the "wien tian" or "circulating the candle", which forms a part of major religious ceremonies, such as Visakha Pucha Day — the full-moon day in May which commemorates the birth, Enlightenment and death of the Buddha. The "wien tian" also occurs during the preordination ceremony of a new monk — although most of the other features of this ceremony are again of Brahmin origin.

Another Thai friend has given me some written details about "wien tian". "There are three candles in each candle-holder," she writes. "The three candles represent the Buddha, the Dhamma and the Sangha. Altogether three holders are used, and the "wien tian" is performed for three rounds — again for the Buddha, the Dhamma and the Sangha.

"In royal ceremonies," she continues, "five types of holders are used: glass, gold, silver, a gold-silver alloy, and copper. In provincial ceremonies they may use bronze, wood, banana-leaf and so on."

The Monkhood in Thailand

Life in Thailand today, as throughout the past, would be unthinkable without the Buddhist faith, and without the monkhood which is the cornerstone of that faith. The 250,000 or so quiet men in orange robes seen throughout the length and breadth of the land are an essential part of the inner fabric of Thai society at all levels, from the richest to the poorest, from the heart of the Metropolis to the remotest upcountry village.

Almost every aspect of daily life, and especially every ceremony, needs the presence of one or more Buddhist monks. While the monks themselves begin each new day at 3.30 a.m. their first encounter with the lay public is between 5.30 and 6.30 or 7 a.m. when they parade with their alms bowls on their "bintabat" or alms round, walking singly or in small groups along the streets and roads, lanes and footpaths among ordinary folks' homes.

For the layman or laywoman, the orange figures emerging out of the pre-dawn gloom in winter, or in the early morning sunshine (or rain!) at other times of the year, mean the chance to make merit by giving specially cooked food—nothing but the best. The householder first removes his or her shoes, and perhaps whispers some private wish, then puts the steaming-hot rice into the bowl which the monk uncovers by deftly removing the lid.

The monk or his "dek-wat" or temple attendant (usually a young lay boy living at the temple) also carries a "pinto" or stacked series of enamelled-metal or plastic containers into which the householder puts additional savoury dishes to be eaten with rice (nowadays these dishes are usually enclosed in transparent plastic bags) as well as dessert such as fruit or cake.

After this the householder makes an obeisance to the monk,

squatting down with the joined palms of his hands raised before his face in a "wai."

Millions of householders throughout the land make merit in this way regularly every morning; others do so once a week on their birth "day" (the day of the week on which they were born) or on "Wan phra" or holy days — the days of the full and new moon and the quarter and three-quarter-moon days in between. For his part the monk makes no gesture of recognition or thanks whatsoever. During the whole of the process of giving, he keeps his eyes fixed on his bowl, and never once looks at the householder. Nor does he replace the lid of his bowl too hastily after the rice has been put in, because that might imply that he didn't approve of its quality! After the "wai" the monk and the householder may perhaps exchange a few friendly words—especially if the monk happens to be the householder's son.

So, plying the streets and lanes in front of folks' dwellings early every morning, the monks play their essential part in Thai society by providing householders with the opportunity to make merit. And for the Westerner who temporarily or permanently enters the monkhood in Thailand, the daily alms round is a rich and moving experience.

Every monk walks barefoot, and at first the "tenderfoot" foreign monk may suffer a little from sharp stones; also, as the bowl is gradually filled with rice it may become a little heavy and hot against the body. But these are only minor discomforts, and one soon gets used to them.

But the early-morning "bintabat" is only one of innumerable opportunities for Thailand's society as a whole to make merit. A poor farmer or even poorer farm labourer may invite a solitary monk into his home in order to offer him a special, carefully prepared meal — and perhaps seek the monk's advice on some personal problem.

At the other extreme, there is a continued round of royal merit-making ceremonies in which Their Majesties the King and Queen and other members of the Royal Family take part — such as the casting of a new Buddha statue, or the raising of the "cho-fah" or gable-end of a new or restored temple, after which they make merit exactly as any other lay person does, by giving food to the officiating monks.

And never a day goes by somewhere in Bangkok and other

parts of the country without a ceremony which needs the presence of monks. Weddings and funerals are two of the more obvious examples.

Perhaps less so are cases such as the farm labourer's problem, which may be a serious one such as a tiny child who is somehow always sickly, never in really good health. In such a case the abbot or another monk from the local village temple may "adopt" the poorly child in a little ceremony which places the child's "kwan" or spirit under the kindly monk's care. Without ever leaving home, the child is usually cured and becomes as robust as his brothers and sisters.

No one would dream of laying the foundation stone or raising the corner-post of a new building without a formal ceremony involving chanting and blessing by monks — or at least one monk, but usually three, five or nine. (Nine monks is the most auspicious number).

The building may be a private house or a high-rise office block or hotel. And when the building is finished, and the family moves into its new home, or the luxury Chinese restaurant or new business quarters of an expanding company have their grand opening ceremony, once again the monks come and chant the words in ancient Pali, and bless the new premises by pouring holy water and anointing pillars and doors with fragrant paste; and once again, merit is made by offering the monks food afterwards.

Ceremonies such as these are always held during the earlier part of the moving, so that the monks' meal may be finished, without hurrying, before midday. After midday no monk may eat until after sunrise the following morning.

Close-cropped hair and betel-chewing

Why do so many elderly Thai women wear their hair short, close-cropped like a man's? And why are they forever chewing betel?

I will deal with one question at a time. As far as I know, there is no connection between the two. And I wish like to make it quite clear that I am by no means an expert on either of them! Although I have lived in Thailand for a good many years now, for some reason it never occurred to me to wonder why so many elderly women wear their hair very short. I think I more or less took it for granted that it was in order to keep cool. (Perhaps you thought that too!)

But it is just as hot and humid in other countries in the region, such as the Philippines; and elderly Filipina women certainly do not wear their hair short.

In fact, a Filipina friend drew my attention to this phenomenon as being peculiar to Thailand, and a Thai friend followed it up by quite casually mentioning the reason.

It is one of those things which every Thai takes for granted, but which Westerners (or this particular writer, at any rate) do not always get to know about.

I discovered that I already knew part of the story — or rather, a particular instance of it — without realising it was part of a general rule. So I will start by relating this particular instance, in the form I have known it for several years.

It happened in the reign of King Rama I, founder of Thailand's present Chakri Dynasty. It was towards the culmination of centuries of running wars against the Burmese; the year was 1785, three years after Rama I had come to the Throne; and the scene was the southern island of Phuket.

An invading Burmese army was on the way, and the Governor

of Thalang (the old name for Phuket) had just died. His widow, Khunying Jan, and her sister Mook had the task of defending the area. They resorted to a typical feminine ruse to confuse and frighten the enemy.

Rounding up all the local womenfolk, they made them cut their hair short to look like men, and dressed them up in soldiers' uniforms. Thousands of coconut-palm leaves were roasted over fires until they became blackened and curled, looking for all the world like the barrels of cannon. (There was only one real cannon in Phuket at the time.)

The mock "soldiers", brandishing their equally mock "cannon", were made to run in and out among the ranks of the real male soldiery of Phuket's rather small army and make as much noise as possible. In this way they managed to give the impression from a distance that the army was many times larger than its actual size, and positively bristling with guns and activity.

They also sneaked back into the town at night and marched out again next day, to give the impression that fresh men had been recruited.

Khunying Jan and her sister did other things too, and finally adopted a "scorched-earth" policy by having every scrap of food as well as all growing crops burnt, after which they gathered all the populace within the walls of the town in a state of siege. The Burmese army was faced with the choice of laying siege to the town and starving to death in the process, or retreating. Discretion proved the better part of valour, and they retreated. But there seems little doubt that the Burmese army's morale had already been severely weakened by the women's close-cropped hair and other male disguise, giving the Burmese the impression of being confronted by a vast army.

The grateful King Rama I bestowed new titles on both sisters. Khunying Jan became Thao Thepkasatree (Dame Goddess Lady) and her sister Mook was made Thao Srisunthorn (Dame Glorious Beauty). If you drive through Phuket province, you will see a modern statue commemorating these two Thai heroines at a crossroads in present-day Thalang District, a few miles before you reach Phuket Town. The story of these two sisters is firmly embedded in Thai history and is known to every Thai schoolchild.

This custom did not end at the time of the Phuket victory; it continued long afterwards. I would guess it continued until about 75 years ago. Since then the habit has slowly died out. More and more Thai women and girls started growing their hair long and silky, as we see it today.

Now for betel. You can still see plenty of elderly Thai woman with their teeth stained red from the continuous chewing of betel, especially in the rural areas.

The Thai word generally used for betel is "mahk" (spoken in a low tone, unlike the falling tone of "mahk" meaning "much"). Betel has always played a major part in Thai culture. "Mahk" is mentioned on the famous 13th-Century Sukhothai stone of King Ramkhamhaeng, said to be the earliest known example of written Thai in its present form.

And among the distinctions historically reserved for a "Chao Fah", the highest rank of Thai prince (the name means "Lord of Heaven" and is said to date back to the founding of the Kingdom of Ayutthaya in 1350 A.D.) were the fact that his betel tray and spittoon, both of them symbols of rank, were of gold with blue enamel; whereas lower ranks of prince had to make do with plain gold.

A common Thai expression for hard times or a period of scarcity is "khao yahk, mahk paeng" — "rice is hard to find, betel is expensive." This shows that rice and betel have long been considered equally fundamental to the lives of the people.

A rather more light-hearted expression is "jaek mahk," literally "to hand out betel" — in other words, to punch someone in the mouth and draw blood, giving them a red mouth like that of a betel-chewer. (The other half of this saying is "jaek waen", "to hand out spectacles" — that is, to give someone a black eye!)

"Mahk" has traditionally always played an important part in rural courtship and betrothal. A young man who wants to woo a fair maid tears off a piece of betel leaf and throws it playfully at her. (Actually, the leaf he throws is called "bai plu"; I will explain this later on.)

And, far be it from me to want to get mixed up in Women's Lib — but I must now point out that in Thailand it is the *groom* who brings the *bride* a dowry.

This is unlike other countries such as India, for instance, where the woman gives the dowry to the man; and in case some readers are confused about the meaning of "dowry" as I was, the Oxford English Dictionary calls it "portion *woman* brings to her *husband*." There's probably a moral somewhere here for Thailand's Women's Libbers, but as I said, I refuse to get involved in it! (Anyway, I seem to have been giving my own wife, Laddawan, vast amounts of dowry ever since we got married, but she calls it housekeeping money.)

The point of all this is that before a traditional Thai engagement ceremony, the groom goes in procession to the bride's house to bring the bride her dowry; and an essential part of this dowry is the "kan mahk" or ornamental bowl containing betel as well as the dowry money. My Thai-English dictionary says "kan mahk" also stands for the settlement demanded of the groom's parents by the bride's parents before marriage.

In fact, the engagement procession includes more than one "kan mahk;" the main one is called "kan ek" and it is followed by a second one, "kan toh." An old song is sometimes crooned plaintively by a forlorn bride to her reluctant groom who has failed to show up for the ceremony: "Eek ghee wan kan mahk ja ma?" ("In how many more days' time will the betel-bowl come?"—that is, "When will you come?") The song goes on, "Mai kan mahk!" ("I'm a betel-bowl widow!")

The "kan" or bowl carried in the procession rests on an equally decorative circular pedestal called a "pahn." Such sets of "kan" and "pahn" are an essential item in almost every Thai household. Each region of Thailand has its own style of "kan mahk," as does each level of society; a rich family will probably have a silver set, a poor one a wooden set or even one made from a coconut shell. Earlier I mentioned "bai plu," the leaf out of which the suitor tears a piece and which he then throws at the girl of his fancy. Now I had better go into some botanical detail, as I feel sure some readers are wondering why I have been calling it "betel" all along, and not "betel-*nut*".

The reason is that it is not "betel-nut." The Thai-English dictionary translates "mahk" as: *"The areca palm; areca nuts and betel leaves* smeared with lime, chewed like chewing gum." A very good description of the rather complex mixture of ingredients that is in fact chewed, and which I'll describe in a minute.

The areca nut and these other ingredients are placed on a leaf called "bai plu" or simply "plu" ("bai" means "leaf") which is then rolled, and the whole thing is popped in the mouth. The dictionary translates "bai plu" as *betel leaves*; the betel pepper, *Piper betel.*

The Oxford English Dictionary supports these definitions. It says: "Betel: Leaf of *Piper betel,* which Indians chew with areca nut parings; *hence by mistake:* betel-*nut,* the areca nut." So when we talk about "chewing betel-nut," strictly speaking we are not quite correct. For areca, Oxford says: "*Areca;* kinds of palms; areca-nut, astringent seed of a species of areca. (Portuguese, from a Tamil word meaning 'close-clustering nut')."

Indeed, the areca nut does grow plentifully in Thailand in clusters on a species of palm tree. But from a Thai friend's description, I wonder why it is called a "nut," for she says it isn't hard at all. It sounds more like a fruit. Here is her description of it and its preparation.

For best chewability, it must be picked at exactly the right age — while it is still green, or else the flavour will be too strong. The fruit is one or two inches in diameter. Preparing it is an art which must be learnt by anyone who chews betel.

First it must be cut lengthwise, either into quarters or into six equal segments. From each piece the hard outer husk is removed along about three-quarters of the length, and the green peel is cut into segments which are bent gently outwards away from the fruit. This reveals the inner flesh which is salmon-pink. It is this that forms the "nut" that is chewed; there is no stone or seed inside.

A large heart-shaped "bai plu" leaf is chosen, about six or eight inches across. The stalk is cut off, and the peeled areca nut is placed on the leaf together with red lime ("bpoon"), strong chewing-tobacco called "ya choon," and occasionally a leaf of "si-siad," which the dictionary translates "cutch, *Acacia catechu*" (neither of which I can find in the Oxford English Dictionary). Then the "bai plu" leaf with all its contents is rolled up and popped into the mouth. The "bai plu" has an astringent taste.

Why is betel chewed?

I asked another colleague to help me by "interviewing" her 75-year-old mother-in-law who lives in Petchaburi Province and is a confirmed betel-chewer. Here are the results:

Q: Why do you chew betel?

A: To pass the time, and sweeten the breath. It's also "aroy"— pleasant to taste — and although you only chew t little by little, you become addicted, and can't stop.

Q: How long do you chew each mouthful?

A: About five minutes. Then I spit is out and mix a fresh lot.

Q: How much does it cost you?

A: About two baht a day. (But that was long ago.)

Q: So how often do you chew it every day?

A: Whenever I feel like it — say 10 times a day.

Q: Does it harm the teeth?

A: No, but some older women with bad teeth put everything into a special kind of mortar first, and pound it up to make it softer.

Q: Can you remove the red stain from the teeth?

A: Yes — we use a special kind of liquid called "ya ploy see" ("medicine to remove the colour") and clean the teeth with a dried areca husk.

Q: How old were you when you started chewing betel?

A: About 40 — and I'm still chewing away!

Q: How does one carry all those ingredients around with one?

A: In a basket, a cloth bag, a box, or sometimes even a leather bag.

Q: Do more women than men chew it?

A: Oh, yes — lots and lots of women.

So that briefly is what betel chewing is all about. In the 1940s, when Field Marshal Pibulsongkram was prime minister, he tried to abolish it by making it illegal. This was part of his overall ""modernisation" drive which included the compulsory wearing of hats and Western-style trousers and shirts for men instead of the traditional "pa-kao-ma." The trousers and shirt have remained but not the hats. As for betel-chewing ... Well, I suppose the truth is that you cannot keep a pleasant and apparently harmless habit down for ever!

Now that I've described the cutting and removal of the areca peel and the folding of the betel-leaf on which it is placed, I must expand on what my other friend told me: She said that the cutting and folding of the areca and betel for placing in the ceremonial "kan mahk" as part of an engagement ceremony is quite an art, like flower arrangement or garland-making, and one must be specially trained to be able to arrange a "kan mahk" properly.

She also mentioned in passing that "mahk" is used as a mordant in dyeing, to make the dye stick to the cloth.

Let me end as I began, by stressing the great importance of "mahk," or areca-plus-betel, in Thai culture. In "Esahn" or Northeastern Thailand, "mahk" has traditionally held the broader meaning of "fruit" in general. Over the centuries this became shortened to "ma" elsewhere in Thailand, and this now forms the prefix for some 40 plants with edible fruit or leaves — including such well-known names as "ma-muang," mango; "malagor," papaya; "maprao," coconut; "ma-keua," egg-plant; "makeua-tet," tomato, and "makok," the hog plum, from which came the name "Bang-makok," Hog-plum village, later shortened to "Bangkok."

Songkran in the old days

Some 60 or more years ago, it seems, the Songkran festival was celebrated in much more robust fashion than today, as has been wittily described by M.R. Kukrit Pramoj in some amusing recollections of his childhood days.

In those days, strictly speaking there was no New Year celebration as such. The official New Year's Day, on which the year changed from, say, B.E. (Buddhist Era) 2462 (AD 1919) to B.E. 2463, was April 1; but that day was not celebrated. All celebrations took place on "Wan Trut," which means "the day for saying goodbye to the old year", and on Songkran Day, which marks the welcoming of the new year.

Songkran falls in the middle of the fifth lunar month (that is, in April) when the Sun is in Aries; but Trut comes at the end of the fourth (or beginning of the fifth) month. So there are several days in between.

But as far as the people were concerned, they didn't pay too much attention to these technicalities. The entire period was simply regarded as an occasion for stopping work, merry-making, being more kind than usual to one's fellow creatures, and generally having a good time. "Sanuk", that wonderful Thai word for which "enjoyment" is just a pale echo, was the key idea.

The Trut period always began with a great deal of "tam boon" or merit-making. Everyone in every home went to the local temple to offer food to the monks. This was done on a truly lavish scale—not just ordinary trayfuls of food, but complete "hahps" (pairs of large baskets slung from shoulderpoles such as street vendors use), one pair of baskets filled with the main course plus rice, and another pair with dessert. M.R. Kukrit remembers walking to the "sala parien" or sermon hall at the temple along a path made sopping wet and slippery by food spilt out from the baskets.

In those days a typical large compound would have a lot of servants, all with families and hordes of children. Another big feature was the flinging of coins from a "kan" or bathing-bowl from an upstairs window down into the compound. In even earlier times the coins used to be put inside limes (rather as the traditional threepenny piece was put inside the English Christmas pudding), but this custom had been abandoned as a waste of time (and lime?). The coins flung down were the "ath" (one-sixty-fourth of a baht), the "los," one-satang, five satang and 10-satang pieces. A "saleung" or 25-satang piece was considered too valuable to give away.

Scrambling and fighting for the coins was all part of the "sanuk." The younger children spent all their time dashing from house to house to capture the scattered coins, enjoying themselves so much that they never noticed the bruises and scratches they accumulated from being almost trampled underfoot by the older ones.

The favourite way of spending the few days' holiday between "Wan Trut" (the end of the old year) and Songkran (the start of the new) was gambling. In even earlier days there had been many different games of chance, but the Government had stopped all of them except cards, and even for these a permit was needed.

So at Trut-time there were card games in practically every household. Everyone was dragged into the game and in each house there would be several games going on at once, with perhaps seven or eight players in each game. The games lasted not for hours but for days on end—anything from three to five days and nights non-stop.

This form of "sanuk" was taken very seriously indeed. Players took only the briefest time off to eat, sleep, or go to the restroom, and even then they'd ask a friend to sit in for them at the game. No one took a bath—it wasted too much valuable time! Most people just called for a bowl of water to wash their faces.

Although there was plenty of liquor circulating, there was hardly ever any trouble with drunkenness because everyone was so intent on the game. There was lots of food, too— more then enough for all the players, spectators, and children who were forever hanging around waiting for the chance of a "handout" or gift from winning players. There was usually a light meal in the afternoon, followed by rice soup late at night. The householder in whose home the games took place collected a small percentage of the winnings to help pay for all this food, but such "levies" were usually very small because the whole idea was for the householder to offer hospitality to his friends.

Card-playing in those days wasn't just for the purpose of winning money, but was a genuine social occasion. There was a good deal of chit-chat, banter and raucous laughter — it was a really happy time, especially for the children, who were allowed to stay up as late as they liked without being chased off to bed.

The cards, by the way, were the long narrow packs of 120 cards used in Thailand's most popular card game, "poi tong." This is not unlike whist or rummy, with the winner being the player holding the highest number of "tong" or tricks of three cards.

The card games provided a rare and subtle way for a young man to win a young lady's heart. He would carefully arrange things so that he was sitting in such a position that he had to play his own card immediately before the girl played hers; for what could endear him more to her than when he placed the winning card ready for her to play!

Besides card games, people upcountry played many other games in the evening at Songkran-time, and often well into the night, by which time the games usually turned into singing and dancing.

When trying to visualise those bygone festival-times, an important thing to remember is that there was no electricity! Not only did this mean there were no lights; there were also no neon signs—and no microphones or loudspeakers! Whatever took place in the way of communal games and dancing had to be within the small circle of light cast by a lamp or bonfire, and within earshot of the singing.

In the old days people hadn't yet recovered from the effects of "Trut" by the time Songkran began. During Songkran the merit-making which had begun during "Trut" continued, but on a somewhat smaller scale, with the releasing of birds and fish, as is done today.

In those days, curiously enough, there was no water-throwing, with which Songkran is associated in most people's minds today. This was a Burmese tradition which had originally come from India, where red powder was thrown. From Burma the water-throwing custom reached Chiang Mai, but at that time there was no rail connection between Chiang Mai and Bangkok, and therefore little communication between the two cities. So Bangkok folk had little or no contact with those Chiang Mai and their customs — hence water-throwing was unknown in Bangkok.

However, young people used to take a "panung" and a shawl and some perfumed water, and visit respected elders over the age of 60. Having entered the elders' house and performed the graceful and respectful prostration still know as the "grahp," they poured the perfumed water over the elders' hands and then presented the two pieces of cloth. The elders then blessed the young visitors.

The general feeling seemed to be that "Trut", being the end of the old year, meant the casting away of everything—especially one's inhibitions! So the public mood was very free and easy. Songkran, on the other hand, was the start of a new year, and when one starts something, one must be less carefree. (It all sounds rather like New Year resolutions in the West, doesn't it? And some of those last longer than others...)

As is still done by many people today, the first duty at Songkran-time in those days was the annual spring-cleaning of one's house. The idea was to start the new year with a clean slate. Songkran was also a special time for making merit on behalf of one's ancestors. If the ancestral ashes were at home, they would be brought out for the ceremony of "rot nam Songkran" or pouring the Songkran water.

This included pouring water over the tip of one's finger into a bowl as is done today after a Buddhist religious ceremony, while making a wish or reciting a special prayer. The water in the bowl was later poured onto the ground (as it still is) near the base of a large tree.

Families whose ancestors' relics were kept inside a chedi or pagoda at a temple would make merit at that temple, and would take the opportunity at the same time to clean up and repair the chedi. This was also part of the Songkran "spring cleaning" tradition.

On Songkran Day, monks would be invited to one's house in

the evening to "suat mon" or chant mantras as they still do today. (The Thai word "mon" comes from the Sanskrit "mantra"). In the morning, writes M.R. Kukrit, we would offer food to the monks and then give them new robes, also on behalf of our ancestors. In some households everything was done on the same day — chanting, offering food for the 11 a.m. meal followed by the giving of the robes.

The robe-giving was a way of repaying our ancestors for all they had done for us. Merit-making on behalf of the dead was supposed to bring "siri mongkol" or good fortune to the house for the whole year, because at the same time the monks would sprinkle holy water on the house and everyone in it.

In those far-off days there was a well known but strange phenomenon every year at Songkran-time. This was the mysterious appearance of a certain kind of creature, known for want of a better name as "the Songkran creature".
They were in fact a kind of worm, and appeared in hundreds of thousands in rivers and klongs throughout the Kingdom. They were about the size of "khanom jeen" — the thin white noodles made of boiled rice flour which are such a common feature of Thai cuisine.

The only thing was, they weren't white; they were all the colours of the rainbow. The huge shoals consisted of individual worms in a great variety of bright colours — yellow, red green, blue, purple and so on. Incessantly wriggling, the heaving mass of "Songkran creatures" produced a vibrating spectrum of colour not unlike the effect of a Van Gogh painting.

But the strange and inexplicable fact was that if you took them out of the river or klong and put them in a bucket of water, the brilliant colours immediately vanished and they looked like perfectly ordinary black worms.

At night during the Songkran period there was also a regular and terrifying occurrence — the intermittent firing of deafeningly loud cannon. This was known as "ying peun atana". M.R. Kukrit wryly remarks that it was not unlike the late-night horror movies shown on television today.

The cannon-firing was connected with the special Songkran prayer meetings which used to be held in the Grand Palace. The chanting began in the evening and went on all night. The purpose of the prayer meetings was to bless the Thai Kingdom and bring happiness and prosperity to the whole country. The prayers, or more correctly chants, recalled the merits of the Buddha and called on the Lords of the Four Worlds to confer happiness and prosperity on the nation.

After the monks had finished chanting, several cannon fired simultaneously, each one several times. They made a really fearful din. It might not have been so bad during daytime — but, like all loud noises, they sounded a great deal louder at night!

Most people believed the cannon were fired for the purpose of driving ghosts out of the city, which at that time was clustered in the area around the Grand Palace. On the night when the monks chanted, many people became very scared of ghosts, believing the latter would be disturbed by the cannon and by the chanting, and would therefore be dashing about all over the place. Children and, indeed, anyone with weak nerves, would pull their blankets over their heads and quake with fear every time the cannon went off. (Perhaps you get the same feeling whenever a loud thunderclap directly overhead sets all the cutlery and glassware in the house jangling, as well as your nerves; I certainly do!)

Ghosts include the spirits of one's own ancestors and, during the cannon-firing, most people were particularly worried about the welfare of such spirits. They were afraid their late loved ones might injure themselves while running from the noise of the cannon. So people built special kinds of first-aid stations beforehand in the compounds of their houses at particular spots where it was believed the ancestral spirits might pass by.

The first-aid stations took the form of a branch usually cut from a "dton makahm" or tamarind tree. The branch was stuck in a plant-pot or sometimes directly in the ground. M.R. Kukrit describes how they used to tie "khao pohk", cones made from banana leaves filled with cooked white rice and small bamboo containers filled with water, on the branches. On the plant-pot or on the ground, they placed banana leaves containing "kap khao" — the various Thai dishes normally eaten with rice — and dessert. So when the spirits of their ancestors arrived, tired after running away from those dreadful cannon, they would stop, eat, drink and rest awhile until they had regained enough strength to rush off again the next time the cannon roared.

Some turmeric and red lime paste (the kind chewed with betel) was also left so that, when the spirits arrived with elbows and knees bleeding from stumbling and falling over in the dark, they could treat their own wounds with the mixture. Strips of cloth were also hung on the branches for the spirits to use as bandages.

...Just think, muses M.R. Kukrit, summing up these recollections of his childhood Songkrans — how kind-hearted the oldtime Thais used to be! They were really lovable. Having been born a Thai, he adds, and having lived in Thailand and loved his country for 65 years (that was written a few years ago) he knows that even after he dies people will still worry about his welfare.

How dates are reckoned

I'd been trying to find out the answers to two questions:

(1) Why does the FIRST lunar month ("deuan ai" in Thai) start in DECEMBER, and not in APRIL, which is the start of the old Thai new year? (April 1 was the official start, but I believe in even earlier times the New Year began around the middle of the month — not always on April 13 which is Songkran Day, but round about that date; the astrological "jor sor" years still do so today).

(2) Why did upcountry Thai folk as recently as 30 years ago (and maybe even today) reckon dates by "wan phra" (Buddhist holy days) which follow the phases of the moon, when there was (and of course still is) a perfectly good seven-day week dating back to the Buddha's time and probably before?

For the benefit of non-astrologers, let me explain a bit more. The first question doesn't need much explaining, really; it's simply that I've always thought it strange that the old Thai new year should start in the FIFTH lunar month, and not, as might be expected, with the FIRST lunar month!

The second question comes from what my wife has told me about her own childhood upcountry where she was brought up by her grandmother.

In those days neither she nor her grandmother nor anyone else paid any attention to the ordinary days of the week — Sunday, Monday and so on. Every day was reckoned by the phases of the moon; days were known as "the 10th day of the waxing moon of the second (lunar) month," "the third day of the waning moon of the seventh month,"; and so on. (And if the year was mentioned, it was according to the 12-year cycle — the Year of the Tiger, Horse, Goat or whatever).

A child's birth was written down in this way and it was then converted to the day of the week, date of the calendar month and year of the Buddhist Era (equal to A.D. plus 543). This was done presumably so that the birth could be registered at the amphoe office.

The even-numbered lunar months have 30 days — 15 days of the waxing moon, the15th day being full moon, followed by 15 days of waning moon; the odd-numbered months have 29 days, with only 14 days' waning moon. The Buddhist "wan phra" or holy days fall on the eighth and 15th waxing-moon days of every month, and on the eighth and 15th or 14th days of the waning moon depending on whether the month is even or odd.

My wife says that every "wan phra" was a school holiday, and there were also occasional holidays on the day before "wan phra", known as "wan goan" because it's the day on which monks shave their heads afresh. — (She can't remember which "wan goan" were school holidays and which weren't).

So in upcountry Thailand life revolved round the phases of the moon because it was geared to the tempo of the"wan phra" days on which merit was made. And in parts of Thailand, as I said, I think this is still true today.

The day of the full moon, "wan phra" in Thai, is a special day on which fall important festivals, Buddhist and secular. In the third month (February) there's Makha Bucha, commemorating the day on which 1,250 disciples independently and miraculously visited the Lord Buddha. In the sixth month (May), Visakha Bucha or Wesak is the day on which the Buddha was born, attained Enlightenment, and died. Assalha Bucha in the eighth month (July), on which he preached his first Discourse in the deer park at Varanasi (Banares), which is also the day before "wan khao phansa," the first day of the Buddhist Lent. "Wan ork phansa" or the end of Lent, in the 11th month (October); and Loy Krathong, the predominantly Brahmin festival of lights and water in the 12th month (November).

And yet... There remain those seven days of the week which seem to have been used since the earliest times and which bear absolutely no relation to "Wan phra" or the phases of the moon.

These days of the week were known not only to the ancients in more western parts of the world but also since very early times in Thailand.

At least three separate phenomena show this: The wearing of

"colours of the day" — red for Sunday, cream for Monday, pink for Tuesday and so on — by former Thai kings and other commanders-in-chief when going into battle; and the even earlier association of the days of the week with Buddhism evidenced by traditional styles and attitudes in Buddha statues dating from very early times and assigned to specific days of the week,

Sunday's attitude is known as "tawai netr" ("give eyes"); Monday's, "hahm samut" ("forbid the ocean"); Tuesday's, "saiyat" ("reclining"). The latter is possibly because an ancient Pali text states that the Buddha died and attained Parinibbana or Nirvana on a Tuesday. For Wednesday, "oombaht" ("holding the bowl"); for Thursday, "nang samathi" ("sitting in meditation"); Friday, "rampeung" ("pondering"); and Saturday, "nahk prok" ("with a naga or seven-headed serpent over his head").

But I said THREE separate phenomena, didn't I? The third one is a simple Thai word, "sapdah". It means "a week," and it comes from the Sanskrit "saptar" meaning seven. ("Saptar" came from the same Indo-European root as the Latin "Septem" and the English "seven").

Then I received a telephone call from my friend M.R. Ayumongol Sonakul, who pointed out what I should have realised; Songkran or the ancient New Year has to do with the SUN, not the Moon; it marks the transition of the Sun from the Zodiac Sign of Aries into that of Taurus ("Rasi Meen" to "Rasi Mayt" in Thai).

The lunar months are concerned with the MOON, of course — they have nothing whatever to do with the Sun.

Now I shall describe the connection between the names of the days of the week in Thai, English and other European languages. I've made a table, which shows several interesting things. The direct derivation of the Thai names from the Sanskrit is very obvious, with the possible exception of Saturday.

In Latin, Sunday has become the Christian "Lord's Day," while the modern Italian, Spanish and French names for Sunday are in turn derived from the Latin; but in English the name has kept to that of the Sun.

The English name "Saturday" comes directly from the Roman god Saturn, after which the planet Saturn was also named. But the German, French, Italian and Spanish names for Saturday come from the Latin "Sabbatum," which came via Greek from the Hebrew "Shabbat", the ancient Jewish Sabbath Day which is still the weekly rest-day in Israel.

Monday is "Moon Day" in all the languages shown in the table.

The names of the other four days in the "Latin" languages come from the Roman gods Mars, Mercury, Jupiter and Venus; names also given to the five planets (including Saturn) known to mankind since Babylonian (or Ban Chieng) times. Mars was the god of war; Mercury, the god of eloquence and commerce (a good salesman, evidently!); Jupiter, king of the gods; Venus, goddess of love; and Saturn, the god of agriculture.

And so to the most important point of all. The THAI names for all seven days of the week are also the Thai names for the Sun, Moon and the *same* Planets, day for day, as the WESTERN ones. Why?

For the answer, we must go back to the earliest civilisations. To the ancients, the Sun, Moon and five known Planets WERE gods.

Says the Encyclopaedia Britannica, "When one gazes at the planet Mars glowing in the sky like a red danger signal, it is easy to understand why the ancient people identified this object with the god of war — the Romans with Mars, the Greeks with Ares."

And, the writer might have added, the people of ancient India with the Sanskrit Mangal. For thousands of years, then, the Sun, Moon and these five Planets have been associated with the same set of gods.

The NAMES of these planet-gods changed from culture to culture, from language to language; Mercury, for instance, was Hermes to the Greeks.

The early people known as Aryans or Indo-Europeans split into two broad groups, one group migrating westward to form the civilisations of ancient Greece and Rome, while the other moved eastward to the Indian subcontinent. Each group evolved their own names for the same planet-gods. But ancient cultural interchange between East and West, especially through Indian astrology, ensured that no matter what names they were given, the Sun, Moon and five planet gods remained attached to the same days of the week in both East and West. And that's why the Thai names for the days of the week are also those of the

Sun, Moon and the same five planet-gods as in the west.

The Thai word for Friday incidentally, is "wan sook." The "sook" has the same sound as the Thai word for "happiness" (though it's spelt differently). So, for Thai people. Friday is the day of happiness...

And most Westerners, too, feel happy on Friday... It'll soon be the weekend!

P.S. Ayumongol followed up his phone call with a letter: "There seem to have been two rival calendars going, rather like a House of Representatives and a Senate, from time immemorial.

"The moon is of course easy to watch, because it gets pregnant and aborts itself with the regularity of the 8 p.m. TV restarting time.

The sun, on the other hand, fools us by going up and down each day but does funny things behind our back throughout the 365-day cycle.

"The funny thing the sun does is to arrange the seasons, which even the most moonmad farmer must have noticed, since he was after all trying to plant his crops for a living as well as study moon and mythology.

"The astrologers also had to depend on the sun. So in fact we have really held two different calendars simultaneously.

"On moon calendars, Siam Rath and a few dailies still publish the lunar date on their back page every day. All the dailies used to, but some seem to have dropped it, which is a pity because it was something of a tradition with the Thai-language papers."

DAY	THAI NAME	SANSKRIT	LITERAL TRANSLATION OF THAI AND SANSKRIT	LATE LATIN	MODERN ITALIAN	MODERN SPANISH	MODERN FRENCH
Sunday	Wan athit	Aditya war	Sun Day	Dominicus Dies (Lord's Day) or Solis Dies	Domenica	Domingo	Dimanche
Monday	Wan jan	Chandra war	Moon Day	Lunae Dies	Lunedi	Lunes	Lundi
Tuesday	Wan angkaan	Mangal war	Mars Day	Martis Dies	Martedi	Martes	Mardi
Wednesday	Wan put	Budh war	Mercury Day	Mercurii Dies	Mercoledi	Miercoles	Mercredi
Thursday	Wan pareuhat	Vrihaspati war	Jupiter Day	Jovis Dies	Giovedi	Jueves	Jeudi
Friday	Wan sook	Shukra war	Venus Day	Veneris Dies	Venerdi	Viernes	Vendredi
Saturday	Wan sao	Shani war	Saturn Day	Saturni Dies	Sabbato	Sabado	Samedi

Magic from the mouth of the pot

I was once at a small farewell party for some visitors from a nearby Asian country, at which a charming young lady in a yellow classical Thai costume with orchid petals in her hair was demonstrating her Thai culinary magic. Water was boiling in two metal pots on twin gas burners in front of her. I asked a Thai friend the name of the little delicacies she was preparing so deftly.

"WHAT?" he said. "Do you mean to say you've never seen *khao kriab pak mor* being made before?" Feeling a bit foolish, I admitted that I hadn't.

Of course I know what "khao kriab" are. They're those delicious pale-pink, crispy shrimp-flavoured things which I munch at parties until I'm so full I can't eat the buffet dinner. But these were quite different.

Let's take a look in the dictionary. "KHAO KRIAB": thin slices of rice flour crisped over an open fire, there being several varieties..." which are then described — but there's no mention of "khao kriab pak mor." "Pak mor" means "mouth of the pot," and these dainties were neither crisp nor prepared over an open fire.

Briefly, the operation was as follows. The young lady scooped out a ladleful of liquid rice-flour paste (a suspension of fine rice-flour particles in water) from a large bowl, and spread it out thinly on the cotton muslin stretched across the top of the right-hand pot.

She then removed a conical metal cap from the left-hand pot and placed it over the right-hand pot, rather like a conjuror about to produce a rabbit.

After completing her magic on the left-hand pot (as I'll describe in a moment for the right-hand pot) she removed the conical cap and replaced it on the left-hand pot. And, hey presto! What had been liquid was now semi-solid — a transparent, wafer-thin pancake on the stretched muslin.

The young lady put a dab of filling in the centre of this "pancake" — a mixture of minced pork, sugar and peanuts — and then took a flat wooden spatula with which, in the lightest and most delicate fashion, she scraped up the thin, fragile "pancake" and folded it over the filling. She then placed the completed morsel on a tray with the ones she'd already made.

And so it went on, alternating from the left-hand to the right-hand pot and back.

(A Thai friend tells me this process is usually done with earthenware pots, and the conical cap is made not of metal but of "bai toey" or screwpine leaves.)

Now, many years ago I graduated in Physics from London University. So I ought to be able to explain just why that film of liquid becomes solid, oughtn't I?

I asked various people, all of whom seemed to take the process for granted — as did the smiling young lady magician herself. "It's the heat," was the usual answer.

But... Surely the steam inside the airtight conical cap would build up pressure, which would tend to PREVENT the water in the rice-flour paste from evaporating?

Could it be that the muslin was acting as a filter, and the water was escaping downwards into the pot, allowing the heat to coagulate (or bake?) the powder into a solid film? "Yes, that's right," said someone else to whom I put this suggestion.

I suspect it's really a combination of both processes — evaporation and filtration. (If any technically-minded readers are wondering how on earth I ever got that Physics degree, the answer is "No comment".) As I write this, another Thai friend tells me "It's just the same as poaching an egg."

But looking more closely, I saw that the cotton muslin stretched over both pots had a hole in it. At first I thought this was just due to wear and tear, but I now believe these holes play some mysterious fundamental part in the solidifying process.

Anyway, I was invited to have a try at scraping up the flimsy "pancake" with the wooden spatula. It was extremely difficult, and my hamfisted attempts caused much uncalled-for mirth...

As I took my hand away, my forefinger accidentally passed

just above the hole in the muslin, and was struck by an invisible jet of steam. At first I thought I'd received a second-degree burn: but the pain soon wore off, and I remained there gawking at the young lady's practised magic, and wondering how it worked...

Cloth design and weaving in Northeast Thailand

I have very kindly been given permission to make use of a fascinating little book which came into my hands a few years ago, called "Esarn cloth design." The author is a young lady named Vimolphan Peetathawatchai, herself a native of a village in the Northeast. The text has been ably translated into English by Mom Rachawongse Poutrie Viravaidya, and the book, partly in Thai and partly in English, was published in 1973 by the Faculty of Education of Khon Kaen University, with financial support from the Ford Foundation. To all of them I would like to say " thank you" for this opportunity of giving readers a glimpse of life in the Northeast, even if only at second hand. The book is dedicated to her late Serene Highness Princess Vibhavadi Rangsit.

In her preface the author states: "...I feel elated because I have done something worthy of being born in the Northeast... I am used to the rural life with its dependence on nature... I have never forgotten the rice paddies at sunset, the boys with their buffaloes, the soft lullabies from distant huts, the fishermen, the women at their looms, and the porches filled with youngsters surrounding their elders telling their fascinating folk tales under the light of the full moon..."

In the Northeast, weaving is traditionally considered a woman's task, and the village women use their free time after the rice harvesting to weave cloth for household use or for presentation to monks at various Buddhist temple ceremonies. The designs of the cloth for household use are based on patterns found in nature, and the exquisite handiwork is seen in such everyday articles as pillows (of the rather hard, square shape typical of the region), mosquito nets, blankets, pasins (women's ankle-length skirts), pakao-ma (men's loincloths) and pasarongs (men's ankle-length skirts.)

Silkworm breeding and cotton planting begin in May or June, and after the rice has been harvested in January a traditional ceremony called "Long Kuang" is held to usher in the weaving season. This ceremony is usually held on a fullmoon night, when villagers gather to spin cotton into yarn. During the afternoon of the auspicious day young girls gather fuel and after the evening meal they assemble near a tree or in the compound of a house to build a bonfire. In some villages the bonfire is made on a mound of earth in the middle of a special wooden platform one or two feet high.

Sitting around the bonfire the village women spin, spin, spin... Stopping every now and then to chat, warm themselves (yes, it's cold in the Northeast in winter) and eat roasted tamarind pips. Meanwhile the young men take the opportunity to "len sao" or court the unattached girls or the girl of their choice. The courting dialogue is in picturesque rhythmic prose, producing a pleasing effect on the listener. In English, the dialogue goes something like this:

YOUNG MAN: I would like to ask you about the fish, about the fields, about the rice. I would like to ask you whether you already have a husband or perhaps a lover?

GIRL: My answer is that I am as pure and fresh as a newly cloven banana leaf. Ever since I grew up I have never had a suitor to court me and I may be compared to a young sapling free from encircling vines. But I wonder whether you have entanglements like a tree entwined by vines.

YOUNG MAN: If your answer is that you have no suitor, then it is our great fortune, for I would like nothing better than to have you as my loving wife, to be by my side.

GIRL: I have always spoken the truth and never been a coquette. In all sincerity, I have never tried to deceive anyone.

There is also a lullaby sung by widows to send their children to sleep so that they can attend the spinning ceremony. The words seem to indicate that folk in the Northeast are pretty much the same as other humans the world over:

Sleep, my child, while I sing to you.

Sleep in this cradle while I rock you.
I will go and spin yarn under the full moon and talk with the young men.
I will find you a step-father to care for you until you are fully grown.
Your uncles and aunts, your father's relatives, have deserted us.
Although we are neighbours, we are ignored.
They eat "pla beuk" (a nearly extinct Mekong River fish) the size of a ship's stern,
but not a morsel will they share.
they eat "pla seua" (a fish with stripes like a tiger) the size of an elephant's head,
but not a morsel will they give.
All we receive are the tiny "pla khao" (white fish) which the villagers give as alms.
The sky is lonely and vast with the stars and moon.
Oh, who will cut grass to thatch the roof so you will live to care for me when I am old?

The Northeasterners plant cotton in May or June, and by November the bolls of the common type known as "fai noi" are ripe for picking. While the bolls are left to wither on the plants, the cotton is dried in the sun for four or five days and then ginned in a "heeb fai" or roller gin to separate the cotton from the seed, a process called "eew." The tangled cotton fibres are then put into a "gradong," a round flat shallow winnowing basket woven from strips of bamboo, for carding. This is done with a device rather like a hunting bow; the bow-string is plucked rapidly to make it vibrate sharply against the mass of cotton so as to fluff up the fibres. The cotton is then rolled round a wooden dowel, resulting in long, cigarette-like tufts to be spun into yarn.

Spinning is done by placing one of these long tufts on the spindle and turning the hand wheel to rotate the spindle and the attached cotton. The fingers of the free hand are used to pluck and pull a few fingers from the revolving mass. The quick rotation of the spindle twists the fibres and picks up other fibres to form a continuous thread of yarn, which is then taken off the spindle and put onto a "bpia" or stick with capped ends, about a yard long, before dyeing the yarn. After dyeing, the yarn is wound round a "gwag" or one-foot-long takraw-shaped rattan spool and then wound onto bobbins.

For the dyeing of both cotton and silk the Northeasterners have traditionally used natural dyes derived from roots, berries, insects and the soil. The lac insect gives a reddish colour, the Indigo plant provides blue; black comes from the "grajai" berry, yellow from the "talaeng" root and green is made by dipping cloth already dyed in indigo into a "talaeng" solution.

The lac insect, its droppings and nest are collectively known as "kee krang". This is a popular source of dye as the insect colonies are very plentiful In the Northeast. The "kee krang" is dried In the sun and ground in a mortar and the resulting powder is soaked in a tamarind paste and water solution in an earthen pot for a day and then put on the fire to boil. The cotton or silk yarn previously soaked is then immersed in the boiling liquid for 30 minutes before being rinsed and hung to dry.

Indigo plants are about a metre high with leaves like the tamarind. They are usually specially grown in rice paddies or orchards because the wild indigo gives poor colouring. When mature, the indigo plants are cut down made into bundles and packed in an earthen jar filled with water for three days, after which they are thrown away. In the meantime the villagers gather snails which are burnt with the bark of the "pleuang" tree; special shells are also wrapped in banana leaves or put in earthen jars to calcify into lime.

When ready, the lime is mixed with the indigo-water in special proportions, and after the sediment has settled the water is carefully decanted into another vessel where it is mixed with ashes of the Cassia Siamea tree. Again the sediment is allowed to settle, and the solution is drained into an earthen pot and put on the fire. Three pulverised chunks of sugar cane, three crushed carambola fruits and the indigo residue are stirred into the solution and well mixed, and the yarn is then dipped until the desired colour is reached.

It all sounds very scientific and involved... Or is it rather like a witches' brew? At any rate, the ingenious and hardworking villagers of the Northeast have discovered successful and effective ways of using local natural products to make the vivid colours which they weave into beautiful designs in cotton and silk.

As I mentioned, black dye is produced from berries of the

"grajai", a tall tree which grows in the forest of Northeast Thailand. The crushed berries are soaked in water for 30 minutes and strained. The cotton (or silk) yarn to be dyed is first soaked In water then dipped in the black liquid, rinsed and hung to dry.

All these northeastern dyeing processes are considered highly secret, so whenever yarn is to be dyed the villagers fence off an area some distance away from the village. There's also a local superstition that if a woman in the early stages of pregnancy passes close by the dyed cloth, the dye will immediately fade and become useless.

Although the Northeasterners have many methods of weaving cotton the one known as "gep kit" or "gep dork" (embroidery while weaving) is widely used in weaving cloth for household pillows, presenting to monks, weddings and various other specific purposes.

The 19 most popular designs mentioned and illustrated in Miss Vimolphan's book are based on local flowers, trees, animals and insects. Some designs are reserved for use by household guests, others for presenting as a sign of respect to one's elders, for decorating a prospective son-in-law's room, for ordination ceremonies and so on.

Compared to the cultivation, spinning and weaving of cotton, sericulture (to give it its posh name) is much longer and more difficult, mainly because rearing the silkworms on mulberry leaves calls for great care in protecting the tiny creature from heat and sunlight.

Yet the northeastern women and girls carry out every stage of this ancient and involved process right up to production of the finished articles — "pasin mee" (women' s tie-dyed ankle-length skirts), "pa sarong" (men's ankle-length skirts), and " pa-kaoma" (men's loincloths).

The silk cocoons are boiled in earthen pots. They are considered to be ready as soon as the chrysalids can be heard rattling when the cocoons are shaken. The top of the pot is straddled by a flat strip of wood with a hole drilled in the middle and a reel fitted a short distance above it. The filaments of the boiled cocoons are unravelled by passing them through the hole and winding them onto the reel.

The coarse filaments from unselected cocoons, known as

"mai leuab," are uneven in thickness and colour when first reeled; they are unsuitable for weaving and are sold in the market. Subsequent reelings produce filaments which are thin and of uniform size known as "mai luad." These filaments are reeled into a basket to await winding onto a "leng" — a cylindrical affair made of four pieces of wood. When the thickness reaches an inch, the hook is rewound on to a "koog" — a device made of four pieces of bamboo fixed at right angles — then back again onto a "leng" to twist the yarn to the correct thickness. The process is repeated until the desired thickness is reached, after which the yarn is wound into a "jai" or hank ready for dyeing.

Before dyeing, the silk thread must be rinsed in a solution made either from spinach, from the trunk, leaf or stem of a banana tree, a palm-tree flower, or the leaves of the "peka" tree. These must be sliced thin, dried and burned, and the ashes are then mixed with water in an earthen pot (earthen pots seem to crop up all over the place, don't they?). After the solution has settled the sediment is thrown away and the silk is soaked thoroughly in the pot and then boiled and dried. The process is repeated until the silk is clean. Another lengthy soaking in "ke" solution made from a thorny jungle vine, lasting three days, is also necessary before the silk can be dyed.

The dyes used for silk in the Northeast are similar to those for cotton although the whole silk process is so long and complicated that nowadays some villagers are turning to chemical dyes which are sold throughout the region.

Special mention must be made of the tie-dyed or "mut mee" silk, which Her Majesty the Queen has done so much to promote in order to help the villagers in the Northeast to increase their incomes. ("Mut" means to tie while "mee" is the word for very thin noodles like vermicelli).

The procedure for making "mut mee" silk is to wind the correct length of washed and bathed silk to make a "pasin" (or whatever other article is required) onto a frame consisting of two parallel wooden dowels set at opposite ends of a rectangular board the width of a "pasin" (one metre). Strings made from banana fibre are then tied to the silk threads in the desired pattern. The silk yarn on its frame is then dipped into dye of the background colour, rinsed and hung to dry. When the threads are completely dry the banana fibres are cut off, and the undyed parts of the threads are dabbed with other colours. (It's really a similar principle to the making of batik).

During weaving, of course, care must be taken to line up the separate threads correctly so as to reproduce the desired pattern.

So, all in all the production of silk in the Northeast and especially of "mut mee", is a very long and complex job. But the often very poor village women and girls continue to produce it with the same expert skill with which their forbears have done so for generations, reproducing the intricate patterns from memory.

Gift-wrapping

I believe the art of gift-wrapping is something specially Thai, and doesn't only become evident during the New Year season; its done whenever gifts are presented throughout the year — at birthdays, anniversaries and especially at weddings. Gift-wrapping is a special skill which seems to be handed down from mother to daughter or passed on from one school-friend to another. I think it is an example of the general delicate manual dexterity of the Thais, which finds expression in so many other art forms such as woodcarvings, gemstones, furniture and lacquerware. (Have you ever watched a maker of lacquer bowls at work in Chiang Mai, using his thumb as a template for the frieze pattern going round the bowl, and ending up full-circle at exactly the right place?)

In its own small way the craft of gift-wrapping may also produce what can almost rank as minor works of art. (Gift-wrapped parcels are known in Thai as "hor kong kwan.") It's mainly the ribbons, with their ends looped into graceful coils and worked into rosettes, that produce this decoratively frothy effect.

If you've ever bought a present in Bangkok (and if you've spent Christmas here you have probably done so) you may know that you can have it gift-wrapped in this typically Thai fashion for free — no matter whether you've bought it in one of the big department stores or in the little shop down the street. All it needs is a little patience on the buyer's part; the wrapping process may take up to 10 or 15 minutes. After all many salesgirls take just as much pride in their particular skill as the lacquerware maker does in his.

In the larger stores one usually doesn't see one's purchase being gift-wrapped. It's whisked away to a special wrapping department somewhere in the inner regions of the establishment and when it reappears it's all dolled up in its gift wrapping, just like an actress emerging from her dressing-room in all her stage finery and make-up.

But perhaps, as I have, you've watched salesgirls in humbler, smaller shops going through the delicate business of gift-wrapping what you've just bought. Sometimes they do it in pairs, especially if they're younger and less experienced than average.

First of all the object to be wrapped is considered carefully from all angles — mentally sized up as it were. Awkwardly shaped articles such as teak elephants are usually put in cardboard boxes to make wrapping easier. Then a drawer is opened and a selection of gaily patterned wrapping-paper, perhaps with classical Thai motifs, is offered for your inspection.

When you' ve chosen the one you like, the girl pulls it out — and as often as not she finds that someone else has already cut a large square chunk out of it, making it just a fraction too small to cover your purchase. In reasonably good English she says "Ne'min', Sir — how bout dit one?" and offers you a second choice and more, until you finally agree on a pattern you like.

Now begins the elaborate process of measuring and folding the paper in a trial run, unfolding it again, snipping off a piece that's a bit too long, refolding, deftly sticking down the edges and flaps with tiny pieces of scotch tape already cut and held ready by the other girl. The two of them may then go into a huddle as to how best to set about the all-important wrapping process.

(By the way, have you ever wondered what they used before scotch tape was invented? I asked my wife, and she said "Oh, there have always been different kinds of glue around. Sometimes in the old days they just used a grain or two of sticky rice!")

Then comes the finale — the ribbon. Nowadays this is usually plastic, but at the more expensive shops it's the real thing, woven of silk or cotton. Either way, the delicate procedure begins: Pass under, over, across — it's almost a ritual, demanding intense concentration, and also something of a conjuring trick. The ends of the ribbon are left long, and the tips neatly cut into a "v." And now comes the bit of what I consider pure Thai magic. Drawing one blade of the scissors across the last few inches of free ribbon with exactly the right amount of pressure somehow produces those beautiful elegant coils.

I couldn't do that to save my life. I once asked a salesgirl where she had learned to do it so expertly. At school, she answered matter-of-factly. I think this craft of making "hor kong kwan" is taught mainly at domestic science schools. My wife says she can't make a "hor kong kwan," but both her nieces, Apple and Mook, are quite expert at it. Apple has to be able to do it properly, being herself a salesgirl in a big department store, but her younger sister Mook is almost just as skilled at it — and they certainly don't teach it at her secondary school; she says she picked it up by watching a friend.

During Christmas and the New Year, I expect your house has glowed with colour from these lovely gift-wrapped parcels, as mine has. But have you ever seen the pile of gifts at a *wedding?* I'm sure the bride and groom must feel pangs of regret, even for only a moment, when they destroy the grace and beauty of those parcels by opening them.

CHAPTER FOUR
LANGUAGE

Thai-English "word-pairs"

Thailand has a city called Chanthaburi; England has one called Canterbury.

The two names sound rather alike — and incidentally, both places have cathedrals. (I believe Chanthaburi cathedral is the largest in Thailand.)

As a newcomer to Thailand in 1965, one of the first things I noticed — simply by looking at the map — was that the names of quite a few Thai towns end in "-buri": Thon Buri, Saraburi, Ratchaburi, Chonburi, Chanthaburi. Change the "i" into a "y", I thought, and they might almost be English or American place-names: Sunbury, Salisbury, Rothbury.

A great many place-names in English-speaking countries end in "-bury", and many more end in "-borough" or "-burgh", such as Peterborough (which sounds rather like Petchaburi), Edinburgh and Roxburgh.

Those English endings all mean "a town or city." The same goes for similar endings in France (Strasbourg), Germany (Hamburg), and Sweden (Goteborg); the Italian word "Borgho" also means a town.

So perhaps I was not too surprised to find that the Thai word "buri" also has the same meaning of a town or city. (I can only think of one Thai town that *starts* with "buri" — Buri Ram. And I only know of one similar place-name in Britain: Bury St. Edmunds.)

Yet I felt it was surprising to find this similarity in the Thai and English words for a town or city, because the Thai language seems so very different, so utterly remote in every way, from English or other European languages.

At the time I made the discovery, I didn't think about other Asian place-names such as Singapore (or Singapura as it is also known), Anuradhapura in Sri Lanka, or Nagpur in India. All of these and many more have endings similar to "-buri" or "bury". I just made a mental note that it seemed strange to find such a familiar-sounding and very common place-name ending as "-buri" so far away from my native England; and that some time I must try to find the reason for it.

What finally set me actively on the trail was a chance conversation about two years later. A Thai friend asked me what the letters "E.R." on British stamps stood for. "'E' stands for Elizabeth, the name of our Queen," I answered, "and 'R' stands for 'Regina', the Latin word for a queen." Then, just to make sure my friend had understood, I added the Thai word for "queen", I said, "You know — 'Queen' means 'rachinee'..."

My friend nodded — but even before I'd finished speaking the full force of what I was saying hit me smack between the eyes: The Latin word "Regina" sounds very similar indeed to the Thai word "Rachinee"!

Immediately I was reminded of my "buri/bury" problem. This time, I did more than just think about it; I talked to an English friend who had lived in Thailand much longer than I had, and who was also something of a Pali and Sanskrit scholar.

He told me that the secret lay tucked away in those two ancient languages of India, and suggested I consult a Sanskrit-English dictionary. I did so, at the central library in Chulalongkorn University.

Sure enough, I found the Sanskrit word for a queen was "rajni". Obviously the Thai word "rachinee" has come direct from the Sanskrit word. Equally obvious seemed to be the connection between "rajni" and the Latin "regina." At least they sound alike. But the reason for this connection was something I still had to find out.

From the Sanskrit dictionary I also discovered (as I should have guessed, but didn't) that "rajni" is the feminine of "raj", meaning "great, powerful, a ruler." We find this word in the Indian "rajah," and of course we meet it every day here in Thailand in such names as Rajdamnern Avenue, Rajdamri Road, Ratchaburi and Si Racha; for it means "royal" or "a king."

And what about that English word "royal"? It comes from the French "roi", a king, which in turn comes from the Latin "rex". And surely "raj" and "rex" are cousins of some sort? Just what

WAS going on?

I eventually found the answer when another friend lent me a very clear and highly readable book by an American professor, called "Historical Linguistics: An Introduction." The answer is well known to all experts in linguistics, but such an expert I am definitely not; so it was quite new to me. Briefly, it is as follows.

Some time about 5,000 years ago, a language or group of languages was spoken which the experts have called "indo-European." As far as I could gather, the region where it was originally spoken is believed to have been somewhere in Central Europe, between the Rhine and Central or Southern Russia. I also gathered that no traces of any written Indo-European language have ever been found.

From Indo-European there sprang other language groups, still very ancient. One of these is known to linguists as Indo-Iranian, from which came the languages spoken and written in Northern India, of which the two most important were Sanskrit and Pali.

Meanwhile, at about the same period in history — roughly 2,000 years ago — another branch of Indo-European developed and gave rise to the ancient European languages Latin, Greek and Germanic.

Because they all came from the same great-great-grandparent language, all these languages have similarities. Latin and Sanskrit, for instance, have close resemblances not only in their words but in their whole grammar and syntax.

Thai is not in itself an Indo-European language; but it contains many words which have come from Pali and Sanskrit. Some of these words came into Thai through the Mon and Khmer languages, and others directly, through the spread of Buddhism whose sacred Dhamma or Teachings were recorded in written Pali.

As for the language in which you are now reading this — almost every English word comes either from Germanic, Latin or Greek. (Many English words in fact come from Gothic, but this itself came from Germanic).

The same is true of nearly all modern European languages. "Buri," "borough," "burg" and "pura" or "puri" all come from a common origin. So do "rachinee," "regina" and the French "reine."

Here are some more examples of Thai-English "word-pairs" which have a common origin in prehistory.

There aren't a great many of them; to date I've found about 70 or so. Because of their Sanskrit or Pali origin, most of the Thai words in these "pairs" are not the ones in everyday use, but tend to be either poetic or technical.

According to the latest edition of the Concise Oxford Dictionary, the English word "tooth" has come from the Gothic *"tunthus,"* which itself came via a Germanic word from the inferred Indo-European roots *dont-* or *dant-*. (This reference to Indo-European in the latest edition of Oxford shows how rapidly this area of linguistic research is growing; there are absolutely no references at all to Indo-European in the previous edition, 10 years earlier.) "Inferred" means there's no direct recorded evidence, but the experts have a pretty shrewd idea that it's more or less correct — and Oxford, like all good dictionaries, always errs on the cautious side!

Readers will, no doubt, recognise those two Indo-European roots, or should we say tooth-roots, "dont-" and "dant-", in such modern words as orthodontist, which comes from Greek, and dentist which comes from Latin, as does the French word *"dent."* In Swedish, Danish and Dutch the word for tooth is *"tand."*

So what do you suppose the Welsh word for a tooth is? Why, *"dant!"*

And the Pali? *"Danta!"* One is tempted, out of curiosity, to search for a similar-sounding Thai word. The ordinary Thai word for a tooth is *fan* or *fun* (the sound is somewhere between the two), so there's not much help there. But wait... The Thai word for a dental surgeon gives us the word we're looking for; *"tantaphaet!"* It comes, of course, directly from the Pali *"danta."*

Consider now the English words "youth" and "young." Oxford traces these back through Gothic and Germanic to the inferred Indo-European *"juwnkos."* Clearly, "juvenile" and the French "*jeune*" both come from the Latin *"juvenis,"* and this must be descended from the same Indo-European root. And so is the Pali *"yuva"* — from which comes the Thai word *"yuwachorn,"* meaning young people in general.

At the other end of the scale, "age" comes from the Latin *"aetas,"* while the Thai word for age, *"ayu,"* comes from the Pali, which is also *"ayu."* These must surely also share a common

Indo-European origin, although Oxford doesn't tell us what it is in this case.

It doesn't help us with "navy," either — beyond telling us that it comes from the Latin *"navis,"* a ship. It is with a little shock of surprise then, that one learns the Thai word for navy — *"na-wee"!* This is no relatively modern borrowing, as might be thought; *"na-wee"* comes from the Pali *"nava,"* a ship — and the similarity with the Latin *"navis"* is too obvious to need confirmation from an Indo-European word, for there surely was one.

But Oxford does give Indo-European great-great-great-grandparents for father, mother, daughter and brother — all of which have similar-sounding equivalents in Thai.

First let's take a look at "father and mother" in a few other European languages: *"père, mère"* in French; *"padre, madre"* in Italian and Spanish; *"Vater, Mutter"* in German, and *"vader, moeder"* in Dutch. All of them are very similar, aren't they? And English schoolboys used to refer to their parents with the Latin words "pater" and "mater" in years gone by. The similarity between all these words shows their common Indo-European origin, conveniently provided by Oxford as *"p'ter* and *mater."* And on the Asian side, these became the Sanskrit words *"pitar"* and *"mata"* — from which have come the formal and legal Thai words for a father and mother, *"bidah"* and *"maandah."*

There's also a charming and poetic Thai word for daughter; *thida* (pronounced *tida*). This occurs in the name of one of Bangkok's temples, Wat Thepthida, and in the word *"kulathida,"* a girl of good breeding. At first the similarity between the Thai and English words isn't quite so obvious — until one find that *"thida"* comes from the Pali word *"duhita"* — and both this and the English "daughter" come from the inferred Indo-European word *"dhugheter."*

"Brother" is interesting too. It comes from the inferred Indo-European *"bhrater,"* which is exactly the same as the Sanskrit word. Obviously the Latin *"frater"* (as in fraternal greetings), the French *"frère"* (as in Frere Jacques) and the Italian *"fra,"* a priest (as in Fra Angelico), all come from the same hoary old ancenstral Indo-European "bhrater." And from the Sanskrit word for brother (which, as I just said, is the same, *"bhrater")* come the Thai words *"paradorn"* and *"parada,"* also meaning brother — with the special sense of a Christian (usually Catholic) priest.

Next, let's look at a few numbers. Once we start on this particular hobby-horse, there seems to be no end to the Indo-European connection.

Those Thai tones, which have so often proved my undoing, are indicated by tone-marks in the written script, known respectively as *"mai-ek", "mai-toh", "mai-tree"* and *"mai-jattawa"* — or Tone-marks One, Two, Three and Four. (These endings are also used to denote ranks in the military). Leaving aside "one," let's just note in passing the similarity in sounds between *"toh, tree"* and "two, three." There's a connection there all right. The *"jattawa"* isn't so obvious, until we look in Oxford for the origins of the English word "four." It comes via a string of Old English, Old Norse, Gothic and Germanic words, from the Indo-European *"quetwa"*. From this also comes the Latin *"quattuor"* which gave rise to the French *"quatre"* and the English "quarter," and on the Asian side of the family comes the Sanskrit *"chatura"*. So **that's** where the "jattawa" comes from...

(Incidentally, although a little beside the point as far as Thai is concerned, from the Indo-European "quetwa" also came the Greek *"tetra-,"* as in "tetrahedron," a four-sided solid figure.)

Let's go back to "three" for a moment. This English word, like its counterparts in all Western European languages, comes ultimately from the Indo-European *"trejes."* Think of the various English words beginning with "tri-": triangle (three sides), tripod (three feet), tricycle (three wheels) and so on. This prefix "tri-" meaning "three" is both Latin and Greek, coming from *"tres"* and *"treis"* respectively. The corresponding Sanskrit word for three is *"trayas."* All of these come from the Indo-European *"trejes."* And the Sanskrit word explains why when the Thai people present a temple with a set of **three** monk's robes in order to make merit, they call this set of robes a *"pa-tri."* ("Pa" is cloth, and *"tri"* is pronounced exactly the same as in "triangle.") Also, the cornerstone of the Buddhist faith, the Triple Gem (note the word "triple") — that is, the Buddha, the Dhamma or his Teachings, and the Sangha or all Buddhist monks — is known in Thai as *Tri-rat"* or *"Ratanatri."*

"Five." Again, this comes via a chain of Old English, Old Norse, the Gothic word *"fimf"* and ultimately from two alternative Indo-European roots, *"pempe"* and *"penque"*. Either one will do, for they both could have given rise to the Greek *"penta-"* as in that well known five-sided establishment, the Pentagon. On the Sanskrit side, "five" became *"panca"* (pronounced "Pancha") from which comes the Indian word for a special drink made of five ingredients, *"panch,"* or "punch" in English. And — have you seen the beautiful old Royal Thai ceramic ware known as "pentachrome" because it is decorated in the **five** primary colours? In Thai this is called *"benjarong"*. The Thai prefix *"benja"* meaning "five" also comes from the Sanskrit *"panca";* and we can see it too in the Thai name of the Marble Temple in Bangkok — "Wat Benjamabopit" — because it was built in the **Fifth** Chakri Reign...

"Seven." Ultimately this English word comes from the Indo-European *"septm",* as does the Latin *"septem"* (September was the **seventh** month in the Roman calendar) — and the Sanskrit *"sapta,"* from which comes the Thai word for a seven-day week,*"sapdah"*.

The English word "eight" (and its German, Dutch and Scandinavian counterparts) comes from the Gothic *"ahtau"*, related to Latin *"octo"* as in "October" and "octagonal", related in turn to Pali *"attha"*... Is there any Thai word like that, meaning something to do with "eight"?

Why, yes, indeed there is: An *"att"*, meaning "one-eighth; an old coin worth one-eighth of a "feuang" or one sixty-fourth part of a baht.

"Nine" is perhaps even more interesting because in Sanskrit, Pali, and poetic Thai it is the same as "new".

On the Western side of the family, the English "nine" is related to the Latin *"novem"* (as in November), while the Latin for "new" is "novus" (as in novel and novice), which incidentally explains why the French word *"neuf"* also means both "nine" and "new".

All these Western words are very similar to the Sanskrit/Pali/poetic Thai *"na-va"* (pronounced "na-wa"), meaning "nine" (as in *"nawarat"* or *"naovarat"* — Nine Gems — and *"naowaloha"* — an amalgam of nine metals) and also "new" (as in Nava Nakhon — New town). It is strange that "nine" seems to be identified with "new" in places as far apart as Thailand and France.

"Dekm", the inferred Indo-European word for "ten", became "dasa" in Sanskrit and Pali, so that in Thai there are various poetic or technical words beginning with *"tossa-"*, such as "

tossaniyom", the decimal system; and "decimal" itself comes from the Latin *"decem"*, as in December, the 10th month of the Roman calendar.

A "cent" is the **hundredth** part of a dollar; a *"satang,"* the **hundredth** part of a baht. The Latin *"centum"* and Sanskrit *"satem"* both come from a common Indo-European root too.

"Baht" incidentally, also means "a foot," as in Phra Buddhabaht, and in fact *"baht"* and "foot" do sound vaguely similar. *"Baht"* comes from the Pali/Sanskrit *"pada"*, which is obviously related to the Latin *"pedis"* (as in "pedal" and biped") and the Greek *"podos"* — which is where the "-pod" in "tripod" comes from! The French word for a foot is *"pied"* (as in *"pied-à-terre"*), and the Oxford Dictionary seems to think that the English word "foot" comes from a Germanic word *"fot,"* related to the Latin and Greek words. So *"baht"* and "foot" are indeed distant cousins...

Now for a brief look at another subject which depends very much on numbers: Astrology.

In fact, astrology depends on time — the time when a person was born. Time measured in "hours" — a word which comes from the Latin and Greek *"hora"*, a season or hour. And so we have "horoscope".

Now it just so happens — have you guessed? — that the Sanskrit word for time or hour is also *"hora"*. So perhaps by now you will not be too surprised to learn that the Thai word for astrology is *"horasat"*.

"Maatr" or *"maatra"*, a measure or a table of figures (as in *"maatrataan"*) comes from the Sanskrit *"matra"*, related to the Greek *"metron"*, from which come the English words "metre" (a measure of length), "meter" (a measuring instrument, such as a parking meter) and "measure" itself. *"Sataan"* or *"satanee"*, a station (police, railway or bus) is from the Sanskrit *"sthatar"*, cousin of Latin *"stationem"* and so of English "station" (and also "stand").

"Taan" (a donation), from the Sanskrit "danam", is related to the Latin *"donum"* and so to "donation".

And have you ever noticed that the Pali and Sanskrit prefix for "great", which is *"maha-"*, is rather like the Greek one, *"mega-"?* Again, they both come from a common Indo-European origin. We find *"maha-"* in the Thai words *"Maharaj"* (a great king), *"mahawitayalai"*, a university, and many more. As for *"mega-"*, well we use a megaphone to make a great sound.

The Thai words *"haan"* (goose) and *"hongse"* (swan, as in the *"Suphanahongse"* or the Royal Barge with its prow in the form of a swan) surely both come from the Sanskrit *"hamsa";* and far, far away to the west, in Germany, there is the word *"gans"* (goose), which is very similar. Remembering dimly from my schooldays that the Latin for a goose is *"anser"* (crossword fans may have met the English word "anserine", meaning "of or like a goose; silly"), I could see the resemblance between this Latin word and the Sanskrit *"hamsa".* My good friend the Concise Oxford Dictionary says the English "goose" comes via old Germanic *"gans"* from that same Latin word *"anser".*

Sometimes the Thai word is absolutely identical with its Western counterpart. The best example I can think of is *"sala"* (a hall or pavilion in a temple). *"Sala"* is itself a Pali and Sanskrit word. In Italian, Spanish and Portuguese, *"sala"* also means a hall. We have a very similar word in English (well, actually we have "borrowed" it from the French); we can find it in the beauty "salon"!

Another word which is pronounced exactly the same in Thai as in German and Dutch is *"nahm"* or *"naam"* (the choice of spelling is yours) — which of course means "a name." In Thai *"nahm"* usually means a noun in grammar, but we also meet it every day in *"nahm sakul,"* meaning a surname. The Thai word comes from the Pali *"nama,"* while the Latin is *"nomen."* (When we "nominate" someone, we name him). The English, German and Dutch words for "name" all come from Germanic *"namon"*, a cousin of the Latin word. (*Nom d'un nom!* as the French say).

My astrologer wife is always talking (quite cheerfully) about *"morana"*, the poetic Thai word for death. It comes from the Sanskrit *"marana"* which is related to the Latin *"mori"*, "to die", and *"mors, mortis"*, death. If this sounds a bit "morbid", well — none of us is "immortal"!

The Thai equivalent for "the man in the street" is *"kon sahman"* or *"sahmanchon".* In fact *"sahman"* means "common". It comes from the Pali *"samang"* meaning "equally or evenly", and this surely is related to the Gothic *"sama"* — which means "the same"!

Many Thai personal names begin with *"Som-"* meaning "fulfilment", such as Somchai, Somboon and Somporn. *"Som"* comes from the Pali *"samma"* meaning "perfected" as in *"Samma Sambuddhasa,"* the Completely Self-Awakened One, that is, the Buddha. And I've more than a hunch that *"samma"* is related to the Latin *"summus"*, "the highest", from which comes the English word "summit".

In Thai there are various words for a god or an angel; *"Theva," "Thevada"* and *"Thep"* (as in Krung Thep, the City of Angels) are the most common ones. They come from the Pali words *"deva"* and *"devata"*. These are obviously related to the Latin *"divus"* or *"deus"*, meaning a god, from which come English words such as "divine" and "deity".

What about life itself? The word "life" looks as if it's connected with the Latin *"vivus"* meaning "alive", and *"vivere"* to live *(Vive le Roi!)* — and anyway, the English words "vivid" and "vivacious" come straight from the Latin. The Sanskrit word for life is quite similar to the Latin - it's *"jiva"*. And from *"jiva"* come the two Thai words for life — *"chiwit"* and *"chiwa"*.

"Montri" is the Thai word for a high government official. It comes from the Sanskrit *"mantrin"*, a counsellor. There's nothing remarkable about that; but from *"mantrin"* there also comes — via Hindi and Malay — a **Portuguese** word, *"mandarim"*. And from this Portuguese word has come the English word "mandarin"! It's **not** a Chinese word — according to Oxford, anyway!

Now we come to the more "poetic" Thai words; words whose connection with their English counterparts more or less speaks for itself. *"Nasik"*, a nose; *"waja"* or *"waji"* , a voice; *"swaht"*, sweetness; *"madhu"*, honey (from the same origin as the English "mead").

The Thai word for "automatic" is *"attanomat"; "wittaya"* means "knowledge or wit" (in its earlier English sense, as in "unwittingly"), and its Sanskrit origin *"vidhya"* or *"vid"* is connected with the English words "wisdom" and "vision". The man's name Vira (also spelled Veera or Weera) means "virile"; *"pastraporn,"* clothes, comes from Sanskrit *"vastra"* — and English "vest"; *"boon"* (the Thai word meaning "good deeds" or "merit") is probably related (via Sanskrit *"punya"* and Latin *"bonus")* with "boon", the English word.

Whenever you come across a Thai word which sounds even remotely like its English equivalent, the Thai and English words more likely than not share a common Indo-European origin some five thousand years in the distant past. You may even form the habit of tracking down Thai-English word-pairs yourself; it's quite catching. All these words form a cultural link between our two languages; a link which is all the more valuable because it brings back to us so forcefully the common origin of all mankind.

"Romanising" Thai names

Thai surnames, as well as first names, names of streets and towns, and especially names of shops, may cause some difficulty to native English speakers when spelt in Roman characters. There are several reasons for this.

First, it is not always possible; the exact Thai sound sometimes just cannot be rendered in English spelling. This is one reason why the same name, especially first names, may be spelt in a bewildering variety of ways in Roman characters.

To take a few examples of the difficulty of rendering Thai sounds in English spelling, the short Thai vowel "a" is halfway between the English "a" as in "cap" and "u" as in "cup"; it is almost exactly the same sound as a north-country Englishman utters when he says "Th'art a BAD LAD" or "On Ilkla Moor baht 'AT". So Thai names such as Pan, San and Aranya are sometimes spelt Pun, Sun and Arunya.

Two Thai consonants have no exact equivalents in English (and are therefore very difficult for a native English speaker to pronounce when they occur at the beginning of a word). The first is half-way between "d" and "t" and the second is halfway between "b" and "p". I have tried to overcome this difficulty by writing them as "dt" and "bp" respectively, for instance, in the "Tod Pa Bpa" ceremony.

Many of the 48 Thai vowels and diphthongs are also difficult to express in Roman characters in such a way that a native English speaker can produce the right sound, although one or two correspond very closely to French vowel sounds.

Consider the northern suburb of Bangkok commonly spelt "Bangsue". Many native English speakers have no idea how to say the second syllable, and settle for something vaguely rhyming with the word "clue". After all, Sue is a very common girl's name in the English-speaking world, and the obvious thing is to pronounce Bangsue in the same way.

But the actual sound is a bit closer (only a bit, but every little helps) to "Bangsir". For those who speak French, the vowel sound in "seul" is very close to the Thai sound, and if the name were being spelt for native French speakers, "Bangseu" would produce almost the right result. But this spelling might confuse a good many native English speakers.

With very few exceptions, Thai pronunciation is much more logical and consistent with the Thai spelling system than English. (Pity the poor Thai student struggling with the English language; how about these groups of words for sheer inconsistency? Bomb, comb, tomb; or bough, cough, rough, though, thought, through!) But once you can read Thai and know the rules of Thai spelling, you can pronounce pretty well every Thai word correctly, without necessarily knowing what it means. This at any rate has been my own experience.

But many Thai proper names come from ancient Sanskrit or Pali, and this is reflected in their Thai spelling. Their pronunciation still follows the Thai rules, often modified by the use of a kind of cancellation sign known as a "garan" placed above a letter, which makes that letter silent. However, when transcribed into Roman characters the "silenced" letter is often kept there (because it was there in the Sanskrit), sometimes supported by an "a" before or after or both.

And there are other ways, too, in which the westernised spellings of Thai names have kept to the old Sanskrit form, giving results which suggest a pronunciation different from the correct one.

For instance, take the government-run handicrafts shop in Rajdamri Road. The actual Thai spelling of this shop is Narain Pant (I have changed the Thai letters into their nearest Western equivalents). But in the Thai spelling, the final "n" of "Narain" and the final "t" of "Pant" are both "cancelled" by the "garan" mark, and are therefore silent. So the correct sound when spoken is "Narai Pan".

The first part of the name is that of the god whose Sanskrit name is Narayana (another name for the Hindu god Vishnu). And in Roman characters the Sanskrit spelling has been kept, with the result that the shop's name appears in print as Narayana

Phand. When pronounced at its face value by an innocent Westerner, this can lead to misunderstanding in conversation with Thais, especially taxi drivers.

To take another example, everyone knows Suriwongse Road. But many foreigners especially those new to this country, again take this spelling at its face value and pronounce the final "se" with great finesse and a fine flourish of the tongue. Foiled again! In the Thai spelling the final "s" (there is no "e") is silenced by the "garan," and the correct pronunciation is therefore Suriwong (or Surawong).

As I said, these Romanised spellings are a result of the desire to indicate the Sanskrit origin of a name.

When King Rama VI gave surnames to certain families, he leaned towards the Sanskrit spelling of these names in Western characters. Their descendants have in many cases kept to this spelling. It represents a great honour besides preserving a cultural link with the past.

However, many of the modern generation of Thais, especially those who have gone overseas to English-speaking countries for study, have often come up against the spelling pronunciation gap themselves. Frustrated by their American, English, Australian or New Zealand friends persistently mispronouncing their names, they have changed the westernised spelling to make it more phonetic for an English speaker.

Two of my colleagues have the same surname. The pronunciation is identical; so is the spelling in Thai. But in English one spells her surname in the Sanskrit style — Dasaneeyavaja, while the other lady prefers the form "Tassaneeyavej", which is closer to the pronunciation. If spelt so as to approximate as closely as possible to the pronunciation, I would say it should be Tassaneeyawed.

There is no "V" sound in the Thai language; there is only "W", a consonant which occurs widely throughout the language and sounds identical with the English one. Yet countless individuals, companies and shops change the "W" to a "V".

This is just one example of the random state of affairs in the westernised spelling of names. It is a free-for-all. A brief look through the English version of the Bangkok telephone directory provided the following forms of the same name: Dhawatchai, Thavatchai, Tavatchai, Thawatchai and Tawatchai.

All are spelt the same way in Thai, but in Western spelling only the last version gives a more or less correct rendering of the pronunciation.

It came as quite a surprise to me to discover that the Thai spelling of "Chulalongkorn" begins with a consonant which to me has always sounded very nearly the same as the English "J". Evidently I had not been listening carefully enough over the years. Just as an experiment, I asked a Thai friend to say Chulalongkorn and then the English word July. Listening carefully and repeatedly first to one word and then the other, I could detect no difference in the first syllable.

Then I changed "July" to "choose" and again asked him to keep repeating "Chulalongkorn" and "choose". To me, the first syllables sounded quite different. Listen carefully to a Thai saying "Chulalongkorn" and try to write down how you think it ought to be spelt from the pronunciation. My own version is Julah-long-gorn.

Other examples of words which I feel could be spelt more in accordance with their actual pronunciation (my suggestions in brackets) are: Kanchanaburi (Ganjanaburee); Chanthaburi (Jantaburee); and Thailand' s famous boys' secondary school Suan Kularb (Suan Gulahp).

I suggest to everyone staying in Thailand for, say, longer than two years that it is worth learning the Thai alphabet; just enough to know the rules of pronunciation so that when you see a name in print or the name above a shop, you know more or less how to say it correctly rather than following the not necessarily reliable westernised spelling.

You will get a lot of fun out of trying to decipher advertising signs and shop names during those interminable waits at traffic lights. Come to think of it, that is how I first started learning to read Thai!

Teaching English

Somebody once coined the witticism: "*Speech was given to us in order that we might conceal our thoughts.*" These words have a subtle double meaning if you have ever tried to teach English to Thais (and to Japanese) or to learn to speak Thai.

During the past 25 years I have been trying to do all of those things. (In one rather strange case I even found myself trying to teach Thai to an English teenage boy for a few months — see next section.)

It all began when I was teaching something quite different (how to make 8mm educational films on a shoestring) at Chulalongkorn University. The head of the Science Faculty's English Department asked me if I would like to help out by teaching English, since after all I *am* English.

Certainly, I told him — I would be delighted to give it a try; but I pointed out that I had no language-teaching qualifications or experience whatsoever. Never mind, he said, he was sure I would manage all right. And so I started.

Perhaps luckily for me in my first attempts to teach our highly complex and utterly illogical English language, all my Chula students were a quiet, well-behaved and hard-working lot. And to be honest I thought I did quite well, even if my teaching methods were a bit unorthodox.

As I said in the previous section, we native English speakers have no fewer than six ways of pronouncing -"OUGH". And our verbs have 14 (yes, fourteen) different tenses — and we use all of them in everyday speech.

The "Chula" lecture rooms were quiet; those that weren't air-conditioned were usually surrounded by a decorous academic hush, and even with my rather weak voice I had no diffculty in making myself heard. But my voice doesn' t carry well across a room and this led to a rather disconcerting experience later.

A friend told me about a language school which needed another English teacher for evening classes and could be a source of extra income for me. The school was situated on the third floor of a building at a very busy intersection in Chinatown's Yaowarad Road. None of the classrooms were airconditioned and the noise from the traffic was almost unbelievable. The school principal asked me to give a trial lesson to a cheerful and pleasant class of young businessmen and women. I did my best and — whenever they could hear me — they were very responsive, laughing at all my jokes and so on. But my voice very soon became hoarse from shouting above the traffic and from time to time what was left of it was completely drowned out by a gale of laughter from the next classroom. Students at that school evidently enjoyed their English lessons in spite of the pitfalls in our language.

When my lesson was over, the principal paid me for it, shook his head sadly and said "I'm sorry but you are totally unsuited for teaching at this school. Your voice isn' t nearly loud enough!"

Later I taught part time for two or three years at a large and prosperous commercial college where every classroom had the luxury of a microphone and speaker system. Although the classes were enormous — anything up to 75 boys and girls — it was sheer bliss; I had only to whisper and my voice thundered English irregular verbs into every corner of the room.

At about the same time I began giving private lessons in my home to students in ones and twos. The length of time during which a student kept these lessons up varied from one single lesson to seven years.

The students who have come for their first and only lesson, and then thought better of it, are usually those whose English isn't very good but who are blessed with a wildly optimistic nature. They think I can turn them into perfect English conversationalists in one or at the most two months. When they find out that they have underrated the complexities of the English language and overrated my ability to teach beginners — well, that's it. I'm at my best when teaching intermediate or advanced students. Even so, 12 years of trying to teach my mother tongue has made me realise just how difficult English can be; and it has also given me a sense of great admiration for all my Thai friends and colleagues who can speak, read and write it so well. I have to keep reminding myself how poorly my own knowledge of Thai measures up in comparison.

One of the things I've discovered over the years is the importance of correct stress. The main reason why my Thai students can't always understand me is that they're unused to the English way of stressing certain syllables, and to the fact that the very short unstressed sound "-UH" is by far the commonest vowel-sound in spoken English.

Similarly, the chief reason why I can't always understand their English is that they are usually stressing the wrong syllables. To correct this, I give them a drill to make them distinguish between the sound of TWENTY and SEVENTY. At first, many Thais tend to pronounce these two words almost identically: "Ta-WENTY" and "Se-WENTY"...

Another difficulty I soon came up against was that there are TWO broad categories of English spelling, pronunciation, meanings of words, and grammar: "British" and "American".

During the first eight of my 12 years" teaching, I must have told hundreds or perhaps even thousands of Thai students that the way to pronounce "advertisement" is NOT "adverTYZE-ment." "The correct way to say it is ad-VER-tissment!" I told them. "You must remember to say it like that."

Then one day I heard an American colleague at the Bangkok World say "adver-TYZE-ment"... "WHAT did you say?" I asked him. He repeated it. "Goodness, is THAT how you say it in the States?" I asked, horrified. "Sure, how else would you say it?" he replied. I hope all those thousands of Thai students have forgiven me for my misguided and uncompromising "Britishness"!

In fact, the mixed usage of "British" and "American" English in this country has led to what I call "Bangkok English" or "Mid-Atlantic English," because roughly half of all English-speaking Thais have learnt it the British way and the other half the American way. So I have to explain that they can say, for instance, "I spent 50 baht ON that book" (British) or "I spent 50 baht FOR that book" (American). Or that to a British housewife "washing up" means cleaning the dirty dishes after a meal, whereas in the United States it means washing one's hands and face and tidying up one's appearance after a journey or something of the kind. And if my Thai students say "By the time I had GOTTEN home..." I can hardly say that's wrong, can I? All I can do is to point out that if they're visiting Britain, they should remember to say "By the time I had GOT home..."

English isn't the easiest of languages to learn, and having two basically separate varieties must surely make it even more difficult for Thais. Yet they master it in their thousands, some to perfection. How many "farangs" can say the same about Thai?

Understandably enough, most Thais who come to learn English at my home want me to teach them how to TALK English. They can read, and most of them can understand me when I speak; but when it comes to speaking themselves, they're tongue-tied. "Poot mai ork!" — "I can't speak it out!" — is their usual description of what I suspect is largely a mental block. Many of them are afraid of being laughed at for "saying it wrong" — a quite unjustified feeling, but one with which I can fully sympathise when I think of my own wife's hearty peals of laughter whenever I've said something wrong in Thai (which is nearly every time I open my mouth).

So I gradually coax my students into speaking, syllable by syllable. By now I know most of the usual mistakes which Thais make when speaking English — mistakes which are surprisingly universal from student to student. One of the commonest is to answer "Yes" when we English speakers would expect the answer "No." This happens as a result of our awkward negative statements which are really questions: "You're not coming tomorrow, then?" we ask, and receive the answer "Yes" — which really means "Yes, that's correct!"

Another common habit is to say "Is mean..." instead of "It means..." My job when teaching English is to try to make my students lose these wrong but often deep-rooted habits.

I have also taught, and continue to teach, a few of Bangkok's Japanese community. Here my problems are rather more serious, for whereas I can always drop into Thai to explain things to my Thai students, my knowledge of Japanese is more or less limited to "Sukiyaki," "Samurai" and "Sayonara."

Once, a good many years ago, a delightful young Japanese couple came to learn English with me. On that first evening, I said, "Now, I must find out how good your English is." An innocent enough remark, I thought, but all it produced was silence and a blank stare. I spoke a bit more slowly: "How well can you speak English?" I asked, enunciating each word in my best BBC-announcer voice. Another blank stare.

"CAN...YOU...UNDERSTAND...ME...?"

I asked, leaving a pause of several seconds between each word. I was still met with utter incomprehension.

A feeling of wild panic swept over me, and I had a violent impulse to leave them sitting there and go to bed... But all was well; I soon discovered that (a) they could READ English quite well, but apparently had never heard it spoken by an Englishman before; and (b) they both spoke good Thai! The rest of that lesson and all future lessons (which went on for about six months, after which the young Japanese wife had a baby and that was the end of that) were conducted in Thai.

At the time of writing I have another Japanese student whose knowledge of English is only marginally better than my knowledge of Japanese. Again, we simply have to communicate in Thai. Luckily we also share a similar sense of humour, and our lessons are often hilarious.

The other evening we were discussing types of question and answer, and I pointed out that a simple question like "Are you coming?" can only be answered with "Yes" or "No." But a question such as "WHY aren't you coming?" must have an answer beginning with "Because..." I wrote down an example of such a question and answer in his notebook. (Here again, he can read my handwriting quite easily). He seemed to understand; he nodded, and we went on to something else.

After a minute he touched my arm. "Excuse me," he said (in English), and pointed to my written word "Because." "Because? Because?" he asked, and then lapsed into Thai: "Passah Thai wah arai?" ("What does it mean in Thai?") That was when I first realised he didn't know the meaning of the English word "Because". "Proh-wah!" (the Thai for "Because") I answered. "AH!!!" He shouted. 'Proh-WAH!" It was almost like Archimedes shouting "Eureka!" as he leapt out of his bath. Immediately, he wrote down in his notebook, next to my written word "Because", the JAPANESE word for "Because"!

Learning Thai

A "farang" friend of mine, a lady who was attending Thai language classes, was a bit startled when the teacher asked her (or so she thought) whether she was wearing panties...

Why, yes, she answered. But...?

It turned out that the teacher had asked her whether she had a map (of Bangkok). The Thai word for a map is "paen-TEE".

I thought this anecdote typical of the sort of misunderstanding that occurs when foreigners start learning Thai, and I asked my friend if she had any more funny stories about her Thai classes. She could not think of any, but she asked her husband, who has private lessons at home. "I can't think of anything special," he said rather glumly, "except that whenever I say anything at all in Thai, my teacher always bursts out laughing." He has my sympathy; I have the same experience with my wife.

With me, it is usually a case of forgetting the correct tone. I have yet to ask a men's tailor, "How much is that tiger in the window?" ("seua" with a rising tone) when I mean, "How much is that shirt?" ("seua" with a falling tone); but when I order my lunch in a restaurant, I always manage to ask for a "North steak" ("neua" with a rising tone) instead of a "beef steak" ("neua" with a falling tone).

Another subtlety that trips me up is the difference between a mechanic and an elephant. The first is "chang" in a falling tone, the second is "chang" in a high tone...

In spite of difficulties such as these, I would like to suggest to all foreigners who are staying two years or longer in this country (or even less, if you are really keen) that it is well worth making the effort to learn Thai. It will make your life here so much more enjoyable, even if you are not the world's most brilliant linguist.

A Thai friend helped me to do this during my first few months here. Later I decided to teach myself — a rather ineffective way of going about it, but I used what I still considered the best textbook I know, "Fundamentals of the Thai Language." In this way, and by talking to people in the course of my daily life, I gradually picked up a smattering of Thai.

Then one day, after I'd been here four years, a friend told me of a good, inexpensive Thai teacher who held classes conveniently near my apartment, and at a suitable time, too — 5.30 p.m. I decided to enrol. The teacher, Khun Boonsiri, was a woman of about my own age. Apart from her considerable charm, she was an excellent teacher with a delicious sense of humour — an asset which she often needed with her rather absent-minded pupils, of whom I was one of the worst offenders.

Our classes were very small, fluctuating between three and seven students — and looking back, my impression is that there were different students each time, apart from a few "regulars" such as myself. The star performers were two Filipina women married to Thais, with Thai children born and raised in this country. These ladies told me their children were a bit ashamed of their mothers" poor standard of spoken Thai, so they were trying to improve it. I could never understand what they were worried about; their Thai seemed far, far ahead of mine.

I think my favourite classmate was an ex-GI whom I'll call Bill. If it hadn't been for Bill, I would always have been bottom of the class. But, bless his heart, Bill's memory was even worse than mine. He was a detemmined trier, but no matter how hard he gritted his teeth, clutched his brow or rolled his eyes, he never seemed able to carry any Thai word in his head for more than two minutes. I always felt grateful to Bill for making even more mistakes than I did...

Khun Boonsiri hardly ever spoke any English in class, except for such basic words as "verb," "adjective or "classifier" (something I won't go into here; you'll find out what a "classifier" is as soon as you start learning Thai!) She started us off straight away reading aloud from a Thai book — not as difficult as it sounds, because the book was a Prathom I (first primary grade) Thai Reader for Fairly Tiny Tots. The print was large and clear, there were plenty of simple illustrations, and the subject was a basic one — hygiene.

Week after week we took turns at reading aloud Thai sentences such as "If we wash behind our ears every night we will grow up strong and healthy." What had seemed difficult at first gradually became easier, until one day we found to our surprise that we had actually finished the whole book.

Then we began a new book, one of a series specially produced by the Ministry of Education for adult illiterates. Its print was quite easily legible, although smaller and rougher than in the Tiny Tots book we had started off with. The stories and articles were short, varied and interesting. They dealt with topics ranging from Thailand's historical heroes such as King Naresuan the Great, to more practical matters.

I remember one particular story about Nai Dam and his wife Nang Daeng. Nai Dam didn't know how to tell the time, and went to the station to catch the once-a-day train for Bangkok only to flnd it had left half an hour before. When he returned shamefaced, Nang Dang roared with laughter. Moral: It is useful to be able to tell the time.

After we'd finished that book, we found ourselves — rather to our astonishment — reading aloud from a Thai newspaper. The ex-GI, Bill, once had to read a Thai word which none of us seemed to have met before. Painfully Bill worked it out, syllable by syllable: "OR-SER-TREH-LIER." "That's right," said Khu Boonsiri encouragingly, "go on." But Bill — and the rest of us — looked puzzled. Suddenly Bill let out a triumphant roar of laughter as he realised that he had just read "Australia!"

Khun Boonsiri always encouraged us to write a few Thai sentences of our own, as homework. We used to bring our efforts into class each week and she would read them out and correct them.

One day we had learnt about the passive, which is used only occasionally in Thai. Anyway, this made me embark on a rather ambitious Thai sentence involving the passive, as part of my homework: "If we don't use a mosquito-net, we shall be bitten by mosquitoes." However, I had somehow failed to grasp the finer details of how to use the passive in Thai; and when she read out my sentence in class, Khun Boonsiri was suddenly overcome by an uncontrollable fit of laughing. What had I done wrong?

When she had wiped the tears from her eyes, she announced

to the class that I had written, "if we don't use a mosquito-net, we shall bite the mosquitoes..."

Our classes were certainly full of merriment, and at the end of eight months my Thai had improved a lot — for which I'll always be grateful to our excellent teacher, Khun Boonsiri.

About two years later, an English friend, Pamela, phoned me to ask if I would give her teenage son Richard THAI lessons.

"WHAT??" I asked, unable to believe my ears. "Are you crazy, Pamela? I'm no expert in the Thai language — it would be like the blind leading the blind! Why don't you send him to Khun Boonsiri? She's marvellous."

"No," said Pamela very firmly. "Richard wants YOU to teach him. PLEASE."

And so it was arranged, and for the next few months Richard came to my house twice a week to "learn Thai." It was a dismal failure. Richard was a nice boy, but he had an appalling memory. Most of our lessons consisted of him saying "Er.." and clicking his fingers trying to remember what I had told him five minutes before. I don't think many of the words or rules I taught him remained in his mind afterwards...

But there was one Thai word which Richard knew well. He had known it before starting "lessons" with me. The word was "NGOO," which means a snake. Most Westerners find if difficult at first to pronounce any word beginning with the sound "NG," and Richard was no exception; but although he couldn't say "NGOO" correctly, he knew what it meant — and what's more, he could actually WRITE it in Thai.

Richard told me the story of how he learnt this word. The family has been spending the weekend at Pattaya, and they'd taken a boat out to Koh Larn island. There, Richard wandered off by himself and started climbing a trail which led up through the jungle towards the top of the hill. Halfway up he came to a sandy clearing, where he sat down for a rest.

A few minutes later a Thai boy of about Richard's age, a native of the island, appeared from the surrounding jungle and greeted Richard with a friendly grin. Richard grinned back, and the boy sat down beside him. Somehow they struck up a friendship — heaven knows how, since neither could speak a word of the other's language.

Suddenly there was a sharp rustling sound in the undergrowth.

"NGOO!" said the Thai boy. Of course Richard didn't understand, and the blank look on his face must have said as much. The other boy picked up a twig, and drew a lifelike picture of a snake in the sand. Immediately, Richard understood.

The boy then wrote"NGOO" in Thai characters in the sand, and said the word again. Richard tried to imitate him, but all he could manage was "UN-GOO."

I don't know how long this went on, but the result was that the word, its meaning, and its Thai spelling became firmly etched into Richard's memory.

As I said, those "Thai lessons" with me as the teacher didn't make much headway — although both Richard and I tried hard. Whenever he couldn't remember a word I'd just taught him, Richard would comfort himself by murmuring "UNGOO"; at least that was one Thai word he knew — even if he couldn't pronounce it quite right...

That was a long time ago, and I've lost touch with the family. By now Richard is grown up, perhaps even married (to a Thai girl, I hope!) But whether he went on learning Thai or not I don't know. Yet I feel almost certain of one thing: For the rest of his life, Richard will never forget that one Thai word, "NGOO."

Bridging the communications gap

"Bye!" I said to a Thai colleague at Chulalongkorn University one Friday evening. "Have a nice weekend." "Oh," he replied, pulling a long face, "I have to come in to work all day tomorrow." "Oh, dear," I murmured sympathetically, "lecturing, I suppose?" "No," he answered, "pottering."

...Pottering? It seemed a strange reason for spending all day Saturday at a university.

"Yes,' he answered, seeing my puzzled look. "We have examinations all day. There's no one else available. So I have to potter."

Slowly it dawned on me what he was saying: proctoring! This is the American term which we British call, rather clumsily I think, "invigilating." It means supervising an examination, seeing that there is no talking or cheating, handing out extra sheets of paper when needed, explaining questions that examinees do not understand, and so on.

That little word "proctoring" is typical of so many English words which are a pitfall for the unwary Thai speaker — and for the native-English-speaking listener — and which may result in a temporary communication gap with foreigners. My Thai colleague had dropped the "r" after the "p" (as it is so often dropped in spoken Thai conversation, but with absolutely no loss of intelligibility: for instance, "pla" (fish) often becomes "pa"); and he had also made the difficult "-ct" sound into an easier-to-say "-tt". Thus "proctor" became "potter".

So if you cannot always understand your Thai friend's spoken English, remember, he is probably having just as hard a time pronouncing our extremely difficult language as you are in understanding his words; perhaps even harder.

Any foreigner who has been in Thailand more than a day or

two has probably come across the less-than-articulate waiter who offers "fly lie", and has learned to recognize this as "fried rice". There is also the classic and perhaps apocryphal story of the Bangkok-based Englishman who lent his car and chauffeur to an English friend when he left Thailand on a short business trip abroad. The friend promised to meet him personally at Don Muang airport when he came back.

On his return, however, the owner of the car was surprised to see only his chauffeur waiting for him at the barrier. "Where's my friend?" he asked. The chauffeur replied, "Your fend, he die!" "WHAT!" gasped the horrified Englishman. "This is terrible! What happened?" Just at that moment his friend came bustling up, all apologies. "Sorry I'm late, old man," he said. "I was just parking the car." The man turned to his chauffeur in confused amazement. "You see?" said chauffeur triumphantly, pointing first to himself and then to the English friend. "I not die. He die." It took the two Englishmen quite a few seconds to realise the chauffeur was not saying "die" but "DRIVE".

The "communciations gap" is part of the way of life for many foreigners in Thailand. The gap is caused by the tremendous differences between Thai and English. It is an unavoidable feature of life for the non-Thai — but it is also part of the fun of living in Thailand.

I once tried to explain the supreme importance of Thai tones to a newly arrived English friend. "If you change the tone, it changes the meaning," I said. "Yes, well, it does in English too, doesn't it," he replied. "I mean, one can sound surprised or angry, or sorry, or pleased, simply by changing the tone." "No, no!" I remonstrated. "It's not like that at all! Take the Thai word 'ma'. If you say it in an ordinary tone, it means 'come'; if you say it in a rising tone, it means 'dog'; if you say it in a high tone, it means 'horse'." "Oh!" he said, a dazed look on his face, and added hastily, "Well, I won't be staying here very long, anyway — it's hardly worth learning Thai, is it?"

All I can say is that this attitude seems a pity, because life here can be so much more enjoyable if you can speak and understand even a little Thai.

I often wish I were one of those relatively few fortunate Westerners who have really mastered the Thai language. I suppose such people are mostly either foreign service volunteers who have lived for longish periods with Thai families or in rural villages, or else scholars or semi-scholars with a natural gift for languages, which means a good ear for subtle nuances of sound and a fantastic memory. (Thais say that such foreigners speak Thai *"bpen nam lai fai dap"* — "like water flowing enough to put out a fire" — a delightful idiom.)

At the opposite extreme are those foreigners who cannot speak Thai at all, either because they have only just arrived on their first visit to this country or because, though they may have lived here for many years, they are simply 'tone-deaf", as one such Westerner expressed it to me.

In between these two extremes is a whole gamut of semi-proficiency in Thai, such as mine. In my own case, I can carry on a phone conversation with the telephone operator or a secretary in a company or government department in the course of my work — as long as the talk is limited to fairly simple stuff such as "When will he be back?".

I often put my linguistic foot in it with those oh-so-subtle Thai tones. Even after many years in this country, I once fell headlong into one of those many pitfalls for the unwary and careless foreign listener.

The occasion was the wedding reception of Sasithorn and Andrew. Sasithorn, who is now Dr. Sasithorn after gaining her PhD at the University of East Anglia in England, was an absolutely adorable person bubbling over with high spirits and with more than her share of the Thai sense of humour. I had known her for years, since her undergraduate days at Chulalongkorn University when she was a student of mine. Andrew, whom I had known for precisely one week, was English and was a fellow-PhD student of hers. (They got married in England, but for career reasons they could not make it back to Bangkok for a proper Thai wedding reception until a year later.)

The wedding cake was brought in, and Andrew asked me how to say in Thai "Please help yourself to cake, everyone!" I told him, innocently but I thought correctly: "Kor chern rapratahn kanom cake." I was really careful about getting the proper rising tones on the "kor" and "kanom".

The trouble was I used an *ordinary* tone when saying "cake" — and Sasithorn, who happened to be passing at that moment, overheard me. She burst into huge peals of laughter and rapped loudly with her knuckles on the table. Apparently that is what "cake" in an *ordinary* tone means — "to rap loudly with the knuckles". To produce the meaning of the English word "cake", you have to say it in a high tone. Oh, well, I thought to myself, that is another new Thai word I've learned — cake: "to rap loudly with the knuckles." And I suppose it was nice to have added a small and unintentional touch of entertainment to an already very lively and enjoyable evening.

It is not only wrong tones that can cause misunderstandings between the foreigner who fondly imagines he or she is speaking faultless Thai and his or her Thai listener... there are also those two extremely tricky consonants that are halfway between a "d" and "t" and between a "b" and a "p", which are really very difficult indeed for a **Westerner** to pronounce. Notice I say a Westerner, because Asians from other countries usually have much less difficulty with these particular sounds than Westerners do. (The reason, I think, is that these sounds also occur in other Asian languages.)

There is a story about an American woman who had lived for several years in the country and spoke passably good Thai — but on one occasion not quite good enough. She kept ducks in her garden in Bangkok and one day she noticed that one of them was missing. She telephoned the local police to report the fact, speaking to the duty officer in Thai, and the ensuing conversation went something like this: "Yes, Madam. Could you please describe it for me?" " Well let's see, it's about average size, brownish-grey with white tail-feathers and a rather long beak..."

"What??" gasped the astonished police officer at the other end. Unfortunately the lady had said "pet" with a full-blooded "p" instead of "bpet" with that dreadfully tricky "bp" sound. And "pet" means a diamond, not a duck.

As I said earlier, I use my own spelling system and I hope readers are not confused by this. The word for "duck", which I have spelt "bpet" is more commonly spelt "pet" and the word for "diamond", which I spell "pet" is normally spelt "phet" (as in Phetburi or Phetchaburi, "the City of Diamonds"). My reason for adopting my own spelling system is that I have so often been misled in the past (or "phast"?) by the Romanised spellings of Thai words, leading me to mispronounce them for perhaps years until I chanced to see them written in Thai, that I now tend to spell the sounds of Thai words as I *hear* them. (See chart)

But those tones... They certainly give my wife a good laugh when I get them wrong — which I usually do.

"Pen kai, " I sometimes complain when I am feeling a bit off colour. What I intend to say is "I've got a fever." Unfortunately when I do have a fever, I usually do not feel well enough to get the right tone; instead of pronouncing "kai" with a sharply falling tone, I say it in an ordinary flat tone — and it means "I'm an egg".

Then there was the time I was telling my wife a long story about our friend Khun San, whose name means "peace". I was so interested in the story that once again I forgot to get the tone of "San" right: it should be a rising tone, but I just said it in an ordinary tone. I became aware that she was not following the story at all, but was chuckling away quietly to herself. "What's wrong?" I asked and she mimicked me "Khun San" in an ordinary tone and pretended to shiver violently. Then I realised I had been talking about "Mr. Shivering". (The Thai for "malaria" is "kai jap san" or "the fever that seizes you with shivering".)

Years later she still has a good laugh over that.

If you are a newcomer to the Thai language, you may be interested to know that the sound which native English speakers would write unhesitatingly as "cow" can be pronounced in **nine** different ways in Thai, all with different meanings. The commonest meanings are "rice", "white", "he, she or mountain", "enter", "news" and "knee". Similarly "ya" can mean, according to the tone, "grass or grandmother" (the same tone for both), "medicine" or "don't".

Talking of grandmothers, in winter when the sun's daily path across the sky is at its lowest, I have problems with staying in the shade on my verandah during the afternoon. I have to keep moving my deck-chair and other sundry garden furniture such as the table with its load of Thai-English and English-Thai dictionaries and so on.

One day, as usual, I bellowed for my wife to come and help me shift everything out of the rather-too-warm afternoon sun. I used the Thai word "yai" meaning "to move" (as in "yai bahn" "to move house"). At least I thought I did... Again I could not understand why my wife was laughing quite so heartily; and again it was the same old "tone" trouble: I had said (or rather shouted) "yai" in an ordinary tone and it should have been a high tone...

What I had shouted was "Please come and help me maternal-grandmother my chair!"

I have always (well *nearly* always) tried to use the transliteration of Thai words which most nearly approximates *to the sounds I think I hear.* The exceptions are where there is a spelling already in widely recognised usage; this includes all personal names and surnames.

In the list on the next page I have left out those consonants and vowels where I think there is no ambiguity.

THAI	ENGLISH	EXAMPLE(S)	MEANING	REMARKS
ก	G	กบ GOP	A frog	But "Krung Thep"
ข	K	ขาย KAI	To sell	But "khon" (masked drama)
ค	K	ครัว KRUA	A kitchen	But "Khun"
จ	J	เจ็ด JET	Seven	
ฉ	CH	ฉาย CHAI	To project (a slide or movie)	
ช	CH	ชัย;ชาย CHAI	Victory ; a man	
ต	DT	ตก DTOK	To fall	
ถ ท ธ	T	ทอง TONG	Gold	But, of course, "Thai"
ป	BP	ป่า PBA	A forest	
ผ พ ภ	P	ผ้า PA	Cloth	
-อ	-OR	รอ ROR	To wait	
-ั	-A-	พัน PAN	A thousand	
-า-	-AH-	บาท BAHT	A baht	But "Chart Thai"
-ำ	-AM-	น้ำ NAM	Water	
-ื-	-EU-	มืท MEUT	Dark	
ุ ู	Usually -OO- This can be a tricky one (or ones).I sometimes add "as in 'foot' " for the first one, and "as in 'boot' " for the second.			
เ-าะ	-OH	เกาะ GOH	An island. (This sound really defies transliteration.I sometimes add "as in English 'NOT' with the 'T' removed"!)	
เ-ือ	-EUA	เสื้อ SEUA	A shirt	
แ-	-AE	แยก YAEK	A crossroads	
โ-	-OA	โกน GOAN	To shave	As in English "loan", "moan"

Idioms and accents

My familiarity with the Thai language, even after 30 years here, is still about as subtle as a sledge-hammer. It sometimes surprises me that Thais can understand me at all. But then, I become just as surprised to find they can understand another foreigner's spoken Thai better than they can my own, when, as sometimes happens, the other foreigner's Thai sounds completely unintelligible to me.

I once had to carry on a detailed conversation with an elderly Japanese restaurant proprietress here in Bangkok. Our only common language was Thai, except that it wasn't really "common" at all, because I couldn't understand her version of the Thai language any better than she could understand mine.

Fortunately there was a young Thai lady present an our meeting who could understand "Japanese" Thai as well as my "English" Thai, and both the elderly Japanese lady and I could understand the young lady's own perfect Thai; so the young lady was able to act as "interpreter" — all In Thai, of course!

During a 10-days visit to Czechoslovakia in 1960 I realised that nothing gives you such a sense of utter helplessness as being in a foreign country and not knowing at least a tiny bit of the language.

So as soon as I knew I was coming to Bangkok In 1965, even (as I then believed) for only a nine-month contract, I began to think about how to learn Thai.

A Thai friend who was on a course in London very kindly promised to give me Thai lessons when we were both In Bangkok. To celebrate this generosity, I took her to lunch in a London pub, where with my usual subtle movement I succeeded in spilling beer all over her dress.

"Oh, please excuse me!" I said; and then a thought occurred to me: "How do you say "excuse me" In Thai?" I asked her.

"Kotord, krap!" she answered. "That is, if a man is speaking; A woman says "kotord, khah".

I gave an involuntary little shudder of apprehension; this sounded even worse than Czech...

However, in the months and then years that followed, I did make an effort, and have been able to pick up enough Thai I get by. (Remarks from taxi drivers vary from "How come a farang can speak such good Thai?" to "How come you speak Thai so badly, yet you've been here 30 years?")

And to be honest, here in Bangkok most Thais are used to "farangs" and the way we speak Thai; their own ingenuity, I suspect, plays quite a large part in their ability to understand our efforts. I sometimes wonder how well (or badly) I'd fare if I were suddenly dumped in a village in the Northeast or the South. I think the puzzled villagers would have to get the headman with his superior education to unravel what I was saying.

I have learnt over the years that colloquial Thai is rich in expressive and often amusing idioms and turns of speech; that at the literary level, Thai is a subtle language rich in poetic and evocative words, mostly derived from Sanskrit, Pali, Mon and Khmer; and — most important to all for a foreigner — if you can't remember the correct tones of each syllable of every word you use, you might just as well be speaking Eskimo.

Hardly a day goes by without my learning at least one new Thai word; so at that rate, my vocabulary should increase at about 365 words a year... But that's reckoning without my appalling memory, because most new words I learn are promptly forgotten again by next day. If only I could remember all those new words which cross my path! How well (relatively) I could speak Thai !

Let me give you an example of one Thai idiom which I do know. It's a very common one, and I've known it for seven years now; as far as I remember, it took me about two years to understand it in the first place! It is *"Joot dtai dtam dtor."*

Please don't ask such a straight forward question as "What does it mean? It's far too subtle for that!

Let's analyse it word by word. *"Joot"* means to light or kindle; *"dtai"* is a torch made of rattan and filled with some kind of tree-resin, something like an Olympic torch; *"dtam"* means just where you're standing and *"dtor"* is a tree-stump. So the whole thing means literally "light a torch, but still stumble into a tree-stump" or something like that.

The best rendering of this idiom's real meaning which I've found is in So Sethaputra's Thai-English Dictionary: "To find oneself actually talking to the person one discusses or criticises; to talk to a person whom one seeks."

I'll give two examples. First, suppose one has gone to a government office to discuss something with a Mr. Uthai whom one doesn't know, having been advised by someone else on the phone that Khun Uthai is the right person to deal with one's problem.

Getting into conversation with a young lady sitting at a desk near the entrance who asks one's business, one discusses one's problem and says one has really come to see Mr. Uthai. "Oh," says the young lady, "that"s me!" (Uthai can be both a man's and a woman name, and of course "Khun" means Mr, Mrs, Miss or even Ms!) So there you are — *"Joot dtai dtam dtor!"*

Example Number Two: you're in an upcountry town where you've never been before. Perhaps you think the streets aren't quite as tidy as they might be, or something else is wrong.
Getting into conversation with a polite and well-mannered stranger in a coffee shop, you eventually confide your criticism to him, and even go so far as to criticise the mayor for allowing such a state of affairs in his town... Only to find that he IS the mayor! *"Joot dtai dtam dtor1"*

Well, how would you translate it? Red face? Mistaken identity? "Touché", as the French say? None of these really fits. No — this idiom is untranslatable, and that's that.

Writing "none of these really fits" reminds me of something else: The comparatively recent adoption into Thai to a few English words, usually with a subtle change of meaning. One such word is "fit."

In English, we talk about a custom-made suit or a ready made pair of trousers as "a good fit" or we may say "it fits perfectly." But when a Thai tells his tailor the new suit "fit", he means something else: it's a bit too tight!

Another word in the same category is "fan". In English, we use this in the colloquial sense of someone who's very keen or interested in something — we talk about a football fan," "a film fan" (though that sounds a bit old-fashioned these days), and "a Rolling Stones fan."

But in Thai, this word, pronounced "fan", has only one meaning: A lover. Whether husband, wife, girl-friend or boyfriend, a Thai almost always refers to his or her sweetheart as "faen".

Other English words have kept their meanings, but the pronunciation has been changed so that Thais can say the word. In a restaurant you ask the waiter for the "bin" when you want the bill — because there's no final "L" sound in Thai. A film is a "feem", ice cream tends to be "eyeteem," a nuisance is "niewsan." And guess what "bo-dai" is? A blow-dry at a women's hairdresser.

I would like to tell you some more Thai idioms; but I don't seem to know any. I've just asked my wife to think of some, but she can't think of any, either.

Well, you know how it is; if someone asked you to reel of some English idioms, just like that, you probably couldn't think of any at all.

And yet in English and in every language, one uses idioms all the time — sometimes without realising it, because the expressions are so common. For several years I've been writing a weekly column of English idioms for Thai students in "Student Weekly," and the way I do it is to open the Oxford Dictionary at random. That way I find lots of idioms, and I then make up imaginary situations to illustrate how each idiom is used.

Let's try doing the same thing with the Thai-English Dictionary. Here we are; 'CHAK.' It means to "draw, to withdraw, to drag, to pull, to haul, to deduct, to convulse, to be subject to spasms."

It also appears to mean "slightly, a bit, somewhat," and in combination with other words, "a flush toilet, to burnish or lacquer, to be slow;" as an idiom, *"CHAK BAI HAI REUA SIA,"* " literally" to pull the sail and spoil the boat," but it really means "to distract one's attention from the matter in hand..." And so on.

My wife has just told me (but very reluctantly, as she's engrossed in a book which I'm sure is full of idioms!) that this idiom about the sail and the boat is quite common.

Foreigners who have been in Thailand even for only a short while will probably have noticed that many Thais find it hard to pronounce an English word which ends in a consonant after a long vowel, because such sound-combinations don't occur at all in Thai. They have difficulty with words like SOIL, HOUSE and TIME, so they simply drop the final consonant and say "SOI", "HOW" and "TAI".

"What time is it?" becomes "What tai is it ?" and this has given rise to a sort of Thai nonsense-saying, *"wat Thai tam dooey it; wat Angkrit tam dooey bpoon."* It means "a Thai temple is made of bricks; an English temple is made of cement." Completely meaningless, of course; it' s just that the first part is a sort of imitation of the SOUND of "what time is it?"

I've managed to teach my wife to say this correctly by getting her to join the "m" in "time" onto the "is" — with the result that (whenever she remembers!) she asks me "What tai MISSIT?"

A student of mine, whose English is quite good, had me puzzled for a minute when she described her English course at university. She told me about the "sow lab." After she had described the "sow lab" I realised that what she thought she was saying was SOUND lab —that is, a language lab. I explained to her — to her great amusement—that a sow is a female pig.

There's one very common Thai word which has come from the West — most likely from France: It 's the word for coffee, which is *"GA-FAIR"*. (That's the spelling which I think comes most close to the pronunciation).

I suspect it had its origin in the French word "cafe"; and probably quite a long time ago, perhaps as far back as the Ayuthaya period.

This Thai word *"GA-FAIR"* has given rise to a kind of jingle or ditty which you may have heard on TV or the radio, or perhaps one of your Thai friends may have hummed it; it's sung to the tune of the Western song "Truly, truly fair," and the first three lines are:

"Dteun gor gin ga-fair,
tiang gor gin ga-fair,
wan yang kam dtong gin ga-fair..."

That's as far as I know the words; they mean:

"Get up, drink coffee.
midday, drink coffee too,

from morn till eve we must drink coffee..."

A Thai friend once told me it's a very old song. I wonder how old? (And I also wonder what effect, if any, it has had on the sales of coffee in Thailand?)

I suppose most people remember the film "My Fair Lady," or the earlier film and play on which it was based — Shaw' s "Pygmalion".

In the story, there was a London flower-seller called Eliza Doolittle who spoke, like many Londoners, with a Cockney accent.

Higgins, a coldly inhuman professor of phonetics, took on himself the task of making Eliza speak like a duchess, with a flawlessly cultured accent; he regarded her as nothing more than a sort of human guinea-pig.

A few years ago I was teaching English to a girl named Atchara. She had recently seen "My Fair Lady" in Bangkok, and there was something that was puzzling her; something that I found very interesting, because it taught me something I hadn't known before about the Thai language.

What worried Atchara was simply this: If SOME Londoners spoke Cockney, then why didn't ALL Londoners speak Cockney?

"In Bangkok, EVERYONE speaks with the SAME accent, whether they're high society, rich and well-educated, or poor," she told me.

That statement needs qualifying. First, Atchara meant NATIVES of Bangkok — not migrants from upcountry, who speak with their own particular regional accent (see below).

Secondly, she was talking only about ACCENT — not the actual words, idioms, slang or grammar spoken by different classes of Bangkokians.

That is, a native Bangkokian working man or servant girl will pronounce an everyday Thai word such as "jot-mai" (a letter) or "gradahn" (a board or plank) exactly the same as a Bangkokian university professor does. This is what might be called the standard or Bangkok accent.

It's also known as the central Thai accent.

To sum up: *THERE'S NO SUCH THING AS A "BANGKOKNEY" ACCENT!*

At the time Atchara told me this, I was commuting by bus every day. So I protested to her — what about the bus-boys who collect fares? Many of them seemed to me to have a distinctly Cockney accent when they shouted "Bpai!" (Go!) because it sounded much more like "Bpoy!"

"Oh, that's different!" she answered. "That's the bus-boys own special accent; they're well known for that."

I never followed that remark up...

Before I go on to regional Thai accents, let me tell you about another incident from my bus-travelling days.

It was a little pathetic, in fact. An elderly Chinese woman in black baggy trousers staggered on board the bus, bent down by a heavy load. In a piercing voice she screamed at one of the two bus-girls, evidently asking where the bus was going. But the girl looked totally blank.

The old woman screamed her question at the other bus-girl, who also looked completely baffled. The two girls looked at each other, and burst out laughing.

The old lady then screamed at all the passengers indiscriminately, but no one seemed to be able to understand her... Until eventually one kindhearted Thai-Chinese passenger managed to make out what she was asking, and reassured her that she was on the right bus.

Which goes to show some of Bangkok's ethnic Chinese community speak Thai with a variety of Chinese accents.

I've been told, in fact, that people of Chinese blood born in Bangkok and who can't speak Chinese, usually speak with the standard Bangkok accent; but those who can still speak Chinese in one or other of its various forms — for instance, business people who speak Thai in the office, but Chinese at home among the family —have a distinct accent of their own.

That's all I know about the kinds of Thai accent spoken in Bangkok — except, of course that migrants from upcountry still speak with their own "regional accent"; for like every country, Thailand has its own accents peculiar to different parts of the country — and special words and idioms too.

The same girl, Atchara, herself a native Bangkokian, was a student at Kasetsart University, and she told me there were some students from southern Thailand in her class. When two of these southern students were carrying on a conversation together,

Atchara found she couldn' t understand a word they were saying!

(Well, I' ve had the same experience myself in Britain. The Birmingham accent is notoriously unintelligible to non-"Brummies"; and I once had a Scots girl-friend up in bonnie Dundee in World War II whom I found difficult to understand at the best of times, and totally nonsensical when she was excited or upset).

I asked Atchara if she could tell me any more about Thai regional accents. Well, she said, the unintelligibility of her southern classmates was due to a combination of their southern regional accent, and strange words and idioms — and moreover, these southern words vary from province to province in the South.

She also told me there are four main or basic Thai accents, corresponding to the country's four main regions — North, Northeast or "E-sahn", Central, and South. Of these, the southern is definitely the hardest for Bangkokians to understand.

I often found taxi drivers hard to understand, and I started asking nearly all drivers whether they came from "E-sahn", because I gradually came to recognise that particular accent. Invariably they answered yes. In fact one northeastern taxi driver told me that 90 per cent of Bangkok's taxi drivers come from "E-sahn"!

I wouldn't be surprised, either.

Poetic and evocative words

The Thai language has a rich fund of literature and of poetic words, phrases and poems which evoke deep emotions in the Thai reader or listener. I shall try to give some small idea of this aspect of the Thai language, although for non-Thai readers it must be admitted that much of the subtle meaning and feeling is lost in translation.

First I'll give the example of a famous Thai song which someone asked me to translate into English. This song is called "Sadu Dee Maha Racha" — "Praise to the Great King" — and it is one of the songs adopted by Thailand's Village Scout Movement. It contains many of the rare, poetic and — for Thais — highly evocative words.

I asked several Thai friends and colleagues, all with a sound and thorough knowledge of English, to give me a rough translation of the song as a working guide. One by one, each of them considered the Thai words carefully, and then said the same thing: "I'm sorry — it's impossible."

Not a very promising start! But never one to take "no" for an answer, I finally said to one of my colleagues, an older man and a senior translator who knows the exact English meanings of a great many Thai ceremonial words and phrases. "Well, then, suppose I have a go at translating the song myself, would you then correct my translation for me? That'll surely be easier, won't it?" And, very good naturedly, he agreed to do that.

So, armed with three dictionaries, I started work at about 9.30 a.m.

By lunchtime I had made a very rough and highly inaccurate translation of the song. It took my Thai colleague and myself the rest of the day to remove the inaccuracies and mistakes, and produce something which he felt conveyed some faint echo of the original — perhaps as much as could ever be conveyed by anyone other than professional scholars. Here, then, is our translation:

Praise to the Great King (Sadu Dee Maha Racha)

May it please Your Majesty our leader, King Bhumibol, be loved by the Thai people.

Our great Ruler, shelter of all the Thai people, widespread as the shade of the Bodhi Tree —

May it also please Your gracious Majesty our Queen, his meritorious consort, perfection of the Chakri Dynasty which resounds to heaven:

Your most gracious and Royal Majesty, our King, I praise you with a humble heart.

O Supreme King of Royal lineage, beloved of all the people radiating merit as befits your majestic mien.

I humbly beg to prostrate myself, worshipping with joined palms, and offer praises to our great King and our great Queen.

The difficulty which my Thai colleague and I experienced in translating that song is typical of classical Thai poetry. Its beauty and charm cannot easily be appreciated by foreigners, of whatever race.

I have also translated another, much easier song, the "Pleng Chart " or National Song.

This should not be confused with the King's Anthem, "Sansern Phra Baramee". which is played at the beginning of every cinema performance and every night when TV and radio stations close down. I have already printed a translation of that song in the book "Thai Ways". The National Song is a brisk, lively melody which schoolchildren throughout the land chant at the start of every school day. (That's how I first became familiar with it, when I lived in an apartment which overlooked a large girls' school. I used to listen to their lusty young voices belting it out at the top of their lungs every morning; it made a pleasant accompaniment to my breakfast). The National Song is also played by all radio stations when they start broadcasting at 6 a.m.

This proved much easier to translate than the other song.

Here, first, is a transliteration of the Thai words:

Pratet Thai ruam leuat neua chart cheu Thai
Bpen pracharat patai kong Thai took suan.
Yoo damrong kong wai dai tang muan
Dooey Thai luan mai rak samakhi.
Thai nee rak sangop
Dtae teung rop mai klart
Ekarat ja mai hai krai komkee...
Sala leuat took yart bpen chart palee.
Talerng pratet Chart Thai tawee mee chai. Chaiyo!

If you've heard the tune on the radio and can remember it you might like to try fitting those Thai words to it — and the best of luck!

Here's the English translation (which I really don't think can be fitted to the tune, no matter how hard you try!):

The National Song

Thailand — the flesh and blood of the Thai people
United into a nation, with every part of the land truly Thai,
So that the whole remains steadfast and strong:
For the wish and aim of all Thais is to be united.
We Thais love peace,
But when it comes to fighting we are not afraid.
We will not allow our sovereignty to be violated:
We will sacrifice every drop of blood for our country's cause,
To raise the Thai nation to ever-increasing prosperity.
Hooray!

One of Thailand's respected men of letters and a former Prime Minister, M.R. Seni Pramoj, wrote a booklet to celebrate his 60th birthday in 1965, entitled "Interpretative Translation of Thai poems," published by SEATO Publications. M.R. Seni pointed out that literal translations would be impossible and often meaningless. Rather, he tried to convey the spirit and meaning of each poem — and he also managed, very ingeniously and successfully, to preserve the metrical verse form of the original works.

The reign of King Narai the Great in the 17th Century AD is considered the golden age of Thai poetry, wrote M.R. Seni. And a Court poet named Sri Praj (pronounced "See Praht") was the most skilled of all poets of that time. Unfortunately he had a mischievous habit of composing love-poems to the ladies of the Court, a weakness for which he was banished to Nakhon Si Thammarat in the south of Thailand. King Narai ordered the Governor of the province to look after Sri Praj, but to punish him for any further poetic offences. However, the King expressly forbade the Governor to execute Sri Praj under any circumstances.

It wasn't long before Sri Praj, true to form, composed a poem in praise of the Governor's mistress. The Governor — who, wrote M.R. Seni, had neither an appreciation of poetry nor a sense of humour — disobeyed the King and ordered the poet beheaded.

Sri Praj was accordingly tied to a stake on the beach. Before the executioner's sword fell, the poet wrote these last immortal lines in the sand with his toe, in the classical four-line verse form known as a "Kloang":

Be ye my witness, o sand.
God's image, though I stand at stake.
If wrong I gave, land true this sword.
If wrong here I take, strike back the striker.

Today, 300 years later, these words form a song known to every Thai. (My wife has just sung it to me.)
(Incidentally, Ayumongol points out that "God's image" is not a Thai concept).

Meanwhile, back in the capital, King Narai urgently needed Sri Praj's help with some poetry, and ordered him recalled from Nakhon Si Thammarat. On learning that the Governor had disobeyed his orders, the King, immediately ordered him beheaded in turn. And so the last line of Sri Praj's poem came true: the sword struck back at the striker.

M.R. Seni also gave examples in his booklet of the work of other Thai poets, and especially of the most famous of all, Sunthorn Phu. He is often called the Shakespeare of Thailand, perhaps because he came nearer than any other Thai poet to understanding his fellow men and women. Sunthorn Phu's direct contact with the common people had an immense influence on his poetry, and through his work can be seen the whole panorama of Thai life 150 years ago; the people's loves and hates, joys and sorrows, their homes, occupations, customs, beliefs and superstitions.

Here are two short examples of Sunthorn Phu's work as translated by M.R.Seni in his boooklet:

Though the earth may end and the sea,
Eternally go on love and life.

And :

A woman is sought for being chaste.
Likened unto jade without impurity.
Once it's cracked on unwise frivolity.
The quality is damaged beyond repair.

But as with all classical Thai poems, one has to hear the original Thai spoken or sung to appreciate their full beauty. And even then, only a Thai can do so fully.

The next section deals in greater detail with one of Sunthorn Phu's well known works.

How to be a good wife

Sunthorn Phu lived from 1786 to 1656 AD, so his life spanned all the first four reigns of the present Chakri Dynasty.

A Thai friend kindly gave me an oral translation of part of Sunthorn Phu's set of verses called "Supasit Sorn Ying," or "Maxims for Teaching Women." Because it seemed fitting, I tried to rephrase this in the form of Shakespearian blank verse.

Here. then, is Sunthorn Phu's advice on how to be a good wife.

***

If your husband loves you, don't be stubborn;
honour him every day; do not be wilful.
When it gets dark, you should not stray away
but light the lamp, go and see to the bedroom,
make and clean the bed, sweep away dust.
And every night when he retires to bed
crouch at his feet and pay him homage. Never forget!
If he is stiff with aches and cramps, ease them
with soothing massage. When you go to sleep,
be decorous; don't let your hands and feet
stray over him while you are asleep.
If you sleep thus your goodness will shine forth.

***

Don't go on sleeping till the sun is high;
you should get up before your husband, and
prepare water for him to wash his face.
Then do the cooking and prepare the tray

of dishes to give a beautiful effect,
along with the spittoon, polished and shining.
Make sure no dust is in the drinking water.

***

And if you know he has to go somewhere
but find that he has not yet woken up,
then gently get him up without delay
to eat his food. Sit near him while he eats,
in case anything lacks; don't give him cause
to shout for it. Pay careful heed until
he's finished eating. Then you yourself may eat.
Don't eat before he does; it is not seemly,
and he won't like it.

***

If your husband is in the Royal service
and must go in and out the Royal Palace,
then you must prepare his carrying-case
with betel and tobacco. Always try
to wait on him, serve him, as a friend would do.
If you thus serve your husband without fail,
then you will prosper and rise in others' esteem.
A true-born lady always shows her nature;
don't throw your good behaviour to the winds.
It is not good to be half-man, half-woman,
and no one will admire you for that.

***

And if your husband should rise up in anger,
you should abase yourself to quench his wrath.
Do not allow yourself to raise your voice
and answer back.
If he is fire, you should be as water
sprinkled on him.
If both of you are aflame, the fire will spread —

anger which then can never be suppressed.
Your private conjugal feelings will escape,
to become known to all the world outside.
What neighbours didn't know, they now will know.
So therefore, don't indulge in your own wrath.

***

Be pleasing to your husband; he will love you dearly.
Never fail to do the household chores.
And if he should fall ill, do not disturb him
but smile, console, be pleasing as before;
talk to him only when he's well again;
tend to his needs and pander to his mood.
Whatever he doesn't like, you shouldn't do.
Guard your speech, and don't be talkative;
keep your own counsel, don't show your feelings outside.

***

All the bad things forbidden by your husband
you should avoid; your manners should be thus.
Do not be stubborn and neglectful; speak
only with sweetness.

***

But if you have a quarrel with your husband,
don't spread tales of the quarrel behind his back.
Always suppress your own emotion
and keep it to yourself; don't let the quarrel
linger on; banish its shadow. Then
you will be called one who uses her brains
and knows how to conceal all evil things.

***

Do this, and those who know you will admire you
and think you clever. And your husband will be pleased.

***

Another Thai friend suggested it might be interesting to compare Sunthorn Phu' s advice with that of Shakespeare in "the Taming of the Shrew". So here is what the once tempestuous Katharine says after she has been reformed:

A woman mov'd is like a fountain troubled,
muddy, ill-seeming, thick, bereft of beauty
and while it is so, none so dry or thirsty
will deign to sip or touch one drop of it.
Thy husband is thy lord, thy life, thy keeper,
thy head, thy sovereign; one that cares for thee,
and for thy maintenance commits his body
to painful labour both by sea and land,
to watch the night in storms, the day in cold,
whilst thou liest warm at home, secure and safe;
and craves no other tribute at thy hands
but love, fair looks, and true obedience;
too little payment for so great a debt.
Such duty as the subject owes the prince,
even such a women oweth to her husband;
and when she's forward, peevish, sullen, sour,
and not obedient to his honest will,
what is she but a foul contending rebel,
and graceless traitor to her loving lord?
I am ashamed that women are so simple
to offer war where they should kneel for peace,
or seek for rule, supremacy, and sway,
when they are bound to serve, love and obey.
Why are our bodies soft and weak, and smooth,
unapt to toil and trouble in the world,
but that our soft conditions and our hearts
should well agree with our external parts?

***

Is it coincidence that both Sunthorn Phu and Shakespeare were men...?

CHAPTER FIVE
SOME FRUITS AND FLOWERS

Durian: endurable or unendurable?

A few years ago in April, Bangkok suffered a severe rainstorm with high winds. One of the casualties of those winds was the row of outbuildings in the grounds of my (rented) house in a quiet soi off Sukhumvit Road. They were completely flattened — utterly demolished — when the giant banyan tree at the back of our house blew down.

Unaware of this (the telephone line had been dragged down together with all the electric power lines), I arrived home to be greeted by my wife with "The house has fallen down!" Just the thing to restore one's spirits after a day's work...

Fortunately, the main house itself was intact, albeit powerless. Even more mercifully, no one had been injured. But my in-laws' personal belongings were dumped all over the place and the lounge was in a dreadful mess.

And as luck would have it, that day someone had bought a durian, which was parked on the dining-room table.

A bit dazed by the wreckage all around, the thing that penetrated my consciousness most clearly of all was the smell of that durian. Fighting back incipient nausea, I asked my wife, "Do you think you could put that durian somewhere else, out of smelling range?" So she parked it inside her son Jiap's Fiat, out in the driveway, and closed all the car's windows.

Yet, such is the all-pervasiveness of the durian's aroma, I could still smell the wretched thing...

They say that's one of the advantages of durians: Expensive they may be, but it's virtually impossible to steal a durian and hide it — its smell gives it away immediately!

The durian is indeed a strange fruit. In spite of its smell, which has been compared (unfavourably!) to that of garbage, very over-ripe Camembert cheese, or decaying fish, it is one of the most coveted of all Thai fruit.

There are even tales of people getting into debt in order to buy one — for the prices are something fantastic. A durian may weigh from two to five kilogrammes and can cost anything up to 600 baht or maybe more.

A colleague in the office, an Englishman like myself, says when he first tried durians he didn't care for them much, but later they grew on him (if you see what I mean) and he came to be quite fond of them. Now he's gone off them again. His wife, who is Thai, however, got a craving for them during the later months of her pregnancy, the sort of "pregnancy-craving" common to women all the world over. It was just his bad luck that her craving was for durian; the poor fellow had to buy one every day for three months, and it cost him something like 4,500 baht! Fortunately for him, after his daughter was born his wife's craving duly ceased, and now she doesn't care much either way about durians.

I wish I could say the same for myself. Long years ago when I was new to Thailand, someone offered me a piece of durian "just to try." I was rather put off by the smell, so I tried holding my nose while biting into the creamy-yellow flesh.

Ugh!!! I rushed to the window, spat it out, and sank into a chair where, as far as I remember, I was finally brought round with smelling-salts... And in all the years since then, I've never dared try it again. Call me unadventurous if you like. I don't care.

For those who've never met a durian face to face, I should perhaps mention that they're dark green in colour, shaped something like a rugby football, and covered all over with very tough, sharp spikes. A Thai friend says if you're unlucky enough to drop a durian on your unshod foot, you're likely to end up in hospital (I didn't ask him if he spoke from personal experience!)

To get at the fruit, two deep lengthwise cuts are made with a very sharp knife, after which the segment of tough skin with its spikes and inch-thick pith is removed, exposing the tender flesh inside — flesh whose flavour has been described by a Western writer as something like a very rich butter flavoured with almonds.

And for readers who may be wondering just why this fruit with its admittedly off-putting smell is so immensely popular and expensive as to be considered a luxury, something to be saved up for, looked forward to and prized, perhaps the Oxford Dictionary's definition may help:

"Durian : A Southeast Asian tree bearing a large oval fruit containing pulp noted for its fetid smell and agreeable taste." And there, perhaps, lies the answer. If one can overcome the Smell Barrier (which I haven't and probably never will) the taste is, they say, out of this world. (But, be it noted, several public places in Bangkok refuse admittance to the durian because of its smell).

Although durians grow wild in Indonesia, parts of the Philippines, Malaysia, Burma and Thailand, the cultivated durians of Thailand are universally agreed to be the best in the world. There's a growing export market for them too, especially in Hong Kong and Singapore. And as far as home consumption is concerned, durians are a multi-million baht business.

Some durian vendors can recite about 70 names of different varieties by heart (there are about 200 altogether). Probably the three most popular are the "Mon Tong" or "Golden Pillow," "Karn Yao" ("Long Stem") and "Chanee" or "Gibbon." There are even specialist shops in Bangkok which sell only durians and nothing else, open only during the season (which is from April to June). They're rather like tailor's shops where one can order a durian flavoured and ripened to measure — almost like a suit of clothes.

Yes indeed — for some reason which I can't (or refuse to) understand, durians are big business in Thailand.

Rambutans: the "hairy-tale" fruit

"The outward appearance of the 'ngoh' (rambutan) is ugly, but the fruit inside is beautiful. One should never be deceived by appearances."

So wrote King Loet La Napalai (Rama II) in his "Ode to Fruit." "Ngoh" is the Thai word for rambutan a local fruit, oval in shape and about the size of a golf ball, whose crimson coloured leathery skin is covered all over with soft, springy yellow-green hairs. The flesh inside is translucent pearly white, sweet and utterly delicious. Hence King Rama II's very concise and apt description.

The word "rambutan" itself is not English, although you'll find it in the Oxford Dictionary. It's a Malay word and not surprisingly it comes from the Malay for hair, "rambut."

The Thai word, "ngoh", is very difficult for most westerners to pronounce; it's like trying to say "not" with your mouth full of toffee! This word has a double meaning: Besides the fruit, "Ngoh" is the name of an aborigine race of people, Negritos who live in the extreme South of Thailand and in Malaysia. The shared name "ngoh" is more than mere coincidence: Both kinds of "ngoh" — the people and the fruit — are dark-coloured and have curly hair.

The "ngoh" fruit is closely associated in Thai people's minds with the story of Sang Thong, the Prince of the Golden Conch-Shell. This folktale, which just about every Thai man, woman and child seems to know, was also written by King Rama II — partly in prose and partly in the Thai verse form called "kloan". But his version was in turn based on a much older legend handed down through many generations.

King Rama II's epic is studied in Prathom 5 (the fifth primary grade) in all Thai schools, which explains why the story of

Sang Thong is so widely known in this country. In order to explain the connection between the story, the aborigines and the fruit, I must just tell you the rudiments now.

Sang Thong was a handsome prince who wore a magic "ngoh" mask over his head. This transformed his whole person, making him hairy, dark and ugly — just like the fruit and the " ngoh" aborigines.

However, the king's youngest daughter in the story chose him as her husband because she was sure he was in reality very handsome and had a noble character. And one night after they were married, Sang Thong removed his "ngoh" mask and revealed his true handsome self to his delighted wife. (See Chapter Six for the complete story).

Now although the "ngoh" in the story actually symbolises the aborigine people of Southern Thailand, it's associated much more with the fruit because everyone knows that the rambutan, like Sang Thong, is outwardly ugly but inwardly pure, beautiful — and good!

Rambutans or "ngoh" are very cheap and popular in Thailand and Malaysia. They're in season from May to September but a lot are canned and therefore available all year round.

The delicious white flesh surrounds a rather large stone. Most Thais eat the "ngoh" in the simplest possible way — by biting into the skin, removing it, popping the whole fruit into the mouth and spitting out the stone. Another easy way is to split the skin open with both thumbs. In fact, spitting out the stone has given rise to another story.

Thailand's most popular variety of rambutan is "ngoh rong rian" or the "School rambutan." The story goes that one day a schoolmaster in the South of Thailand was eating rambutan from neighbouring Penang where some of the most delicious varieties come from. As he ate, he tossed the stones into the school yard. One of the stones took root and grew into a huge tree (rambutan trees can grow 60 feet high) which cross-pollinated itself with a local variety.

From this one hybrid tree there grew further trees which eventually spread throughout Southern Thailand, all providing excellent fruit — and all from one school yard. Hence the name of the variety "ngoh rong-rian."

The trouble with the simple methods of eating "ngoh" by biting into the skin or splitting it open with the thumbs is that even if the flesh is what the Thais call "lon" (that is, if it comes away easily from the stone) a thin layer or husk of outer bark from the stone still remains clinging to the inside of the flesh. This causes a rough sensation on one's tongue and throat. A typically elegant Thai technique is used to carve one's way round this difficulty.

A small delicately curved and very sharp knife is used — the same type as has been in use ever since the Ayuthaya Period by the "Ladies of the Inside" in the Royal Palace for intricate fruit and vegetable carving. With this knife a cylindrical section is quickly and deftly cut out of the flesh including the stone; this cylinder containing the stone is removed and thrown away, leaving a tunnel in the remaining flesh to be eaten. This part is therefore free not only of the stone but also of all the rough bark associated with it. This operation of cutting out the stone is called "kwahn."

Rambutans which have been "cored" (or "kwahn'd") in this way are tender and pure joy to eat. Naturally only cored fruit is canned — sometimes with pineapple chunks embedded in the "tunnels" as an extra bonus, giving a blend of two separate flavours.

G(r)owing bananas...

Whole volumes have been written on Thai bananas... Correction — what I meant was whole volumes have been EATEN.....

However, the subject is quite a weighty (and tasty) one. I've long been vaguely aware that there are many different varieties of banana in Thailand; but it was a letter from a reader of my book "Thai Ways" which finally drew my full attention to this topic.

The letter, in turn, led to another of those long "communication-gap" (but nevertheless fruitful!) conversations with my wife one evening which continued during breakfast next morning.

The reader, an Englishman in Chiang Mai, wrote:
"I have recently bought your book 'Thai Ways' which I am at the moment reading. One thing puzzles me however. You refer to columns made of carved banana-tree trunks.

"If you have ever cut a banana tree you will know it has no wood; in fact bananas are botanically not trees at all, but giant herbs. A carved banana trunk would not support anything and would only last a day or two..."

The letter ended: "I don't know if you can help me in elucidating this. The reason I am writing is that I am trying to compile an account of the uses of Thai plants, and am drawing on as many sources as I can, including your articles. If you can throw any more light on this subject, I should be most grateful."

The columns I referred to made of carved banana-tree trunks were part of an "official" crematorium at a funeral ceremony in which the "mock cremation" is held.

So... That evening after I received the letter I asked my wife about it.

The Englishman was quite right, of course; the section of banana-tree trunk which my wife obligingly chopped in the garden next morning and which I examined while my breakfast got cold, was rather like a cylindrical onion (or perhaps a leek) from which I could peel off layer after layer leaving virtually nothing in the middle.

To go back to our conversation of the evening before. My wife said she thought the carved banana-trunks were probably stuck, nailed or tied onto columns made of actual wood. And the entire structure isn't meant to last longer than one day anyway — the day of the cremation. (A friend tells me that the pillars are also sometimes decorated with carved pumpkins and turnips.)

It's several years since I originally wrote the article in the book; I can't remember whether this was just another of our usual "communication gaps," and whether I never knew the correct details. But as I referred to "banana-wood" a few lines further on, it rather looks that way.

What made our more recent evening's conversation so interesting was all the other things my wife told me about Thai bananas or "gluey". It was almost like a miniature encyclopaedia article. She said every part of a banana plant can be put to good use. The leaves, known as "bai-tong" are used to make "krathongs" or little baskets for holding food and especially sweetmeats — and also the larger, more decorative variety floated on Loy Krathong Day.

The banana fruit is of course eaten; so too is the flower known as "hua plee."

As for the trunk ("gahp gluey"), besides being used to decorate official crematoriums and other objects, very serviceable string can be made out of it. After peeling off a section of the onion-like (or leek-like) stem, a piece of wood (NOT a knife) is used to slit this gently and delicately into thin lengths which are then dried in the sun, and sold to vendors for tying up their customers' purchases.

The soft substance at the very centre of the stem is sometimes used for making curry. Opinions among Thais vary widely on whether this is tasty or not. In my correspondent's second letter he wrote that he asked a Thai friend about it and was told "If you like curried banana stem, it's 'aroy' (tasty); if you don't, it isn't." (Rather like durian, in fact!) This central part is also fed to pigs and it's almost the staple diet of pigs among the hilltribes, though it's mostly wild bananas which are used.

My wife mentioned three main varieties of banana. First "gluey horm" ("Sweet-smelling banana"), the large variety identical with bananas as they are known in the West.

Next "gluey nam wa" — little baby ones which are the most generally useful; their fruit contains the most vitamins, she says, and so it is often fed, mashed, to infants being weaned from the breast in upcountry areas. It was also probably this variety whose stems were used to decorate those crematorium pillars.

The third variety she mentioned was "gluey tanee." According to a world authority, this is one of two species growing wild in Thailand from which have come all the Thai cultivated varieties.

The fruit of "gluey tanee" is inedible because of its seeds, but its leaves make good "bai-tong." It's also well known through the legend of Nang Tanee, the spirit which dwells in its tree.

A few days after this banana-conversation (I know just what you're thinking...!) our office canteen was selling bunches a little yellow-skinned bananas. Seven baht for a huge bunch and absolutely delicious.

On asking, I was told this variety is called "gluey kai" or "egg-banana." It's also made into a Thai dessert with syrup. However, my wife still says the other three she mentioned are the best known — especially " gluey nam wa."

My Thai-English dictionary lists eight varieties as examples. In his second letter my correspondent says he has recorded from various sources over 60 names for various sorts of Thai bananas, though sometimes more than one name is used for the same variety. He says N.W. Simmonds, the world authority on the subject, records 28 Thai varieties...

So there you are, banana-lovers. That's all I know.

P.S. I've just learnt something more. A Thai colleague tells me that traditionally beginners in Thai boxing classes have been taught to use their feet, knees, elbows etc., by attacking a banana-tree as a sparring-partner! It's supple and resilient, "just like a punching-bag..."

CHAPTER SIX
LEGENDS

An episode from the Ramakien: Torapa and Torapee

This episode doesn't seem to be performed very often in public but is very well known to most Thais because they have learnt it at school. It is about two water buffaloes called Torapa and Torapee.

If those names seem confusingly similar, here's a tip to help you distinguish them when reading the story: Torapa is the father, Torapee the son. The one whose name ends in "pa" is the father!

The story as I shall tell it has been taken from a Thai-language school reader for Prathom 7, the highest primary school grade, corresponding to the 12-year-old age group. The verses in this book are the original ones composed by King Rama I; the translation is a joint effort by a Thai friend and myself. (To be more precise, my friend translated it verbally and I put it into the written form which follows.)

Before I start, I would like to repeat what I mentioned earlier: The beauty and poignancy of the classical Thai "klon" verses can only be fully appreciated by Thais themselves: and this is probably also true of the feelings aroused by the stories. In this story there is the feeling of warmth and love which the mother-buffalo Nila has for her baby, Torapee, as well as the loving care which the "thevadas" or guardian spirits show towards the baby buffalo. The friend who translated this story for me says the impression created on her when she was taught this story in class at the age of 12 was so strong that it still remains with her 15 years later, and will probably do so all her life.

Here then is the story.

The water buffalo Torapa had existed in a previous life as a demon called Nontikan who was a guard in Phra Isuan's palace. (Phra Isuan is the Thai name for the Indian god Siva). One day

Nontikan saw a beautiful palace maiden, Malee, and fell in love with her. He tried to caress her, but his advances made Malee very angry because being a celestial maiden she was high-caste, while Nontikan was a demon and therefore low-caste.

Malee complained about Nontikan to Phra Isuan, who, as punishment, condemned Nontikan to be reborn as the white buffalo Torapa. He furthermore decreed that Torapa's son would kill him, and only after this death would the curse be removed so that Torapa could be reborn again as Phra Isuan' s guard.

Torapa was born in the forest of Himawan (the Himalayas). He had an evil disposition, and when he grew up he collected five thousand female buffaloes as his wives. Knowing about Phra Isuan's curse whereby he would be killed by his own son, every time one of Torapa's wives gave birth to a son he promptly killed the baby buffalo for his own protection.

But one day one of his wives, Nila, managed to escape from the herd when she was pregnant. She hid herself in a cave, where in due course she gave birth to her son, a black buffalo whom she named Torapee.

Tenderly and lovingly, Nila suckled and nurtured Torapee, and when he was old enough to understand, she told him why he had never seen his father. But she became afraid that the wicked, lustful Torapa would soon notice her absence from the herd and would become suspicious. So, sadly bidding her baby son Torapee farewell in the cave, she left him there and made her unwilling way back to the herd.

The six benevolent "thevadas" or guardian spirits of the cave felt an overwhelming pity for poor defenceless little Torapee, all alone with no one to take care of him. So they entered his body, thus endowing him with immense strength and power.

So Torapee grew up energetic and sturdy; unfortunately he also became aggressive, swaggering and overconfident. Maybe he inherited these bad traits from his father Torapa, although the story does not say so explicitly.

Torapee knew that his destiny was to seek out his father and kill him. But wisely, even cunningly, he waited until he could be sure he was big enough to do battle with Torapa. The way he measured this is told charmingly in King Rama I's verses. Day after day while Torapee was growing up, he went outside the cave and searched for his father's footprints. Each day he measured his own hoof against the print of his father. At last came the day when his own footprints were as big as Torapa's. Torapee knew he was now big enough to fight — and kill — his father.

Torapee followed the trail of his father's hoofprints until he found Torapa himself. He said, "I'm your son. It has long been my intention to kill you. Now I shall do so!" And the two buffaloes, father and son, entered into mortal combat.

Skillfully Torapee jumped aside to dodge the old buffalo's mad rushes. After a while, Torapee changed tactics and locked horns with Torapa — very much as the bulls do in bullfights in southern Thailand.

Thanks to the hidden power of the six "thevadas" or guardian spirits inside Torapee's body, he was able to kill Torapa. He rejoiced in his victory and the fulfilment of his destiny, and the six spirits shared in his rejoicing.

But now Torapee's pride became overbearing. He actually challenged those six spirits, his protectors to whom he owed his very life, to do battle with him. The spirits, however, refused to fight against a common low-caste animal. At this point Torapee got so much above himself with pride that he rashly challenged the great and mighty god Phra Isuan himself.

As you may imagine, this was an extremely foolish action on Torapee 's part. Phra Isuan was so angry at his effrontery that he immediately put a curse on Torapee, telling him he must now fight a powerful monkey called Palee, who would kill him. After that, Torapee would be reborn as the demon Mangkornkan, the nephew of the demon king Totsakan. Torapee's existence as a demon would only come to an end when, as Mongkornkan, he would meet his death from an arrow shot by Rama.

Torapee, under Phra Isuan's curse, made his way to the monkey-city of Keet Kin, where he challenged the monkey Palee to the pre-ordained fight. Neither animal could gain the upper hand, so at Palee's suggestion they went to a cave where in the narrow, confined space they would be able to come to closer grips with each other.

Before leaving for the cave, Palee told his brother Sukreep that if he, Palee, were killed, bright red blood would be seen flowing out from the cave; but if Torapee were killed, the blood would be dark.

The two animals, buffalo and monkey, fought in the cave for seven days. Again, there was no decisive result. Finally Palee said to Torapee, "Your strength comes from the thevadas inside your body. I cannot win."

Palee reasoned this way because he knew that being a monkey, he was a higher form of animal than a buffalo — he could think and fight at the same time, while a buffalo (an ordinary buffalo, that is) could only do one thing at a time. Therefore Palee should have been able to vanquish Torapee; it was only the hidden power of the six spirits inside Torapee's body that was preventing this.

But Torapee answered "No! My strength is my own!"

This unbelievable ingratitude for all the help they had given him made the six protecting spirits so angry that they immediately left Torapee's body. As they did so, they created a luminous aura around the buffalo's body, so that Palee could see him much more clearly in the darkness of the cave. With one blow the monkey killed Torapee.

This point in the story is always impressed on Thai school children by their teachers. Ingratitude is always bad, and brings its own retribution. Children should love and respect their parents and all those who guard them.

The thevadas joyfully clapped their hands, which caused rain to fall. The rain diluted Torapee's dark blood, making it light red; and Sukreep and his fellow monkeys waiting outside the cave wept, for they thought it was Palee who had been killed.

At this point in this story, the verses in the school text-book from which this translation is taken come to an end. But before leaving the story of Torapa and Torapee, I'd like to mention that two incidents from it have become everyday Thai expressions: A son who defies his parents is called "look (child) Torapee;" and if a subordinate challenges his superior's position, this is called "measuring footprints."

The legend of Phraphum Chaotee

You'll see them everywhere in Bangkok and throughout Thailand. In the compounds of private houses, big hotels and office blocks, even petrol stations, as well as humble farm dwellings.

They are the beautiful little spirit houses set on raised platforms, often looking like sparkling miniature temples with intricate red-and-green tiled and tiered roofs and stately gilt "prangs" or spires, which serve as shrines for the spirit of the land on which the building stands — the "Phraphum Chaotee". The dictionary translates this as "the guardian spirit inhabiting a homestead".

My wife has a big and rather old book called "Prohmachaht" or "The Life of Brahma". It's full of various fascinating items of Thai folklore, legends and the like, and one of these is called "The Legend of Phraphum Chaotee".

I asked a Thai friend if he would be kind enough to translate it for me, as I had tried myself and only managed as far as the introduction, after which the profusion of poetic and Pali words defeated me.

My friend confessed almost as much despair; in fact he frankly gave up on one or two passages. So I have condensed the results into something which I hope readers will find more or less intelligible — and interesting.

Here goes.

Once upon time there lived a king named King Tossaraj, whose queen was Queen Santahtook, and who ruled over a kingdom called Krung Palee.

In due course they had nine sons. When these sons reached manhood they were highly gifted, so King Tossaraj decreed that they should rule over various places as follows:

1. Phra Chaimongkol was to rule over houses, other residences and buildings.

2. Phra Nakornrat was to rule over gates, military camps, outposts and ladders.

3. Phra Thepen, over animal enclosures.

4. Phra Chaisop, over provision stores, rice barns and other storage places.

5. Phra Khontan, over wedding premises and "reuan hor" or homes for newlyweds.

6. Phra Thammahora, over orchards, gardens and farms.

7. Phra Waiyatat or Phra Thevaten, over temples and places of worship.

8. Phra Thammamikkarat, over food grains and cereals.

9. Phra Tasthara, over swamps, canals, streams and ponds.

Later on in his reign, King Tossaraj fell into bad ways, abandoning the Ten Virtuous Principles of a Ruling Monarch and thereby creating great hardships for his people.

Learning of his trouble, the four-armed god Phra Narai came down to earth in the guise of a minor Brahmin and asked King Tossaraj to grant him a small residence where he could meditate in seclusion. Unaware of the Brahmin's real identity, the King gave his royal permission and poured the Water of Royal Dedication from a gourd to signify his assent.

But the King's ill-intentioned counsellor, Phra Sukorn, realised that the Brahmin was actually Phra Narai in disguise, so he used his own magic powers to reduce himself to a very small size and entered the mouth of the gourd, blocking the flow of the Water of Dedication.

Phra Narai in turn knew what Phra Sukorn was up to, and pierced the mouth of the gourd with a blade of grass, hitting Phra Sukorn's eyes and forcing him to flee in pain. Phra Narai then resumed his normal god-like form, after which he drove the evil-ruling King Tossaraj out of his kingdom of Krung Palee and into exile in the Himapan Forest. Here the ex-king suffered many hardships, including starvation.

Eventually the ex-king Tossaraj returned to Phra Narai to beg for his kingdom back. Phra Narai gave his permission, stipulating that henceforth anyone who wished to perform any auspicious ceremony must propitiate and pay homage to Phra Phum with offerings beforehand, as Phra Phum owned the land. After making offerings and paying homage, there would be happiness and prosperity.

This, says the book, is the origin of the present tradition which has been handed down from generation to generation since ancient times. "Learned persons please judge it according to your own opinion."

The book then goes on to specify details of when and when not to set up spirit houses according to the lunar days and months; I will not go into these details, since anyone wishing to set up a spirit house always consults an astrologer about them anyway.

Sang Thong, Prince of the Golden Conch Shell

The hairy-skinned rambutan fruit is associated in the mind of nearly every Thai with the legend of Sang Thong.

This centuries-old Thai folk tale, in the version written by King Rama I partly in prose and partly in the Thai verse form called "Kloang", is studied by all Thai school children in Prathom 5, the fifth primary grade, throughout the land.

There once lived a king named Tao Yosa Wimon. ("Tao " or "Thao" is an old Thai word meaning a king). He had two wives, Nang Chan Thevi (usually just called Chan) and Chantha.

Nang Chantha bore the king a daughter. Later, the King dreamt he would have a son who would become very powerful and a challenge to the throne.

Hearing about this dream, Nang Chantha became jealous, for she saw that if the dream came true the son would become the king's heir and her own daughter would be disinherited. Nang Chantha therefore persuaded the court astrologer to tell the king that should he ever beget a son, that son would have an evil nature and the king should immediately get rid of him .

Not long afterwards the king's other wife Nang Chan bore the king a son, who emerged from her womb encased in a conch seashell. This was extremely embarrassing for the king and Nang Chan; moreover, it gave the court astrologer the perfect excuse he needed. "I told Your Majesty that if you had a son he would be evil," he said. "And what could be a worse omen than a son born inside a seashell?"

So Nang Chan and her infant son, still inside the conch shell, were banished. They went to live with an elderly couple in a hovel in the forest. Here every day Nang Chan helped the old couple by chopping wood and going out to find food . She did all the cooking, and planted a vegetable garden outside the hut.

And all the while, her son whom she had named "Sang" meaning a seashell, remained inside his shell.

But one day when the child was five years old, while Nang Chan and the old couple were out of the hovel, Sang at last emerged from the shell. Looking around him, he decided to help his mother by doing some of the housework and chasing away the wild chickens which were eating the cooked rice Nang Chan had put outside to dry. Afterwards he went back inside his shell again.

When Nang Chan returned and found the house spick and span, she wondered who was responsible. So next day she pretended to leave the hut, but instead hid herself so that she could see what went on inside. To her utter astonishment she saw Sang come out of his shell and start tidying the hut. This was the very first time she had ever set eyes on her son. Wanting him to be a normal boy like other children, she destroyed the shell, and from then on Sang lived the life of an ordinary child.

Tao Yosa Wimon soon heard the news about his son, and remembered with foreboding his dream and the astrologer's warning. So he sent soldiers into the forest to do away with Sang. When the little boy was all alone in the hut, the soldiers took him away. Sang wept bitterly for his mother, but the soldiers told him not to worry; they said that if he went to sleep they would take him back to the hovel.

However, when Sang did fall asleep the soldiers tried to carry out the king's orders; but Sang woke up and pleaded for his life. The kindly men were also in tears, but they knew they had to obey the king's command. But when they tried to stab the boy with knives and spears, one by one the weapons broke without harming him. So they took him to the king.

Sang did not yet know who his father was, and he told the king about his mother Nang Chan and how the soldiers had tried to kill him. The king's own eyes filled with pity, but his second wife Nang Chantha was quick to notice this, and she cast a spell on the king so that he forgot his own identity and ordered Sang to be drowned.

But once again Sang's life was saved, this time by a female Naga (sea-serpent goddess) who took care of the little boy. The Naga decided to send him to live with a giantess called Nang Panturat. So she put Sang in a boat with enough food for the journey and a note forbidding anyone to harm him. Then she sent the boat on its way with a gust of wind.

When Nang Panturat saw the boat approaching she decided to befriend little Sang, although this was against the advice of her astrologer. She ordered her servants to put on their most elegant clothes and greet the little boy. The servants brought him to Nang Panturat's castle, and he lived there for the next ten years.

One day the giantess went on a hunting trip. She warned Sang not to go near either of the two wells which stood one on the left and the other on the right of the castle.

But Sang was secretly curious, and he found the left-hand well contained liquid silver and the right-hand one liquid gold. He dipped his finger in each well in turn, but when he tried to wipe the silver and gold stains off his finger he found he couldn't. So he bound a piece of cloth round his finger, and told his servant he had cut it.

Then he returned to the castle where he found in an attic a pair of glass shoes, a gold cane, and the magic "ngoh" mask which changed his whole appearance, making him ugly all over. Putting on the shoes, he was delighted to find he could fly.

He also realised that his foster-mother was a giantess, so he decided to leave her. One night he crept out to the well of liquid gold and immersed his whole body in it to make himself beautiful.

It's from this point onwards in the story that he is sometimes known as "Sang Thong" rather than just plain "Sang" which means a seashell. "Thong" means "gold."

Then he picked up the gold cane, put on the magic glass shoes and the "ngoh" mask, and flew away. The mask changed his whole appearance, making not only his face but also his body look ugly and hairy like the rough hairy crimson skin of a "ngoh" or rambutan fruit.

When Nang Panturat found that her foster-son had escaped with her magic shoes and mask, she tried to follow him to the top of a high mountain where he had landed. But Sang Thong begged his own mother's spirit for protection, and this prevented the giantess from reaching him. She called to Sang Thong to come down, but he refused. Because of this, Nang Panturat died of grief.

Sang Thong arranged her funeral, and then flew off to a distant land ruled by Tao (King) Sa-mon. Here he settled down to live at the edge of a forest.

Tao Sa-mon had seven beautiful daughters, and he wanted to marry them off. The first six were able to find husbands to their liking — handsome young kings in their own right, all of them. But the youngest daughter, Nang Rochana, was much harder to please. She rejected every suitor presented to her.

So Tao Sa-mon summoned every unmarried man in the kingdom—including the ugly-looking Sang Tong. The king told Nang Rochana to choose a husband by throwing a flower garland to the man she favoured.

To everyone's amazement (though perhaps not to yours!) Nang Rochana threw the garland to Sang Thong, for she was able to see his true golden form, and was sure he was really very handsome and of noble character.

But her six handsome brothers-in-law jeered at Sang Thong for his ugliness. As for the king, he was furious; for not only did the "ngoh" mask make Sang Thong look revoltingly ugly, but he also appeared to be a person of low rank. So Sang Thong and Rochana were banished and went to live in the forest.

One night Sang Thong removed his "ngoh" mask and revealed his real, handsome shining gold self to his wife. Nang Rochana was overjoyed to find her instinct had been right. Moreover, Sang Thong told her he was in fact a prince. Rochana tried to burn the costume, but it wouldn't burn, and Sang Thong wouldn't take it off at all after that. This made Rochana very unhappy.

But Tao Sa-mon wanted Sang Thong to test his prowess against his six brothers-in-law. He ordered all seven young men to go fishing, saying each man must bring him a hundred fish. Any man who failed to catch a fish would be put to death.

Sang Thong put on the magic glass shoes and flew off to a spot on the river bank near where he knew the other six would be fishing. He sat down under a large banyan tree and took off his "ngoh" mask. He then chanted a magic spell which brought all those fish in the river which were fated by their karma to die anyway, swimming towards him. The other six sons-in-law were unable to catch even a single fish, for all the fish were swimming round the area where Sang Thong was sitting.

When the six young men approached Sang Thong, none of them recognised him without his "ngoh" mask on; they felt sure this handsome young man who had attracted all the fish must be a god. They begged him to give them some fish otherwise they would lose their lives, and promised him anything he asked for in return. Sang Thong asked them all to chop off the ends of their noses and give them to him.

The six men had no choice, and in return for their chopped off nose tips Sang Thong gave each man just two fish. On their return to the palace the six were very embarrassed by their truncated noses and paltry offerings of two fish. Sang Thong, meanwhile, produced a hundred fish as stipulated

The king angrily ordered another contest. Each man was to bring him the carcass of a deer, again on pain of death. Everything happened exactly as with the fish, but this time Sang Thong demanded a portion of each man's ear. Each of his brothers-in-law was able to give the king only one carcass, against Sang Thong's twenty carcasses.

I've condensed this story considerably; in the primary school textbook it takes up nearly fifty pages. In the final episode, the god Indra saw that Sang Thong must get rid of his "ngoh" mask for good, and settle down to a normal human life, because Rochana was so unhappy about his "ngoh" costume. Indra therefore challenged Tao Samon and all his sons-in-law to a game of "kli" or polo, with the kingdom as prize. The six sons-in-law were powerless, so the king begged Sang Thong to come to the rescue. Sang Thong agreed on condition he was given a complete set of new royal robes. When he had put these on, he looked so magnificent that no one, not even the king, recognised him. Sang Thong won the game.

On learning who Sang Thong really was — that he was indeed the son of Tao Yosa Wimon — Tao Sa-mon was overjoyed.

Sang was also reunited with his mother, Nang Chan, in a typically Thai fashion. She came to the palace disguised as a cook, and carved the story of Sang's early life on pieces of marrow which she made into a soup and gave to him, so that he knew who she was.

Although this story is deeply loved and firmly embedded in Thai culture, I for one can't help noticing its resemblance in many ways to the fairy-tales I learnt when I was a child. If I were an anthropologist, or a folklore expert, perhaps I could say more about the universal human ideas and ideals that have given origin to such tales. But I'm not — so I can't.

All I can tell you in conclusion is that in this story from that time on, as in all fairy tales, everyone lived happily ever after.

Axe-identally

This story is mainly about axes (the kind used for chopping down trees, not for plotting mathematical graphs).

Axually — I mean, actually — it all began when I was talking to a salesgirl in a bookshop. She said why didn't I write about "theparak"? She began telling me a story about it in Thai, which I couldn't follow. I asked her to tell me in English, and I couldn't understand that, either. The whole thing was a bit disjointed because the shop was full of people, and she kept having to break off in the middle to serve customers.

I asked her if she could write the story down for me some time, but she said she had no free time; even her weekly day off was always crowded, and she never had a minute to herself. A pity; it sounded an interesting story. It was something to do with "theparak" being twin guardians of the entrance to a house, I think; and I believe soldiers came into it, too.

Of course, I asked my wife about it when I got home. She was a bit vague too, but she told me "theparak" meant the spirits who live in trees. The dictionary wasn't much help either. It just says "guardian spirit" — which is more or less obvious from the Thai spelling, "theparaks" with a silencing mark over the "s". "Thep" is a god, spirit or angel (as in Krung Thep, City of Angels) and "raksa" means "to take care of."

I reminded my wife that some years ago she had told me about the old Thai belief that before chopping down any tree a woodcutter must first ask permission to do so from the "theparak" inhabiting that particular tree. He did this by leaning his axe against the tree and leaving it there overnight. If the axe were still in the same position next morning, this meant the "theparak" was agreeable to the tree being felled; but if the axe had fallen down on the ground, this meant "no". Either that, or the other way round — my wife can't remember!

After that, I was talking to another young Thai lady, an office colleague. She told me a charming little story about a "theparak". Here it is.

There once lived in a village a woodcutter who was poor but very honest. One day he went to the forest as usual, and began to chop down a tree at the edge of a pond.

Suddenly the axe slipped from his hand and fell into the pond.

The woodcutter was very upset; he couldn't swim, and losing his axe meant the loss of his very livelihood. He began weeping.

The "theparak" came out of the tree in the guise of an ordinary villager, and asked the woodcutter what the trouble was. On learning the reason, the "theparak" said he would help. Diving into the pond, the "theparak" emerged holding an axe of shining silver. "Is this your axe?" he asked the woodcutter. "No, that's not mine!" the honest fellow answered.

The "theparak" dived in again and this time came out with an axe of pure solid gold. Again he asked the woodcutter if this was his axe, and again the woodcutter said "no".

The third time, the "theparak" came out of the water with the woodcutter's wood-and-metal axe. "That's my axe!" said the woodcutter.

The "theparak" now revealed his true spirit form to the woodcutter. "You are a very honest man," he told him, and as a reward for his honesty the "theparak" presented him with all three axes.

Overjoyed, the woodcutter went back to the village and proudly showed his valuable new possessions to all his neighbours.

The next day another woodcutter from the same village went to the same tree, and deliberately let his axe fall into the pond. The "theparak" again appeared disguised as a villager, dived into the water and came up with a silver axe. "Is this your axe?" he asked, and the dishonest woodcutter said "Yes, that's mine!" Whereupon the "theparak" gave it to him. When the "theparak" dived in a second time and brought out a gold axe, the woodcutter claimed that too; and he also claimed his own axe when the "theparak" fished that out.

"You're a very dishonest man!" said the "theparak", revealing himself; and as punishment for this dishonesty, the spirit took away all three axes.

Moral: Honesty is the best policy in the timber business.

CHAPTER SEVEN
THAI DRAMA AND DANCE

The "khon"

Various kinds of traditional Thai drama and dance were revived after the Ayutthaya Period by the Chakri Kings, and owe much to them — especially Kings Rama I, II and VI (King Vajiravudh).

Here is what I know about the "khon" or masked drama which dates back to Ayutthaya times and is believed to have originated about 400 years ago.

This particular art-form is used *only* to perform episodes from the "Ramakien' (and very, very occasionally for one other story, "Unaruth"). The "Ramakien" story is known to every Thai and considered one of the peaks of Thai culture and dramatic art.

According to the attractive desk-calendar produced by the Siam Commercial Bank for 1981, the "khon" (pronounce "cone" with a *rising* tone!) developed through a gradual refinement of the ancient Thai arts of the theatre such as the "nang yai" or shadow-play and "grabee-grabong", which the dictionary gives as "a fencing contest with swords, clubs or other weapons."

Over hundreds of years these various forms of stage performance were improved, and out of them evolved the "khon" which today is considered a major symbol of Thailand.

According to the same desk-calendar, in earlier days players in a "khon" performance wore masks covering the whole face, called "hua khon". The only exceptions were the comic characters, whose masks covered only the back and top of the head, with the face exposed so that they could tell jokes; all the other characters could neither speak nor sing because of their completely masked face. Instead, they danced in rhythm with the music and singing from the orchestra, their hand and body movements taking the place of speech, as is done today, with the narrators in the orchestra telling the story.

Today the "khon" has changed somewhat; only the giants, monkeys and other animal-characters still wear masks. The "thevadas" or gods, as well as human characters both male and female, wear only headdresses called "chada." But even so, they never talk or sing.

The "khon" masks are very beautiful and elaborate. The making of these masks calls for specialised and expert skills, and all sorts of materials such as lacquer, silver, sea-shells, coloured glass and gold leaf are used.

A Thai friend of mine says the different facial expressions on the masks of the various characters in the "Ramakien" story are particularly interesting. The combination of the colour of the face, the shape of the eyes and mouth and the type of headdress serves to identify each character — especially the monkeys and demons.

As for the "Ramakien" itself, it is ultimately derived from the ancient Indian epic "Ramayana" written by the poet Valmiki about 2,300 years ago.

The story describes the birth of Rama in the kingdom of Ayodhya (correct spelling!), his marriage to Sita (Sida in Thai), the latter's abduction by Ravana or Totsagan to Longka (Sri Lanka), Rama's long struggle to regain her and his ultimate victory over Totsagan.

King Rama I of the present Chakri Dynasty rewrote the first Thai version of the "Ramakien" and it was later partly adapted and rewritten again in classical verse by his son King Rama II. Although the "Ramakien" is effectively the only story ever performed nowadays as a "khon", the converse is certainly not true. Carefully chosen "Ramakien" episodes (there are 138 altogether) are learnt by every child as part of the official secondary school curriculum; they are also performed in other Thai dramatic forms such as shadow-puppetry and so on.

Pictorially and decoratively, "Ramakien" episodes are seen throughout Thailand as mural paintings, wood-carvings, folk tales, music, songs and many other art-forms.

If you see a Thai classical dance performance in a hotel or restaurant, it's an even chance that it will be an episode, or part of an episode, from the "Ramakien" — the story known to every Thai.

Relationships between different drama forms

I've been trying, perhaps rather rashly for a non-Thai and non-expert, to piece together what I've learnt (mainly from books) about Thai drama and dance during the Rattanakosin era (though the history of many of these art forms goes back much earlier).

The task has proved much bigger and more difficult than I thought; however, it seemed a nice idea during Rattanakosin year (1982), and it was also partly a minor research exercise for my own benefit, to try to clear up some of my muddled ideas on the subject.

The questions to which I've been trying to find the answers were: What are (or were) the basic relationships (a) between the different drama forms such as the khon, the various kinds of lakhon, the likay, the manohra, and the shadow-play; and (b) between Thai *dance-drama* and Thai classical *dance "per se"* — if, indeed, the two can be separated.

For this purpose I took the advice of friends and borrowed three books from the Siam Society's library: "The Siamese Theatre" edited by Dr Mattani Rutnin (1975); "The Khon and Lakon" by Dhanit Yupho (1962); and "Souvenir of Siam" edited by Jaivid Rangthong (1954). I also talked to that very knowledgeable man, my friend Ayumongol.

Two short sections from the prefaces of the first two books tell one quite a lot. Dr Mattani writes: "The theatre and dramatic literature have always been, and still are, the keystones of our society. They are spontaneous artistic expressions of our people, reflecting the complexities of our way of life and thinking. Beneath the elaborate dance costumes, or intricately carved puppets, are satirical portrayals of our different social groups, ideals towards which we aspire, reflections of the alternate suffering and happiness of our lives..."

And Dhanit Yupho, formerly Director General of the Fine Arts Department, writes: "The arts of dancing and music are inherent to the Thai people in general, but originally these arts in their classic form were under the patronage of the Kings, royalty and noblemen. The troupes of dancers and musicians were privately owned or supported and performances were given only in the palaces or aristocratic houses... In the reign of King Rama VI and under his personal charge, Thai dancing and music reached the zenith of its development and success. After his reign the court kept only a few artists to perform at royal functions...

"In 1932 the Fine Arts Department was re-established and from 1934 on it was the duty and pleasure of the public and the Government to support the Thai art of music and drama once reserved for the nobility."

Since then the Fine Arts Department has revived and kept alive the old traditional forms through the School of Dramatic Art which continues to train children in the skills handed down by the masters of old.

Thai drama proper can be classified under two main headings — the "khon" (pronounced "cone") or masked dance drama, and the "lakhon" (pronounced "la-corn") which has the more general meaning of a stage performance, play or drama, and has developed into several different forms; I found seven in my literary researches — lakhon nai, lakhon nork, lakhon talok, lakhon chatri, lakhon deukdamban, and lakhon phanthang.

One point to bear in mind is that most of these — and the Thai shadow-plays and puppet performances too — differ from the normal Western play because *the audience already knows the story!* The interest lies in the dancing, posturing, costumes, music and so on.

The first item in Dr Mattani's book is a very clear explanation called "Notes on the Siamese theatre" originally written by King Rama VI in 1911 and published with an introduction by Prince Dhaninivat in the Siam Society's Journal in 1967.

On the similarities between the two main forms, the "khon" and the "lakhon", His Majesty wrote that both are very ancient, and the theatre where both are performed was very simple, with neither stage nor scenery and very little stage furniture.

The chief requirement is a clear space where the dances and actions can be performed, with a wide bench at either side to form thrones for the chief characters. (Today, however, the National Theatre has elaborate scenery, though this is a relatively new feature).

Costumes and props such as weapons and chariots are however very elaborate; the costumes are made to resemble those worn in theatrical shows in Siam in olden times, and have not been changed because they have been found most picturesque and suitable.

In both "khon" and "lakhon", demons, monkeys and other animals wear easily recognised masks.

The music is very important and rather strictly bound by tradition. Standard "action tunes" tell the actor what movements he is supposed to execute — there are a "walking tune" (in fact, several variations; depending on who's walking, adds Ayumongol), a "marching tune," a "laughing tune," a "weeping tune," an "anger tune" and so on.

Songs are not usually sung by the actors themselves, wrote His Majesty, as it is practically impossible to sing and do the elaborate dances and posturing at the same time; so the songs are sung by a troupe of singers.

King Rama VI then turned to the essential differences between the two basic forms; he wrote that in the khon practically all the actors except those playing female parts wore distinctive masks (nowadays only demons and monkeys do so), and all the parts are usually played by men.

Dancing and posturing in the khon require the use of the whole body and a great deal of muscular exertion. Because of this, and the masks, the actors can neither sing nor speak, so the lines are spoken by a chorus.

In the lakhon, masks are confined to the rare demons, monkeys or other non-humans. Both men and women may take part, though usually not together; and grace rather than strenuousness characterises their movements, with hands and arms being used more than legs. The khon emphasises strenuous virility, the lakhon grace of action.

The lakhon may be called a singing drama, but the singing is done by a choir; the actors may, however, speak certain lines themselves. Another big difference is that the "khon " is almost only used for performing episodes from the "Ramakien," while the various types of lakhon tell other well known stories.

Here are some more details about the lakhon, which according to the dictionary has the general meaning of a stage performance, play or drama.

I'll try and present as coherent an account as possible, although slightly bemused by reading three books. My friend Ayumongol has helped to make things a bit clearer in the course of an hour's conversation which should really have lasted three weeks or so to sort everything out properly. If those more knowledgeable than I am find mistakes, please forgive me.

In his book "The Khon and Lakhon" (1962), Dhanit Yupho, then Director General of the Fine Arts Department, says it is possible to divide the lakhon into three major categories: lakhon chatri, lakhon nork, and lakhon nai.

The lakhon chatri was originally acted entirely by men, mainly in the South of Thailand and especially at Nakhon Sri Thammarat. From what I can gather, not only from Dhanit Yupho's book but also from other sources, the lakhon chatri shared a common origin with another type of drama now totally different, called the manohra or nora because it originally presented the story of Manohra, the beautiful "kinnaree", half-bird, half woman. Although they are quite different today, the southern manohra and the central Thai lakhon chatri seem to be interwoven historically, as will be evident from what follows.

According to Henry D. Ginsburg's article on the manohra in Dr. Mattani's book, during the last century many southern manohra troupes came to Bangkok to settle down and perform lakhon chatri; a chatri performance was apparently one of the entertainments at the funeral of King Rama I's father.

Recently the southern manohra has changed almost beyond recognition, influenced by the modern "look-toong".

Ayumongol adds that the manohra is now completely different in movements and costume from any form of drama in central Thailand; the dancing and singing, too, belong specifically to the South.

A French writer included in Dr Mattani's book (the article was written in 1923) said; "The lakhon chatri troupes are strolling comedians who go from village to village. I had the chance of seeing one at Khao Tao.

"They arrived in single file at sunset, covered in dust from trekking along sandy paths, each carrying his bundle of accessories wrapped in a brightly coloured cloth. The little procession entered the village surrounded by children who had run up to greet them, then gathered in front of a farmer's house where there was some kind of celebration.

"That evening they performed an episode from Sangtong (the Golden Conch). Usually, when they arrive unexpectedly, they stop in the liveliest part of the village, normally the market; they set up their musical instruments and beat a tattoo on the drums to announce their arrival.

"Almost invariably, someone in the village has a vow to fulfil or some ceremony to be carried out which calls for a theatrical show; so arrangements are made with the troupe-master. And if by chance nobody engages them, the performance takes place just the same, a collection is taken and everyone contributes either money or food."

It's the lakhon chatri which one sees performed today at shrines where people still come to fulfil vows made to spirits in return for some favour granted — such as the Erawan Brahma shrine, the "Lak Muang" or City Pillar shrine, and further afield at such places as the San Prakan shrine in Lop Buri, and in Petchaburi Province.

When it came from the South to the capital (Bangkok or Ayutthaya, I'm not sure when) the lakhon chatri also underwent changes in the costumes and orchestra, so giving rise to the lakhon nork; "nork" means "outside" or "outer", perhaps because it came from the "outer provinces" — the South.

Originally performed entirely by men, the lakhon nork aims at quick action and humour, with short colloquial lines and plenty of openings for the cast to ad-lib. The acting must be lively and natural. "Sangthong", arranged as a lakhon nork by King Rama II, is a favourite story.

At some time in the past, Royalty may have taken the lakhon nork into the Royal Palace and court, making big changes and turning it into the lakhon nai ("inside"), performed exclusively by ladies of the court. (Other experts think it may have been the other way round!) The lakhon nai still places great emphasis on dancing and on slow, graceful and "correct" movements.

The story performed in lakhon nai is always an episode from

"Inao", based on a tale from Java but now firmly ensconced as a part of Thai literature, having been rewritten by King Rama II in a version highly suitable for stage presentation.

The lakhon nork and the lakhon nai are still performed from time to time by the Fine Arts Department; and the styles have by now to some extent become intermingled, with both sexes performing in both types.

There are several other forms of lakhon, including the lakhon phantang, which means "hybrid", and which Ayumongol neatly sums up as a general term for all forms which can't be fitted into any other category...

... Phew......

Lakhon phanthang stories include Rajathiraj and Prince Narathip's version of another very old story, Phra Law.

As you can see, the various kinds of Thai dance-drama are pretty complicated (at least for a Westerner like me) — and they are also all interrelated.

One of the writers in Dr Mattani's book (1972) says that at least during this century, the manohra's most characteristic features have been (a) the dance made up of stylised attitudes forming basic steps — "the spider weaving its web," "Rahu seizing the moon," "the half-open lotus," and so on; (b) a clever, comic stream of rhyming verse in the southern dialect, and (c) a play, which might go on throughout the whole night.

The 12 stories said to comprise the basic repertoire of the old-time manohra are more or less the same as those performed as lakhon nork in central Thailand — Sangthong, Kawee, Khun Chang Khun Phaen, Phra Aphai Mani, Kraithong and so on.

But nowadays in a typical modern manohra the hero is usually a young government official or professional man, and the treatment is a combination of low-key melodrama and broad comedy, with the hero, heroine and other main characters speaking in central (Bangkok) Thai, while only the comics and country characters speak in southern dialect (ee, boot it moost be soomthing like them comic characters as coom from the north-country in English farce!).

The lakhon chatri of central Thailand also follows the same fashion; certain characters such as the forester speak with a southern accent, to remind the audience of the chatri's southern origins.

There are four or five other kinds of lakhon which I'd like to mention, but space forbids, and I've dealt with the main ones. (My wife has just told me about two more which I've never even heard of: Lakhon yoi, a short sketch or sideshow, and lakhon yok, a toy theatre used as an offering in spirit houses and other shrines).

There's one more dramatic show, the simplest of all: The sepha, defined as "story-telling by the recitation of rhymes previously composed." The rhyme, I gather, is always an episode from the same long classic story — that of Khun Chang Khun Phaen.

For a sepha performance there's no need for a stage, nor for much space. A reciter (more than one, if it's a long recitation) and his castanets plus an orchestra are all that's needed.

When a sepha reciter feels like a rest, he brings a passage of the rhymes to an end by singing it, and the orchestra takes its cue and strikes up the same tune, while the reciter lights a cigarette or goes out for a breather. (This was written in 1940).

Now I'll deal briefly with the "nang" or shadow-play.

"Nang" means animal hide or leather, and it refers to the leather from which the beautiful and intricate characters have always been cut out (and still are).

The words of the "nang" are recited by a chorus, and the transparencies are moved about in accordance with the words by men who are generally accomplished dancers, as they have to dance while they move the pictures.

The figures of each character are drawn, embossed, and painted on large sheets of hide and are mounted on sticks as holders. The story is always an episode from the "Ramakien" — as with the khon.

In fact it seems to be the general opinion that the khon (which is known to be very old) evolved out of the "nang" — which must therefore be even older; for the manner in which the " nang" players have to leap about behind the screen is very similar to the virile, leaping movements of the khon.

This form of "nang" is now known as "nang yai" or "large nang" for a reason I'll explain in a minute; it is still performed from time to time by the Fine Arts Department and Ayumongol says the best place to see it is at Wat Khanon, a temple in Ratchaburi.

Another form is known as "nang talung;" the figures are much smaller (which is why the original form is called "nang yai") and quite different because the arms and legs are movable.

"Nang talung" performances consist of all kinds of light drama; the manipulators are usually singers and comics who evoke roars of laughter from their audience (rather like the likay, in fact). Troupes nowadays are mainly in the South.

Four of the Chakri Kings—Rama I, Rama II Rama V, and Rama VI — made outstanding contributions to the richness of Thai literature which finds one of its main expressions in the stories performed as one or other of the various forms of Thai dance-drama; words which can only be fully appreciated by a Thai.

As I said earlier, these forms are all interrelated — or at least seem so to a Westerner. The apparent similarity in the costumes and movements tend to make all the classical forms of dance-drama look similar; to me, at any rate.

But to every Thai, the differences and nuances between the different forms are surely very marked.

From what I've written already, and if you've seen Thai classical drama performances yourself, it'll be obvious that dances or dance movements usually form an integral part of the telling of the story. Conversely, if you see a short classical dance performance at a hotel, restaurant or similar place, the chances are it'll be a shortened episode, or part of an episode, from one of the Thai literary classics.

In his introduction to Dhanit Yupho's article in "Souvenir of Siam" the late Phya Anuman Rajadhon (also formerly of the Fine Arts Department) says: "Dancing arose with jumping and capering about to express the emotions which stirred one's heart. Later the movements were improved and made beautiful to give pleasure to the spectators. In its original form (called "rabam") the dancing was unconnected with any theme. Later on it was adapted to the interpretation of the story..."

Phya Anuman points out that this adaptation was done to make the "rabam" more interesting; among other versions he mentions the "Praleng" danced in pairs, holding a peacock's tail-feathers in each hand, and the "Dance of the Silver and Gold Flowers," both of which are preliminaries to khon and lakhon performances. During training, the distinction is maintained; beginners first practice the "rabam" or dancing to music alone without any theme, and only later do they learn to interpret stories through dancing.

Dhanit Yupho gives full and fascinating details of 52 separate dance movements of scenes (including seven types of fencing with rapiers, swords and sticks). I'll just outline a few of these, starting with dance scenes which are part of the khon (that is, the "Ramakien" story) and of lakhon stories, and then going on the dances *"per se"* —including the relatively modern ramwong. I must point out that what follows is a very drastic simplification, purely for reasons of space. First, the "Ramakien" includes an important *style* of solo dancing called "chui-chai", used when a character feels pleased with him or herself after having dressed up or changed by magic into someone or something prettier; a male character "struts about," while a female one "minces" — for instance, when Benjakai has successfully disguised herself as Sida, and also just before the demon king Totsakan visits Sida who is a prisoner in his garden.

In fact, it seems to me that every khon performance — that is, every "Ramakien" episode — can really be thought of as one long series of individual "sub-episode" dances such as "Rama bathing" "The capture of Benjakai," "Rama crossing the sea with his army," and "Presenting the Monkey" — in which Totsakan is furiously angry and his dancing is the very opposite of "chui-chai," whereas the white monkey Hanuman, Rama's commander-in-chief, "keeps his cool" and dances accordingly.

Other story-linked dances described by Dhanit Yupho include "Phra Law in the Garden;" "Busaba in the Temple" from the "Inao" story; "Rochana's Garland" from the Sang Thong story, in which Princess Rochana chooses her future husband by throwing the garland at the apparently ugly "ngoh" Sang Thong. All these and many others form an integral part of their respective stories when these are performed as lakhons on the stage. (Perhaps the comparison is not very apt, but I can't help being reminded of the stylised and elegant dances in Gilbert and Sullivan's "The Gondoliers" and "The Yeomen of the Guard.")

There are other dances or sets of dances which are complete stories in themselves, such as "Mekala and Ramasoon" which is about thunder and lightning.

And now to my original query about Thai classical dance *"per se."* Well, as I suspected, there are such dances. Among others,

Dhanit Yupho describes the Flower Pot Dance introduced from Vietnam during King Rama I's reign, and modified into the Lantern Dance by King Mongkut (Rama IV): The Fan Dance, modelled on that of China during King Rama II's reign; "Si-nuan", a delightful and popular folk-dance; and two other beautiful and well known dances from the North of Thailand, the Candle dance and the "Fon Lep" or Nail dance.

Finally, then, to a totally different and much more modern type of dance, the ramwong. I'm including it here because for Westerners such as myself it *is* Thai and it *is* a distinct danceform. Moreover, the book "Ramwong Songs" from which I've obtained my information is published by the Fine Arts Department; and once again, its preface is written by Dhanit Yupho (in 1960.)

He says the ramwong evolved form the ramthone, formerly a popular seasonal entertainment in certain regions of Thailand, in which the instruments were the "ching" or small cymbals, the "krab" or castanets and the small drums or "thones" which provided the rhythm and gave the dance its name. In about 1940 the ramthone spread to other parts of the country, and was danced throughout the whole year; a great many new songs were specially composed for it — invitations to join the dance, love duets, praising of beauty and so on.

In 1944 the Fine Arts Department decided to promote the ramthone and improve it to conform with the art and tradition of Thai dance. The Department also officially renamed it the ramwong (which was what everyone called it, anyway) because the dancers form a chain which becomes a circle ("ram" means "to dance" and "wong" is a circle). After World War II the ramwong grew even more popular — especially among Westerners, says Dhanit Yupho; and as a result it has been introduced into many other countries.

I too danced the ramwong many years ago, soon after I first came to Thailand; it happened on a stage in a restaurant, and — no doubt like many another "farang", before and since — I felt acutely self-conscious...

And quite unnecessarily.

CHAPTER EIGHT
ODDS AND ENDS

A tale of a "bpeeb"

One evening when we were sitting at home my wife suddenly burst out laughing. I asked her what she was laughing about, and she said she'd just remembered something which happened a long time ago.

This is quite a common occurrence; Laddawan suddenly remembers something interesting or funny from the past, which I inevitably put down on paper.

She's not sure how old she was at the time, but she thinks she was about 16 or 17. She had the reputation among her relatives and friends of being what Thais call "ser-sah" or "soom-sahm." I think this can best be translated as "hamfisted."

At this time she and her sister lived in Samrong, between Bangkok and Paknam but nearer to Paknam. An elder cousin of hers, a man called "Phee-Wai", used to deal in sugar. Everyone in the neighbourhood used to gather the sweet liquid from the coconut-palm trees in their orchards and boil it into palm-sugar, which is delicious and rather like fudge. Phee-Wai used to buy the sugar from all the houses in the district, and sell it to a merchant whose place of business was alongside busy Klong Padung Krung Kasem, near the main Hualampong railway station in the heart of Bangkok.

Phee-Wai put the sugar in what are called "bpeeb" — empty kerosine tins. As far as Laddawan remembers, a "bpeeb" full of palm-sugar weighed about 30 kilos, and they used to load about 70 "bpeebs" in Phee-Wai's boat for each trip to Bangkok. That's about 2,000 kilos — or two tons!

The boat was the old-fashioned kind called a "rua jaeo", propelled manually by large oars or paddles fixed to posts, one in the bow and the other at the stern. The rowers worked standing up; Laddawan rowed in the bow.

If you look at a map of Bangkok and its surroundings, you'll see that it's quite a long way by water from Samrong down the canal, Klong Samrong, to the Chao Phya and then up the river to the city.

In fact the route they followed made use of a convenient short-cut which bypasses the enormous loop in the river including the Port of Bangkok at Klong Toey. In English we sometimes call such a canal cut through a narrow neck of land "The Cut," and by coincidence the Thai name for this particular short-cut canal is "Klong Koot!" ("koot" means "to dig").

So what they did was to propel the large, heavily-laden boat down Klong Samrong into the river, then turn left and go downstream for about a mile, then across the river to Phra Pradaeng and along the "Klong Koot."

They always set off on these trips very early, about 4 a.m., and Laddawan remembers the vast expanse of night sky full of stars — including an occasional shooting-star, which rather scared her!

Sometimes, just as they had nosed snugly into "Klong Koot", a huge sampan or junk would come sailing past behind them down the river — and the resulting undertow from the wash would suck their smaller boat right out of the klong back into the river!

From the map, I reckon the total distance they had to paddle their boat with its heavy load was about 14 miles. Anyway, the journey took about six hours — for which Laddawan was paid five baht.

Arriving at Klong Padung Krung Kasem at about 10 a.m., they would unload all the "bpeebs" from the boat onto the jetty. The merchant would take them away, remove the sugar, and dump the "empties" back on the jetty. Laddawan's job was to stay on shore and throw each empty "bpeeb" back to Phee-Wai on the boat.

On this particular occasion, she didn't throw one of the "bpeebs" hard enough, and it fell short into the water, where it floated. Phee-Wai bent down to retrieve it, but he too failed to grab it the first time; he straightened his back, and bent down again to try to fish it out of the water.

Laddawan, who surely couldn't have been concentrating on the job, chose precisely that moment to throw the next "bpeeb". It caught Phee-Wai smartly between the eyes with a resounding thwack, just as he was bending down...

That was the memory which made Laddawan suddenly laugh the other evening at home.

That, and the torrent of abusive language Phee-Wai used, which was quite unprintable. I imagine the Thai equivalent of "You clumsy oaf!!" figured largely in it — or something even less polite...

Laddawan's other chief memory of those long, tiring river trips was the journey home.

Of course the boatload was much less without those two tons of sugar. But it could still be hard work, depending on the direction of the current in the Chao Phya; if the tide was coming in, the return to Samrong could take almost as long as the outward journey.

But sometimes as they paddled out of Klong Padung Krung Kasem into the river, they were in luck: They were able to get a hitch from an engine-powered boat. For this towing service, of course, they had to pay.

...That is, unless they were even luckier and met a string of rice barges. In that case they would hail the rearmost boat and hitch themselves onto it. That way, the skipper never saw them and they didn' t have to pay anything...

Phee Wai had taught Laddawan (or he thought he had taught her) always to loop their tow-rope into several coils, so that when they hailed the engine-driven boat or barge, Laddawan could throw all the coils together. Then the coils of rope would have enough momentum to carry them all the way from their boat to the other one.

But on one occasion she forgot to coil the rope as she had been taught. She just tossed the end of the rope — which of course fell plop into the water, a long way short of the barge.

As luck would have it that was the last barge-string of the day, and once again they had to paddle the 14 miles home under their own muscular power... And poor Laddawan was once again on the receiving end of Phee Wai's sarcastic and colourful tongue.

A story of grit and determination

A few years ago I received a handwritten letter care of the Bangkok World's sister publication Student Weekly, for which I write a regular column on English idioms.

It was an intriguing letter, to say the least. The first thing that caught my eye was the heading "Top Secret!" It began, "Dear Sir. This is my first letter that I write to a man in English.

"I know that my English Grammar is not good enough to write. But I try.

"May I introduce myself first. I am an old Thai girl and am now working as clerk in..." (here she gave me details of her office and the name of her town in Northeast Thailand. She has asked me not to give her real name or her native town because she doesn't want anyone who may read this to recognise her and think she's seeking publicity. I respect her wish and shall therefore change the town to Roi-Et and give her the fictitious name Tanya).

The letter went on to say she earned 1,220 baht a month. "When I'm in trouble I'll write letter to my friend to pretend that I am very happy. No one know that I feel very sad.

"... When I heard some one said that if we need to be good in English not only to read but also to write letter. That why I try to write this letter to you to practise my English.

"And hope that you won't mind to answer this letter to a pen-pal in Roi-Et... Thank you!"

Of course I answered it. I made a photocopy of it, on which I corrected her mistakes, and sent it back to her.

I was curious to know just what she meant by "an old Thai girl," and also the significance, if any, of that "Top Secret!" (I later discovered it was just a joke!)

I asked her to tell me more about herself, and told her a few details about myself too — such as my age, which was then 64.

Her second letter followed promptly — "... You and I are old, why just pretend that we are young enough for the new world. (Young in heart)... I was born in the year 1944. My father had died when I was two years old. When I was five years old my mother married again. — My world has broken down. I couldn't stay with my step-father. My aunt took me to live with her. I feel (she meant "I felt") so bitter, sorry and worry... I finished school (MS 3) when I was 17 years old now I'm 34 years old and studying in MS 5. I have to study English in school too... And now you can help me with my English. And do you know? I am very interested in an old Englishman like you. And hope that you are a good person too..."

I corrected that letter too, answered her queries about grammar, and returned it. And so it went on: I received a dozen or so letters in the two years that followed. I learned that she was working very hard indeed, studying for her MS5 English exam for two and a half hours every evening after a long working day — and all day Saturday too. She was doing very well, getting "A's" and good grade points term after term.

It wasn't long before she telephoned me one Saturday morning at home to say she was in Bangkok for the weekend. I invited her over to my house for the day, and my wife Laddawan and I got to know her quite well. She's a pleasant looking woman, rather with the tough upcountry appearance of a farmer, yet extremely fluent in spoken English, and obviously a person of great sincerity.

That day I learnt about her five children, all at school, her husband who earned a little over 1,000 baht a month as a government driver, and whom she loves and is faithful to. She's a fine wife and mother, and her sole aim in life was (and still is) to better herself so her husband and family can have a higher quality of life. And she has always known that the only way towards a better job was for her to master the English language.

Her letters continued after that first visit. Gradually I learnt about her earlier life. After leaving school at 17 she came, like so many others, to Bangkok, full of hope. "...I was so excited. I stay with my cousin. I begged her to find me a job, so she found me a job working in the house of a Chinese family. I received only 50 baht a month.

" I needed a place to live, so I stayed there for one month. After that my cousin found me another job, this time working for a Thai family. My responsibility was to care for the children...

"I got married when I was 23 years old. I married him because I need a friend to protect my life... He was nice, so I thought that nothing will happen between us, even though we had no money at all after we got married. We worked very hard to earn the living. We used to work in rice-field.

"When I was in Bangkok I had a part time in the afternoon to go to learn typing. I can type both Thai and English that is why I could get the job in Roi-Et government office two years after I got married. My salary was 400 baht a month.

"...I tried so hard because my education was very low. Two years after I was in high school, I finished and my heart leaped with joy. I got 2.90 (grade points). I can't tell how glad I am..."

Immediately after passing her MS 5 exam in English, Tanya was able to get a much better-paid job in one of Thailand's many refugee camps.

She is now much nearer to Bangkok — but, sad to-say, separated from her family in Roi-Et. She started coming to me for English lessons at weekends, and I did what I could to help her further.

Khun Tanya is pushing and struggling ahead with her English because she still doesn't earn enough and needs a better job. I have written about her because to me she seems a fine example of Thai grit and determination to pull oneself up by one's own bootstraps, and succeed — not for herself, but for the sake of her husband and children.

When "Toang" was a novice

Until a few years ago, my wife's sister Sumalee, her husband and her four children lived with us in a series of rooms in the outbuildings of my rented house. Sumalee's husband drove me to work every morning in a battered old Corolla, and fetched me home in the evening.

Then suddenly, for no reason that I ever discovered, her husband died in November 1979, after less than a week in hospital. I never did find out just what he died of. The body was kept at a large temple nearby until the following April (1980), when it was cremated; and on the occasion of the cremation Sumalee's 13-year-old son whose nickname is "Toang" became ordained as a Buddhist novice monk.

There was nothing unusual in this. Young boys often ordain as novices as part of the cremation ceremony of a parent or elderly relative. This is known in Thai by a characteristically simple and picturesque phrase — "buat nah fai," literally "ordination in front of the fire." But usually such entries into the monkhood only last for a few days; in fact my wife says a boy may even ordain on the morning of the cremation day, and disrobe again the same evening.

With Toang, however, it was different. He had long wanted to wear the orange robes and take the vows of a Buddhist novice. As early as 1976 when I was a monk for a month at Wat Cholpratarn just outside Bangkok, and Toang was only nine, whenever the family came to visit me Toang would look wistful and beg his mother to let him become a novice. Sumalee even went as far as asking the abbot what was the earliest age at which they accepted novices, and was told nine years old.

However, Sumalee wouldn't agree, because Toang was so naughty. My wife says he used to come and ask her every day for five baht, and whenever she refused he would fly into a rage and bang his fist on the table or stamp his foot; and he used to steal the occasional 100-baht note left lying on the table. Yet still, he continued wanting to become a novice.

In retrospect, it seemed almost as if he knew of his own shortcomings and wanted to put them right — or, who knows, perhaps he even felt he *must* put them right.

Toang disrobed after nine months. The change in that boy while he was in the monkhood was quite remarkable.

All monks and novices (a man cannot become a full monk until he is 20) are naturally calm, and their outward equanimity may be taken as a sign of an inner peace of mind — though again, no one other than the individual himself can know whether this is indeed so or not. But the new thoughtful look in Toang's eyes whenever he came to visit us, and his willingness and aptitude to learn Pali and the Dhamma or Lord Buddha's Teachings, seemed to indicate that he really was finding a new peace of mind.

On his visits to our house, I used to "wai" to him and he smiled but being in the monkhood he did not, of course, "wai" back.

On his last visit as a novice he sat on a garden chair on the verandah and faultlessly intoned a Pali blessing while his mother and I knelt "waiing" in front of him.

In a way, Toang was probably instrumental in saving his mother's life and that of his sister Mook; for the two of them were at the temple visiting him when the giant banyan tree at the back of our house crashed to the ground in a thunderstorm, completely demolishing our outbuildings. If Sumalee and Mook had been in their rooms, they would almost certainly have been crushed to death. Mook's father, having died five months earlier, was spared all this; but the ancient Corolla was a crumpled mass of metal, and the garage in which it had been parked was a heap of smashed timber and rubble.

On one occasion, Toang brought a fellow-novice of about the same age to our house. This boy was from a very poor family indeed, as the following little incident shows.

The novice (we never asked his name) went to the toilet. Seeing a strange-looking knob, he pulled it... The next second, he was out in the kitchen yelling at the top of his voice "MAEH!!! TOK JAI MOT LEUY!!!" ("COO!!! THAT DIDN'T HALF GIVE ME A

START!!!") The sudden loud noise caused by his pulling the knob, plus all that water gushing out all over the place, had startled him out of his wits. It was the very first time in his life that he'd ever seen a flush toilet!

P.S. While I was busy writing this, sitting on the verandah, I became aware of someone squatting in front of me and "waiing" respectfully. I looked up; it was Toang — dressed in an ordinary white shirt and shorts...

Our eclipse

In 1980 a partial eclipse of the Sun took place on Chinese New Year's Day. This was not specially arranged as part of the festivities; it was, I believe, a purely natural phenomenon.

Eclipses are universal, of course, but there were a few rather Thai features about our eclipse. When I say "our," I mean our private family eclipse, as viewed from our garden.

As readers of "Thai Ways" may know, my wife Laddawan is an astrologer. Perhaps that's why I couldn't seem to get her interested in looking at the eclipse itself. She was far more interested in her astrological books and charts, trying to work out why there should be an eclipse on that particular day, February 16.

Anyway, I am interested in nature in a mild sort of way, and around 4.30 p.m. I realised I should have remembered to get hold of some dark-coloured plastic to look at the Sun, but hadn't done anything about it.

I searched in the drawer in my bedroom, but found only one rather tatty old pair of sunglasses. One quick look at the Sun through them immediately convinced me that that was the way to sure and permanent blindness. I began yelling for more sunglasses. I borrowed Laddawan's, and another pair from her sister Sumalee.

Have you ever tried looking at the Sun through *three* pairs of sunglasses? Dogged to the last, I managed to keep all three pairs on my nose, and — yes, there it was! A neat arc cleanly clipped out from the bottom right-hand edge of the Sun. Excited, I called Laddawan to come and look, but by now she was involved in something far more interesting on the telly.

About 15 minutes later I took another squint, and — yes again, the missing piece of Sun had definitely grown bigger. I asked Sumalee and her daughter Mook to have a look through the sunglasses, and they saw it too; unlike my wife, they seemed quite interested.

As I continued looking every 15 minutes or so, the Sun's missing arc grew larger and gradually shifted upwards and to the right. It was some time about then that I first became aware of The Smell.

It was awful. The whole house and parts of the garden reeked with the stench of burning rubber. A fuse or a short circuit? Were we on fire? Or was someone burning old tyres?

A few minutes later Sumalee appeared and smilingly handed me a large piece of heavily smoked glass. "You'll find it much easier with this," she said in Thai. "Better than three pairs of sunglasses!" So that explained where The Smell had come from. I didn't ask what it was that Sumalee had burnt to produce the smoke on the glass; maybe it *was* old tyres...

Anyway, the smoked glass certainly did make it easier to watch the progress of the eclipse. Sumalee and I were able to follow the missing arc, growing steadily larger and climbing up the Sun's right-hand side.

At one stage, we even lured Laddawan away from her television programme during the commercials. She rushed out onto the lawn, grabbed the smoked glass, took a quick look and said "Yes, yes, I can see it!" "No, you can't — not from where you're standing," retorted Sumalee. "That's a branch of a tree you're looking at!" "Oh, yes, so it is. Well, never mind — I'll take your word for it — "and she dashed back indoors, afraid her programme might have started again.

The best time for viewing the eclipse was just before sunset, when of course the Sun always looks larger — an optical illusion caused by the refraction of the atmosphere or something. It looked just like a quarter-moon.

Next day I got Laddawan to explain what she was trying to find out about the astrology of the eclipse. In a solar eclipse, the Moon comes between the Earth and the Sun. Laddawan was trying to discover whether there was any significance in the fact that on the chart for February 16, the Sun and Moon (number 1 and 2) were both in the same sign of the Zodiac, while Rahu or the Earth (number 8) was in the diametrically *opposite* sign.

In 1978 there was an eclipse of the Moon on March 24.

(Laddawan told me this; I checked in the Bangkok Post files and she was right). In a *lunar* eclipse, the Earth comes between the Sun and the Moon, and it's the Earth's shadow which blocks out all or part of the Moon. The chart for that day again showed the same effect: The Earth and the Moon were in the same Zodiac sign, but that time the Sun was in the *opposite* sign.

It seems to me that this only proves that the true astronomical positions of the planets are shown correctly on the astrological charts — as they should be!

I know just a little bit about the Thai legend of Rahu, or the Earth, Rahu is said to be a giant who puts the Sun in his mouth during a solar eclipse ("Suriyakraht" in Thai) or the Moon in his mouth during a lunar eclipse ("Jantakraht"). Upcountry Thai folk believe that if they can only make enough noise to frighten Rahu away by banging pots and pans and letting off fireworks, he'll go away... And sooner or later, he invariably does!

On being pregnant

My wife has been telling me some old Thai beliefs and superstitions about pregnancy. The usual expression for a pregnant woman is "puying mee tong" — "A woman with a stomach."

...Well, we've all got stomachs, haven't we? But not all of us are pregnant, I'm thankful to say!

However, the Thai expression conveys a straightforward idea (no pun intended) of the state of affairs, and is typical of the down-to-earth Thai way of putting things. It expresses the essence of the matter: Pregnant women have more stomach than the rest of us.

The strongest belief about a pregnant woman is a very ancient and deeply-held one. She should never set foot inside the "bot" or main chapel of a temple when any religious ceremony is taking place inside.

The "bot" is used for the ordination ceremony when a man enters the monkhood and for other types of religious function as well. No matter what kind of ceremony is taking place, if a pregnant woman enters the "bot" while it is in progress it's believed she will have a difficult time during childbirth.

Apart from avoiding this, one way in which she can encourage an easy birth is to eat those rarities, soft-shelled eggs — another delightfully simple analogy! So relatives and friends of a pregnant woman who happen to come across a soft-shelled hen's or duck's egg, always give it to her to eat.

Then there's the belief about elephants. To ensure an easy birth, a pregnant woman should walk under an elephant's belly. My wife thinks this may be because the elephant is a rare, exalted and valuable beast, but she apologises for being a bit vague about the details.

Another well known idea, and surely a most valuable one, is

that a pregnant woman should never harbour feelings of blame, resentment or hate against anyone. The belief is that if she does so, her child will be born with the same characteristics as the person who is hated or resented.

A shopkeeper or vendor is said to be always very pleased when the first customer of the day is a pregnant woman. This is a sign that business will be good for the whole of that day, because, in my wife's words, two pairs of eyes have visited the shop or stall — those of the mother-to-be and those of the unborn child as well! I suppose it's something like having two customers for the price of one.

And talking of two for the price of one, you know those joined-together "twin" bananas which one sees very occasionally? I mean the kind where the two bananas are joined together all the way along, by a common skin. You've probably guessed what's coming... If a pregnant woman eats such a pair of bananas, she'll give birth to — yes — twins! Thai analogy again, at its simplest and most logical.

A Thai friend has also pointed out that taxi drivers are always especially obliging and kind towards pregnant women because of their "condition." My wife has added her usual shrewd and spicy comment to this, too: She says the driver will do his utmost to help the pregnant woman into the taxi as quickly as possible, and take her to wherever she's going as speedily as he can — because he's scared that she'll give birth inside his taxi!

That's all I know about Thai superstitions concerning pregnancy.

And I'm afraid I can't tell you anything special in the way of Thai beliefs about the birth process itself.

However, my wife says that in upcountry Thailand, after a baby is born, the afterbirth or placenta is usually put inside an earthenware pot and buried under a tree or plant. Not just any tree or plant; it must be the particular species in which the mother's guardian spirit lives. And this depends on which year in the 12-year cycle the mother herself was born.

My wife was born in the year of the Tiger — "Bpee Kahn" in Thai. Incidentally, according to her huge book of ancient lore, this means she is a "female sea-ogre," but I can't honestly say she looks or behaves like one! It also means that her guardian spirit lives in the turmeric or "kamin" plant. So after her son

Jiap was born the placenta was duly buried beneath a turmeric plant.

Now here are a few additional details from my wife about birthmarks and moles. A birthmark, Thai people say, is actually a mark made by the undertaker after death in the immediately previous existence. So if a baby has one or more birthmarks, this means it was a human in its previous life.

Moles, like birthmarks, have special significance too — but here again, I'm afraid my wife's information is rather sketchy. She says that a mole ("fai" in Thai) means either good or bad luck, depending on its position on the body, and on its colour. A red mole is better than a black one, and a "white" one (pale pink, that is) is best of all. She gave me two examples: A mole just beneath the eye signifies teardrops — so there will be much weeping throughout one's life. And a mole on the stomach, especially if it's a "white" one, is the best possible kind; it's called "fai racha" — a "royal mole."

A Christmas past

Western readers who have spent Christmas and New Year in Thailand will perhaps have noticed two features which stand out as different from the West: Firstly, Christmas Day in this predominantly Buddhist country is for most Thais a perfectly ordinary working day; and secondly, seasonal gifts are presented at any time between Christmas and New Year's Day.

As those of us who work in offices know, the office is a prime place for present-giving, and throughout the festive season some people's desks are piled with parcels so that one can't always tell whether a person is the giver-to-be, or the receiver. Outside of the office, presents are mostly given during the weekend between Christmas and the New Year, when people have enough leisure time to make rounds of visits to their friends' homes. In Thailand, one gives New Year rather than Christmas gifts — or let's say it's a combination of both. In fact, present-giving continues for several days after New Year's Day.

My own experiences of past working-day Christmases in Bangkok are just a dim memory now, from the days when I taught English and film-making at Chulalongkorn University. But one particular Christmas Day stands out; it's one I'll never forget, because it was so startling and at the same time so typically and delightfully Thai.

I had gone along to give my scheduled English lecture to a group of third-year Physics students in the Faculty of Science. They were a particularly bright and pleasant group, I remember, but on that Christmas Day they somehow seemed even more so than usual. As soon as I set foot inside the classroom they startled me out of my wits by leaping to their feet as one man (and girl) and bursting into violent song. "We wish you a Merry Christmas," they yelled, in perfect tune," we wish you a Merry

Christmas; we wish you a Merry Christmas, AND A HAPPY NEW YEAR!!!"

Then they sat down, all grinning broadly. Still in rather a state of shock from this sudden and unexpected assault on my ears, I could only say "Well, er — thank you very much — and the same to you!" (Does one wish a Thai a merry Christmas. I wondered at the back of my mind? I supposed there was no harm in doing so). My commonplace utterance drew a loud and prolonged burst of clapping. I felt as if I'd just won the Nobel Prize for Literature.

Recovering my composure more or less, I was just turning towards the blackboard — my mind had been on irregular verbs, and there was something important I simply had to tell them — when one young man called out "Sir! Sir!" "Yes, what is it?" I asked. The student got up from his seat and, accompanied by much giggling and whispering among the girls, walked up to me and handed me an elegantly wrapped parcel. "For you, Sir," he said, "Merry Christmas!" Another deafening burst of clapping from everyone. "For me?" I asked — rather superfluously, since he'd just given it to me. I thanked them all profusely, and turned to the blackboard again. But it was not to be... Not yet.

"Open it, Sir!" they called in chorus. Indeed, it was a command. But... Open that gorgeous creation covered in paper bearing a classical Thai motif and decorated with coil upon elegant coil of artistically disposed ribbons? It seemed almost like desecrating a work of art.

However, I did as ordered, hoping that whatever was inside the parcel was even half as beautiful as the outside. I found a plain cardboard box, inside which was a very attractive matching tie and handkerchief in Thai silk. "Oh, this is beautiful! Thank you all very much indeed!" I said again. Then, still thinking of those irregular verbs, I turned once again to the blackboard... Only to be foiled yet again.

"Sir! Sir! Put it on, Sir! Put it on!" Again student authority asserted itself, benevolent but insistent. I had no choice. Standing there in front of them, feeling a bit of a fool but by now grinning as broadly as they were, I undid my tie, took it off and put the gift tie on. At the last minute I also had the presence of mind to tuck the matching handkerchief in my breast pocket. Another burst of delighted clapping. I now felt like the Best-

Dressed Man of the Year.

A little apprehensively, wondering what else was coming — a brass band, perhaps? — I turned to the blackboard for the third time that morning. "And now," I ventured, "do you remember what I told you last week about those special irregular verbs?"

They did — at least, some of them did. And at last they let me get on with the Christmas Day lecture.

"Kamoy!"

Early one morning some years ago my maid came into the second-floor apartment where I was then living, took a look around and called out "Master! Come look quick! Television and stereo gone!"

It was true. The TV set and stereo were nowhere to be seen. The usual hue and cry was raised, with members of the apartment's resident staff rushing about clucking like distracted hens.

My maid touched my arm and pointed silently to the telltale corner of the screen door leading to the balcony outside. The wire screen had been neatly cut away, leaving a gap just wide enough for an arm to be inserted so that it could reach down and unlock the bolt from inside. So much for the security provided by bolts, I though ruefully.

Suddenly someone shouted "Look!" and pointed. Perched on top of the high wall separating our compound from that of the large school next door was one of my twin loudspeakers. A search-party went into the school grounds, and there, nestling snugly against the wall hidden from view, they found the lot — TV, stereo and the other loudspeaker, all without even a scratch on them. I was lucky; evidently the "kamoys" (the Thai word for thieves) had been disturbed during their getaway and had made a run for it, leaving their loot behind to be collected later — which they never did.

The second time I was "kamoy'd" I wasn't quite so lucky. It happened a few years ago, in my house in a quiet soi. My wife, woken up at about one o'clock in the morning by the barking of our dogs, got up and looked out through the window into the garden.

She saw a man walking across the lawn from the fence, over which he had obviously just climbed, towards the back of our house. My wife couldn't make out in the dark whether the intruder had a gun or knife hidden on him, so very prudently she remained where she was, inside the house. "KAMOY!" She yelled at the top of her lungs. "KAMOY!! KAMOY!!!"

But nobody else woke up. My wife waited. The events which followed have become a bit confused in the re-telling, but not long afterwards she heard the sound of a motorcycle revving up and roaring away from our gate. She then discovered that one of the two gas cylinders outside our kitchen was missing.

By this time the rest of the family (with the exception of me!) had woken up, and everyone had gathered in the garden. Peering over the fence, my wife could see quite unmistakably the circular mark made in the earth at the edge of the soi where the kamoy had temporarily rested the stolen gas cylinder — and also one of his shoes, which he hadn't had time to put on before making his getaway.

About an hour later there were again shouts of "KAMOY!" from another house a short distance down the soi. A different man was seen running away. All our lot, including my wife's young nephews and nieces, immediately gave chase. My wife says she really doesn't know exactly what two women and three young children would have done if they had caught the "kamoy"!

Meanwhile the owner of the other house had phoned the police, and soon they caught the runaway "kamoy." They brought him along, handcuffed, in their police car and asked my wife if this was the man she had seen; she said no, it wasn't. The police then asked the "kamoy" why he had climbed the wall into the other house. Without batting an eyelid he replied that he had needed to obey a call of nature — but he said it in rather more basic, down-to-earth terminology.

The police told my wife they had already chased a man on a motorcycle and, while doing so, they had seen an empty gas cylinder lying in the ditch in the next soi. Not wishing to lose sight of their prey, they didn't stop to pick the gas cylinder up, intending to do so later. Their prey, however, got away when a traffic light in Sukhumvit Road turned red at a strategic moment; and by the time they got back to where the gas cylinder had been...Yes, you've guessed it — it was no longer there.

As in other countries, Thai "kamoys" do indeed often work in gangs. I'm told they usually hold a little ceremony just inside the premises they are about to burgle. All I know about this ceremony is that it involves a red rose and the lighting of joss-sticks.

The owner of a private company which supplies security guard services once told me a few details about the psychology of "kamoys" in Thailand, and about his own psychological methods in dealing with them — methods which are typically and charmingly Thai.

He said he trained his guards to make friends with the neighbourhood people wherever they were stationed — also including members of the local underworld. When the guards were off duty they sat chatting with the local kamoys in the coffee-shop — something which would surely be unthinkable in the West.

"Please don't come and interfere with us when we're on duty," the guards told them. "After all, we're only doing our job, and it's our livelihood. We have wives and kids, just the same as you. If you pinch anything from our premises, we'll lose our jobs!" The amazing thing was that this friendly man-to-man approach often seemed to work.

There was however one occasion when this "fraternisation" overreached itself. An off-duty security guard had, it seemed, professed his ardent love for the attractive daughter of a leading local gang-leader.

The gang didn't go along with this at all. It was, they felt, carrying "fraternisation" too far — much too far. They decided to teach that security guard a lesson.

At dead of night they broke into the compound where the amorous guard was now on duty, and beat the living daylights out of him. Just to emphasise their point, they also stole a couple of air-conditioners from the same premises.

Unfortunately their intelligence service had let them down; they didn't know that the guards' duty roster had been changed at the last minute. In the pitch dark, they had beaten up the wrong man...

Next day when they discovered their dreadful mistake, they sent a profuse apology via the grapevine... And, believe it or not, they also surreptitiously sent back the two airconditioners!

A talented little girl

A few years ago I met an interesting and charming little Thai girl who had been in the news. She was Nipa Sae Lim of Wat Sa Bua (Lotus-Pond Temple) School, and she had won an award in the UN-sponsored International Children's Art Contest which took her and her art teacher to Paris.

Having myself read about Nipa and her paintings, I decided I'd like to write about her. So off I went with two Thai colleagues to the school, to meet her and her teacher. In fact, as things turned out, I went not once but three times. At our first meeting I hesitatingly asked if I might borrow four of Nipa's paintings to take back to the office for photographing; the following day I went to return the paintings and ask Nipa some more questions, but she'd gone out with her teacher to receive an award from the Ministry of Education — so back I went on the third day. After that, I began to feel I knew Nipa, her art teacher Mrs Montha and the school itself quite well.

Wat Sa Bua School is surprisingly quiet and peaceful considering it's in the heart of the city, just where Rama I Road crosses over the main railway line from Hualamphong Station. What struck me about the temple compound was the apparently total lack of monks each time I went, although a few white-clad Buddhist nuns could be seen.

The other very interesting sight in the compound was the making of joss-sticks. Groups of finished sticks lay in neat circles on the ground, drying. The way these circles are formed is a fascinating example of Thai manual dexterity: The workers simply place a bundle of sticks vertically on the ground, shaped into a rough cylinder by the middle finger and thumb of each hand — and then take their hands away! As if by magic, the joss sticks fall neatly on the ground in tightly interlocking circles. ("You and I couldn't do that to save our lives!" said my Thai colleague to me. I'll go along with that).

Much larger king-size joss-sticks are also made at the temple, about three feet long and looking more like rockets. I believe they are used in the same way as the giant Lent candles, being large enough to stay alight all through Lent.

The school itself is a primary or "Prathom" school, with about 300 pupils aged from seven to 12. The two-storey school building is elderly and charming, built mainly of wood; the cement gables and cornices have delightful stuccoed patterns on them. Inside, all the wooden floors are polished and spotless. A special corner of an upstairs room had been set aside for Nipa to work in — she came in every morning at 7.30 and painted for an hour before school started — and about 25 of her more than 100 paintings were on display round the walls in a larger room.

I found I was able to talk to Nipa without too much difficulty, except for my rather limited vocabulary. She was neither shy nor swollen-headed by her success, but a perfectly normal and delightful little girl, the youngest of seven children. Her father worked as a receptionist and general factotum in a small hotel in Chinatown; her mother made a bit of extra money sewing up cloth sports caps at home. The family was none too well off, I gathered.

Nipa had been painting since she was six. Her work showed tremendous natural talent; but the development of that talent also owed a lot to Mrs Montha, obviously a gifted teacher who knew how to get the best out of her pupils. She had encouraged and nurtured Nipa's gift for painting by taking her to interesting places, pointing things out to her on the spot — and then leaving the rest to Nipa's own vivid memory and imagination.

Whenever foreign countries organise children's art contests, the Thai Government's Public Relations Department sends circulars round to all government schools. This was how Nipa's paintings first became known internationally; she won awards from India in 1975 when she was only eight, and from Italy and Belgium the following year. In the most natural and straightforward manner, she took me to see framed certificates hanging in the headmaster's office.

Nipa's paintings were sheer joy. Subject-matter, composition, line, and especially colour — all were lovely. Done in oils on standard-size 65x45-centimetre canvasses, they were like a microcosm of Thai life: Markets with vendors, street scenes with figures reminiscent of L.S Lowry's north-of-England milltown paintings, canals, river life, agriculture, Modigliani-like portraits, an ornamental flight of birds, the school playground — and my own favourite, a picture of a woman giving alms to two monks outside a temple. With its flowing lines and brilliant oranges, reds and yellows, this was a little gem.

Mrs Montha also showed me a picture done by eight-year old Charoenchai, who had been painting for only a year and a half. Noticing his lively interest and doodling based on what she was teaching in class, she started telling him about current events. He got hold of the idea that to cut down forests illegally is wicked — and painted a huge red giant with his mouth full of illegally cut logs in the midst of the forest.

An idyllic holiday

It must have been in 1969 or 1970 — I can't remember which. I do remember it was late October and it was a carefully planned three-way, 10-day trip: By sea from Bangkok to Songkhla; by the Transport Company's regular orange bus service from Hat Yai across the peninsula to Phuket; then back to Bangkok by Thai Airways.

And it turned out to be one of the most restful, idyllic holidays of my whole life — especially the sea trip. Unfortunately, the delightful passenger service by sea from Bangkok to Songkhla doesn't exist any more, which is indeed a great pity. It was at that time run by the Thai Navigation Company with three or four coast-going vessels. Ours was the m.v. "Bhanurangsri," a Danish-built diesel cargo vessel with about six passenger cabins.

The two-and-a-half-day sea voyage was almost incredibly cheap: 300 baht per person one-way Bangkok-Songkhla all in, with four meals a day (yes, four — including afternoon tea British-style, brought to us on deck), not forgetting morning coffee. The distance by sea is a little over 700 kilometres — say about 450 miles.

My wife and I boarded the "Bhanurangsri," which was moored on the Thon Buri bank of the river, at about 8.30 on a Sunday morning, and settled into our comfy little cabin. The ship was due to sail at 9 a.m. sharp — and she did. We steamed (or rather, dieseled) slowly down the Chao Phya River... As far as the upstream side of the Krung Thep Bridge. And there we stopped.

And stopped... And stopped...

The trouble, apparently, was that they couldn't raise the Knung Thep Bridge to let us through — because of a city-wide power cut. (It was a Sunday, remember).

No one seemed to have any idea how long the power would be off, but everyone was very "jai yen" ("cool-hearted") about it. We were served a delicious lunch on the top deck, right there in the middle of the Chao Phya River in the heart of Bangkok. It was certainly a rather unusual place to be eating one's lunch...

Finally at about 2.30 p.m., amid mild cheering, the power came back on. They opened the bridge, and we proceeded on our way — only four hours behind schedule.

The afternoon journey (oops, sorry, *voyage*) down-river was pleasant and placid. We passed the colourful bustling waterfront of Samut Prakan or Paknam, and shortly afterwards on the opposite bank, the gleaming white spire of Phra Samut Chedi to which my wife reverently "wai'd."

After a brief squally end-of-monsoon rain-shower near the mouth of the river, we moved slowly out into the Gulf of Thailand just as the sun was setting, with the hump-backed island of Koh Si Chang prominent on the horizon to our left (I mean, to *port!)*

Before I had planned the trip, friends had warned me that the sea would most likely be terribly rough at that time of the year; but for some reason I ignored these warnings. And for once, my instinct was right: The sea was as smooth and calm as the proverbial millpond throughout the whole trip.

Dinner that night was served in the ship's small dining-room (or should I say galley? No, that's the kitchen, isn't it?) We were the only cabin passengers on board, although there were a great many less fortunate than us who were travelling steerage — plus all kinds of cargo, from pigs to brand-new road trucks.

So we had the dining-room to ourselves, and the setting and service were splendid, spick-and-span and shipshape. We dined off spotless white linen tablecloths amid polished teak and gleaming brass pillars, served by very attentive stewards in immaculate uniforms.

The whole atmosphere, and the huge silver sugar-bowls in particular, reminded me of my occasional wartime meals in England in Royal Navy and Fleet Air Arm officers' messes.

All our main meals on the trip were "set meals" — there was no à-la-carte menu. And indeed none was necessary, for the meals were imaginatively planned so that alternate lunches and dinners consisted of Thai and Western food.

We awoke to brilliant sunshine and a glass-smooth sea. A distant smudge away on the starboard horizon indicated the coastline somewhere around Prachuap Khiri Khan. Breakfast in the teak-and-brass-pillared dining room was very English — bacon and eggs, toast and marmalade, and as much coffee as we wanted.

We had the top deck to ourselves (and indeed the whole forward part of the ship), and it was here that I found a peacefulness such as I could scarcely remember before. An awning sheltered us from the sun, and there was absolutely nothing to do but sit in deckchairs and watch the empty, silent sea glide slowly by. (The "Bhanurangsri's" top speed, the elderly captain told me, was 17 knots, or about 19 miles per hour, but we never went flat out; we proceeded most of the way at a sedate 12 to 15 m.p.h.).

Laddawan read a book, and later told my fortune with the cards; there was so little breeze that she was even able to do this without the cards blowing away.

Lunch was tasty Thai food, served on deck by our ever attentive and smiling steward. In the afternoon we passed a green, hilly island covered with palm trees, Koh Phangan.

I spent some time in the wheelhouse chatting to the crew, and learnt that because we were four hours late we wouldn't arrive at the next island, Koh Samui, until nearly dusk.

Hardly had we left Koh Phangan behind than we sighted Koh Samui. In those days it wasn't nearly as well known as it is today, but I'd read about it and was quite keen to see it.

The ship anchored about a kilometre offshore as the island had no proper harbour. A motor-launch was waiting to take us and a few other passengers ashore.

The captain glanced at his watch. "Don't be late!" he told us sternly. "We'll stay here exactly an hour — and if you aren't back in time, we shan't wait for you!"

He obviously meant what he said, and feeling a little like guilty school-children, we promised to be back in time.

By the time we stepped ashore it was dusk, and we couldn't see much of Koh Samui — and anyway there was so little time.

When we were safely back on board, the ship set off southward again, and shortly afterwards we were served a delicious fish dinner on deck.

After dinner Laddawan went to the cabin to read, but I installed myself on the lower deck, right at the front of the ship (in the bow, as we sailors call it). The moon was nearly full, and I began to rub my eyes, for we seemed to be entering fairyland.

In front of us, and on either side, the weird shapes of hundreds of jagged rocky islands loomed up, and we threaded our way between them across the gleaming silver sea. They looked like cleverly lit cardboard silhouettes on the stage. It was pure magic. The phrase that flitted through my mind was "Thousand-Island Dressing"... Perhaps I was still thinking of that delicious dinner.

The magic continued, endlessly it seemed. But I was getting sleepy, and reluctantly went to bed.

The next day was cloudy with a hint of rain. We could see the coast south of Nakhon Si Thammarat quite clearly. The captain said we'd reach Songkhla by midday or soon after.

And so we did, more or less — at 1.30 p.m. to be precise, in pouring rain. We went ashore and were whisked off to the Samila Hotel for three or four more peaceful days by the seashore.

For those who haven't been to Songkhla, I'll just mention three of the many things worth seeing: The miles of quiet sandy beach fringed with tall pines, with views of the two offshore islands known as "The Cat" and "The Mouse"; the park behind the hotel filled with bushes cleverly trimmed in the shapes of animals; and a steepish but quite short climb up a hill not far from the hotel, with a radio mast and ruined temple on top, from which there's a magnificent view in all directions.

It was the first time Laddawan had been so far South. "I like it here," she said, "the people seem so much more relaxed and somehow friendlier than in Bangkok."

We took a taxi to nearby Hat Yai, which was very much less developed then than it is now. In all the streets vendors were selling apples — shiny red beauties at three baht apiece — and cheap umbrellas from Hong Kong.

My other memory of Hat Yai is of banks; there seemed to be at least one branch of a bank in every street. Even in those days it was evidently a very busy commercial centre.

Finally we left Songkhla for a one-night stopover in Hat Yai, and this time just for a change we went by train. The fare was two baht each for the 30 kilometre journey, which had all the charm of small country branch railway lines everywhere, with the train snaking around hillocks and diving in and out of wooded groves.

After our one-night stay in Hat Yai, we got up very early to catch the regular Transport Company's orange bus for the nine-hour cross-peninsular journey to Phuket. (We'd already booked our bus seats the previous afternoon).

On the dot of 7.15 a.m. the large orange bus, fairly full with an assortment of farmers' wives, small-time businessmen and a few baskets of chickens, pulled out of Hat Yai bus terminal.

Very soon we were tearing along a country road through lovely mountain scenery — and shivering with cold from the draught of fresh early-morning air coming in through the open door and windows!

First stop Phattalung — and soon after that the road started winding its way up the aptly named "Khao Phap Pha" or "Folded Cloth Mountain" range, with wonderful views reminiscent of Switzerland. Then down again, rounding more hairpin bends onto the plain and the attractive provincial town of Trang.

On again, mostly over flat country through rubber plantations, but with occasional rugged mountains towering on both sides of the road. The day grew hotter, and we stopped by the roadside while the driver and conductor got out and had lunch. In fact we all had lunch, with a constant stream of food vendors parading up and down inside the bus.

After about 45 minutes the bus crew returned, and we set off again... And drove for what seemed only a hundred yards or so, then stopped for another half-hour during which the crew took a well-earned siesta.

After we had set off once more, the road plunged up steeply into more mountains, looping and winding its way through occasional rain-squalls high above the wonderful setting of Phang-nga Bay far below on our left, dotted with fantastic island rock formations.

And so down to the provincial town of Phang-nga, behind which we could see the locally famous mountain shaped like an elephant's back and head, complete with an eye formed by a natural cave running right through the mountain.

On again over the Sarasin Causeway to Phuket Island, and southward through lush rolling countryside to Phuket town.

We arrived at 4.30 p.m., after a 250-mile journey that called for much skill on the part of our driver, especially in manoeuvring the large bus on winding, wet, slippery mountain roads.

In fact the thing I found most remarkable about that long ride, apart from the wonderful scenery, was that the same driver took us all the way from Hat Yai to Phuket. I was surprised they didn't have a relief driver.

In those days the Thavorn was Phuket's best hotel by far, and here we had a large, comfortable room and lots of delicious local seafood. We stayed two days, during which it rained almost the whole time in a steady drizzle.

We explored the quaint old town with its own special atmosphere, and one or two of the island's lovely beaches, in a damp half-hearted way.

I remember on Hat Surin Beach seeing something new to me — two or three local women on hands and knees making little pointed "chedi's" or spires in the sand, row after row of them. They seemed in a great hurry to finish them before the tide came in and washed their handiwork away. In reply to my query they told me they were "tam boon" — making merit.

On the morning of our third and last day in Phuket — when, of course, the sun shone brilliantly — we flew home to Bangkok.

We were in thick cloud the whole way, apart from a brief downward glimpse of that same glistening white pagoda opposite Paknam Samut Chedi, which my wife had "wai'd" reverently from the ship, 10 days before...

Khru Prateep

"She's just a plain girl who grew up in the slum, but to more than 60 families in the sprawling Klong Toey ghetto she is like a fairy godmother."

So wrote reporter Sumit Hemastol in a newspaper article headed "In a class of her own" in July 1973. He went on:

"For 20-year-old Miss Prateep has turned her run-down wooden shack that is her home into a school where she is teacher to scores of slum children.

"By day she teaches and in the evening she attends a teachers' training college to further her studies."

Sumit ended his article: "Sixty slum children and a dedicated teacher barely out of her teens... Khun Khru, chok dee na krap!" ("Good luck, Teacher!")

In fact, Miss Prateep Ungsongtham (as she then was) started running her school when she was only 16, but not until Sumit's article appeared did the outside world hear about her.

Miss Prateep (now Mrs, see below) has come a very long way since then, and has received worldwide recognition. The 60 children have become more than 5,000 — 1,600 at kindergarten, and nearly 3,000 at primary and secondary levels, not only in Bangkok but also in 14 provinces. Children addicted to drugs as well as those hard of hearing are also being cared for.

She is still pursuing the same aim, with the same singleness of purpose, deep compassion and love for her "brothers and sisters" in the Klong Toey slum which have been her driving force from the start.

I went to see her early in 1982, and she showed me her then latest project, the infants' day-care nursery — of which more anon.

In spite of her fame Khru Prateep is still utterly unspoilt, and her deep sense of commitment is something for which I can only offer my humble admiration.

Here is her philosophy, as expressed in a small booklet she gave me called "MY EXPERIENCE OF SOCIAL WORK IN THE SLUM". I'm quoting from it at some length because she says it so much better than I can.

"PROBLEMS CONCERNING OURSELVES:

"The important one is the problem of deciding how long one can sacrifice oneself for the mass, for children and for the poor. This is the conflict between the common good and the private self.

"People usually start with optimistic evaluation, especially those with little or no experience.

"So when difficulties are encountered, they tend to become frustrated. Dreams dissolve into dependence, and one tends to feel hurt and scared to touch the work again.

"Some people are scared even to analyse the lesson, not daring to blame themselves, but putting the blame on external causes.

"When we start the work, there tend to be many sympathisers and co-workers, but as the work proceeds and becomes harder, there are fewer and fewer helpers. Then we become lonely and ask ourselves 'Why are we toiling, and for whom?'

"After exhausting work we receive no benefit. Finally the idea runs dry and effort is neglected and unfulfilled.

"I myself am continuing the effort because of two thoughts. The first is the pity I have for children with no education.

"I used to be poor before, short of books and clothes. Teachers used to beat me because I did not wear clean clothes to school, and I had to leave school because of lack of funds, even though I desperately wanted to study.

"I had to work since very young to collect money for school fees.

"I pitied other slum friends in similar conditions and made up my mind to become a teacher when I grew up... This is the main impetus when I feel sluggish or despondent.

"The other reason is my conviction that if we persevere and apply the correct method, anything can be achieved. 'Let's see whether this is impossible,' has always been my thought.

"One has to sacrifice a lot when one works for the mass.

"When tired, I would ask myself whether I would be selfish because of some small exhaustion, or would I go on for the sake of the poor and the helpless young...

"Seeing friends of the same generation becoming rich and advancing in social status, I would think back to my relatives, my neighbours. The parents of my tiny pupils. They are still many times poorer than myself. Shall I reap the benefit myself and float away from them, or shall I stay and help them?

"When one is young, one can work for society without thinking much about oneself. Once you reach the age to start your own family, you have to make a clear-cut decision about the future..."

Since she wrote those words, Khru Prateep has been able to solve this problem in her own typical way: she has married a delightful Japanese man who is also a dedicated whole-time social worker; she is now Mrs Prateep Ungsongtham Hata, and they have two healthy young children. They have their own house located in the slum. At the same time, she has vastly expanded her work for the poor and sometimes desperate people in the slum community, by whom she is still regarded with near-adoration as their own "Khru Prateep". Thailand is many times the richer because of her. The Thai word *"prateep"* means "a lamp, a light", and that's what she is for thousands of slum dwellers: a guiding light, a beacon.

Khru Prateep has won two major international awards: The Magsaysay Award for public service in 1979, and the John D. Rockefeller Third Youth Award in 1981 for her "outstanding contribution to the welfare of mankind".

With the money from the first award she set up the Duang Prateep Foundation to carry on her work more effectively; the Rockefeller money she used to set up her next venture, the nursery care centre or Foundation for Slum Child Care, so that pupils who had previously needed to leave school early to look after their younger brothers and sisters could now continue their schooling.

When I visited her, Khru Prateep showed me the nursery care centre, at that time a small two-storey house in a pleasant little garden with swings, where 21 little ones from one month to three years old were being cared for.

Miss Salee, a charming young "nanny" then aged 24, greeted us; she was holding a pale, sickly-looking infant with no hair.

"Two years old," said Khru Prateep. "Malnutrition. But we'll get him right, in time."

With great love and tenderness she then took the poor little thing in her own arms while the smiling Miss Salee showed me the spotless upstairs room with a few more babies in cribs. A slum mother was there, one of the community volunteers who at that time gave two days a month to help in the nursery.

Khru Prateep is now general secretary of the Duang Prateep Foundation, which as already mentioned has increased the scope of its work enormously; and her own life is busier than ever on behalf of the slum community as a whole. The Foundation now has a staff of 130 paid workers and about 200 volunteers to help with the work.

The Foundation has a well established sponsorship scheme through which private individuals and organisations are allocated one or more slum children whose education they pay for at secondary schools, high schools and even at university level — not only in the slum but also through the New Life Project in Chumphon and Kanchanaburi Provinces.

Here is a letter from a seven-year-old slum child to her sponsor. She has one sister, her father is a manual labourer at Klong Toey port who is sometimes out of work, and her mother is also a labourer at a construction site.

How are you, my dear sponsor? I and my family are well. I am writing this letter to have a little chat with you and to say thank you for your support for my education. Now we have an examination and then the school will close for holidays. I will stay at home and study, I do not go anywhere for pleasure. I have many friends. All of them are good as well as my school marks which are "very good".

I wish that Buddha may protect you and your family from being sick or injury and wish you happiness. May your wishes be fulfilled.

This is all for today. I'll write you again and let's have a chat together again.

The foundation now also has many new, large premises to cope with its work. But life goes on; the slum is like a monster, devouring money and help almost as fast as it is poured in. Khru Prateep and her helpers continue relentlessly fighting the monster, the apathy, and they have already made life better for thousands in the slum. What a long way she has come since she started teaching at age 16...

She needs still more help; in cash, kind, services, whatever. If you go and see her, she'll be delighted. And you will surely be touched by her sincerity, the warmth of her personality — and the sheer power of her goodness.

* * *

This section has been updated to 1995.

From Pinewood Studios to Phang-nga Bay

It's all rather a long time ago now. But some of the unfilmed and off-the-record things that happened during Secret Agent 007's visit to Thailand were amusing enough to be worth telling again.

As it turned out, the movie in question, "The Man with the Golden Gun," wasn't one of the major James Bond moneyspinning films; but that's the way it is in movie-making. If every producer knew during shooting that his film was going to be a smash-hit at the box-office, well... There'd be no bad movies, would there?

Anyway, for the location scenes the filming was to be done in Thailand — mainly on one very scenic little island, Khao Ping-gan in Phang-nga Bay near Phuket.

Before Roger Moore, Britt Ekland and the other big names came out here, an advance army of studio carpenters and the like were sent over from Pinewood Studios in England to prepare the "set" and improve on nature by adding artificial boulders, building the master-mind Scaramanga's hideout on the island and so on.

I met one of the advance film crew, a carpenter or "chippy" as they are known in British film studios, lying on the beach on Khao Ping-gan Island and chewing nonchalantly on a leg of chicken. "How do you like Thailand?" I asked him.

He went on chewing silently for a moment, thinking over my question, then said in a Cockney accent, "Mmm...'s not a bad little plice, reely, I s'pose."

My goodness, I thought, some people just don't know when they're lucky. Here was this English studio carpenter, taking it easy in one of the loveliest places in the world — a spot which tourists pay thousands of dollars to come and see — and all he could think of was "not a bad little plice."

I was on Khao Ping-gan ("the hill of leaning rocks") purely by chance that day, on a tourist day-trip from Phuket. I knew, of course, like almost everyone else in Thailand at that time, that 007 in the person of Roger Moore and a whole crew of other actors, directors, assistant directors, sheensifters (sorry; scene-shifters) and other specialists in the art of film-making would soon be descending on Thailand for the filming of the much-publicised "Man with the Golden Gun."

But it wasn't until it was all over, and everybody had gone back to their native mist-shrouded England, that I had an opportunity to hear from the local Thai production manager, an old friend of mine, the curious anecdotes I shall now relate.

Khao Ping-gan, where most of the location shooting for the film was done, is one of those spectacular limestone bluffs that rise sheer out of the sea in Phang-nga Bay. The only way to reach it is by boat, a journey of some 45 minutes (if the boat is a long-tail one) from the nearest mainland point accessible by road, the Old Phang-nga Customs House.

So, naturally, when the local film production crew headed by the production manager were getting everything ready for the time when the people from England would be coming, one of their first tasks was to arrange daily seaborne transport for them — camera crew, director, actors, the lot. All kinds of boats were hired — long-tail boats, charcoal boats, fishing trawlers, even government boats from the Old Customs House.

There were about 40 long-tail boats for hire. And that was when the trouble started; for the film unit found they would only be needing 20, which they promptly hired for the duration of the filming.

The remaining 20 or so unhired boatman were... Well, they weren't exactly overjoyed. During the first day or two of filming, they made their feelings quite clear in the most direct possible way: They jammed their empty boats against those carrying the film people so they couldn't get out of the narrow channel into midstream, and threw in various other harassing and obstructionist tactics as well.

So much precious and expensive time was being wasted that the local production team soon got the message. It was that well known ploy, a protection racket.

"OK," said my friend the Thai production manager to the disgruntled unhired boatmen, "150 baht a day to leave us alone...?"

"No way!" (or its equivalent in Thai), they flashed back. "Four hundred baht!"

This was so ridiculous it was almost funny. Even the HIRED boats were only getting 300 baht a day!

Finally 150 baht was agreed on. "Right, that's settled," said the production manager briskly; he had a thousand and one other things to see to. "Now, how many of you are there?

It seemed no one had a clear idea; estimates varied from 28 boats to 43.

"Well, if you can't even make up your minds how many you are, we shan't pay you anything at all!" snapped the production manager, his patience almost at an end (and he is a very patient man).

And then, do you know, the strangest thing happened — something very Thai.

The unhired boatmen's resentment suddenly vanished, melted away into thin air. They smiled, and accepted— NOTHING!

Perhaps they were simply weary of arguing, and of the whole business; but anyway, from then on they never gave the film people any more trouble at all.

There was another example of this "protection racket": A local businessman owned the concession to gather all the birds' nests on Khao Ping-gan, the main filming location. Not just ordinary birds' nests, of course; these were the much prized and very expensive variety used in that favourite Chinese delicacy, birds' nest soup.

Like practically everybody else in Thailand at the time, this local businessman knew about the impending arrival of Roger Moore, Britt Ekland, Christopher Lee and all the other British film people. As soon as he knew that "his" island had been picked for the filming, he was right there on Khao Ping-gan, waiting to greet the advance Thai production team.

"I must tell you that I have to put up the scaffolding to gather the birds' nests on this island immediately," he told them solemnly.

"But that will ruin the film shots," protested the production manager. "I wonder whether you would be kind enough to wait for just a little while — only 10 days, then our filming will be finished. Do you think you could possibly do that?"

"No, I'm afraid not," came the answer." Surely you know the time for gathering the nests is critical; if we waited 10 days, they'd be well past their prime."

So once again it was the same ploy. A sharp ten-minute bargaining session began on the beach.

The production manager asked the businessman how much he thought the birds nests would bring him in net profits; back, quick as a flash, came the answer: 60,000 baht.

Trying hard to suppress a grin, the production manager asked him to work it out again more carefully; and it appeared there had indeed been a slight slip in arithmetic. The correct value was 10,000 baht...

Finally the businessman settled for a paltry 4,000 baht.

And indeed, he was lucky to get even that; because he knew, and the production manager knew, and he knew that the production manager knew... That the season for gathering birds' nests on the island would not start for at least another two months — long after all the filming was over and everyone had gone back to England!

When I said that the Thai crew were responsible for the smooth running of everything during the filming, I was of course speaking relatively; unforeseen incidents were bound to crop up, but by all accounts the Thai crew did a fine job.

With a mixed Thai and British crew, neither nationality speaking or understanding the other's language, it was absolutely essential to have an interpreter. This was even more necessary down south around Phang-nga Bay, where local people totally unfamiliar with the English tongue were temporarily taken on the film company's payroll.

The interpreter seems to have been a real "Born Loser." He probably had a more miserable time during the filming than anyone else in the team. Whenever there was any argument or misunderstanding, he was always the poor unfortunate in the middle, getting abuse from both sides. Anything that went wrong was somehow always his fault. He was even roughed up more than once by the local men who imagined — quite mistakenly — that he was double-crossing them.

Finally in desperation he bought himself a gun (not a golden one) for self-protection. But even this turned sour on him; in fact, it nearly proved his undoing.

He always carried the gun in his trouser pocket, and one day when he was trying to get the cap off a soft-drink bottle and didn't have an opener, he used a hammer. Unfortunately, on the back-swing the hammer accidentally hit the gun in his pocket... Off it went, wounding him severely in the leg. The poor chap spent the next two weeks in Phuket Provincial Hospital...

In the picturesque provincial town of Phang-nga, where most of the British film technicians were staying during the filming, the crew found to their delight that there were four expert tailors' shops where they could get fitted out with handsome made-to-measure tropical-weight trousers and sports shirts. Prices were very cheap too — only 60 baht for trousers and 40 baht for a shirt (that was in 1974).

Delighted with the high quality of the material and workmanship, and especially with the attractive Thai designs of the cotton shirts, most of the crew bought a new set of trousers and shirt every day!

Perhaps they shouldn't have been too surprised (but they were) when the prices suddenly shot up overnight by 200 per cent, at three of the four tailors...

But those foolish three tailors were also in for a shock; their greed had killed the golden goose well and truly, and their very lucrative "farang" market vanished as quickly as their prices had gone up. The film men simply transferred their custom to tailor number four, who very wisely had NOT put up his prices... He soon made himself a small fortune, as you can imagine.

And when the location filming was finished and it was time for the "farangs" to say goodbye and head back for England, the wise little tailor of Phang-nga took each of them in his car the 35 miles to Phuket airport, complete with his wife and daughters. There were almost tearful "goodbyes" and lots of "wais." Customers who buy a new shirt and trousers every day for several weeks on end don't often come the way of a remote up-country tailor...

Some street scenes were also filmed in Bangkok. As stipulated by British film union rules, morning and afternoon coffeebreaks were provided for the film crew; tea, coffee and soft drinks were supplied by the film company, plus a tempting array of smoked salmon and caviar sandwiches, pastries and what-have-you.

During the first few days' filming in Bangkok, stalls for the coffee-breaks were set up on the pavement conveniently near the scenes being shot. Occasionally it happened quite by chance that the stalls were near bus stops. Passengers getting off buses rubbed their eyes: Evidently some bighearted, public-spirited philanthropist was giving away free food and drink, and very posh stuff too! Without pausing to enquire what it was all in aid of, they joined in the fun and helped themselves liberally to the free food and drink... That is, until the Thai production manager suddenly found out what was happening, and quickly put a stop to it!

Some scenes were shot in front of the Rajdamnern boxing stadium, where a hot curry vendor had his stall; the film people were anxious for him to move because he was blocking the view for an essential scene.

"Do you think you could possibly set up your stall somewhere else?" He was asked politely.

"Sorry," came the answer, "I'm well-known around here; lots of regular customers. If I move, I'll lose a whole day's takings — that's 5,000 baht...."

Once again, as he had done at Phang-nga, the production manager quickly suppressed a grin of total disbelief; but he got the message.

"Would you take a bit less?" he asked. "After all, your food won't be wasted — you can sell it tomorrow."

"No, I can't! Has to be eaten fresh; doesn't keep."

Long sigh. "Very well; we'll pay you 5,000 baht to move. But you must give us all your curry, so we can at least use it for our film crew."

"Not on your life! If you want me to move, you must pay me 5,000 baht AND I'm keeping my curry as well!"

Poor production manager; he knew when he was beaten... Sadly he counted out the money...

Finally there was an unscripted scene at the Floating Market.

A mid-west American sheriff and his wife were supposed to be on holiday in Bangkok, and the script called for a baby elephant to come and cadge for tidbits; the sequence was to end with the sheriff spluttering in the canal as if the baby elephant had pushed him in.

What actually happened was that the young animal became

so genuinely enraged by all the shouting and excitement during filming that it really did shove the actor into the canal good and hard — and much sooner than anyone was expecting. But the cameraman managed to grab a shot of totally unrehearsed flailing limbs that was far better than the director had hoped for!

Out and about

The DATE: Sunday January 3, 1982. WEATHER: Sunny and mild. No — on second thoughts, make that "HOT!"

Since 1977 I've only been outside Bangkok twice; staying at home is easier, safer, and much more comfortable.

The last time was on September 13, 1981, when I went with the Siam Society on an unexpectedly slippery and mudridden safari through the orchards of Thon Buri — the first time I'd been outside the city for four years.

And then I did it again.

In the opposite direction, this time — past Phra Khanong Bridge and out into the wilds of Samrong. Although we were only away from home for two hours, quite a lot of things happened...

The occasion itself was a simple one: My wife Laddawan and I went to donate some money towards the construction of a new "sala" or pavilion at Wat Suan Soam — the Orange Grove Temple which is mentioned in the book "Thai Ways." It's the little country temple near which my wife and her sister were born and brought up, and the only other time I had ever been there was for their grandmother's cremation in 1968. So I was curious to see whether the surroundings had become more built-up, what with all the new factories that have sprung up in the area.

And I also wanted to see the shophouse or "hong taeo" which I bought for Laddawan in 1980, built on land belonging to the same temple, and in which her sister Sumalee and three of her four children have been living since the banyan tree fell down in a storm and demolished their previous living quarters in the compound of our rented house near Soi Thong Lor.

At 2.30 p.m. four of us set off in my stepson Jiap's clapped-out gas-guzzling old Fiat 1800: Laddawan, Jiap, his current girl-friend Tukata, and myself.

Before long we were driving due south, along Sukhumvit Highway towards Paknam. I was sitting in front next to Jiap, and the sun was coming in smack onto us through the windscreen, producing a hot, sticky "greenhouse effect;" during a month of cold weather, I'd almost forgotten that old familiar sweaty feeling...

Anyway, we passed through busy Samrong and a mile further on we turned off down Poochaosamingprai Road, and then along a still very countrified (and bumpy) Soi Suan Soam. We passed only two factories, both of them clean, modern, surrounded by lush greenery and without any sign of pollution, and soon we arrived at Wat Suan Soam.

The little temple was just as rural as I remembered it dimly from 14 years earlier. Trees all around, apart from the tiny village community occupying one soi opposite — and the only chimney in sight was that of the temple crematorium.

We knelt briefly before the Abbot in his quarters, "wai'd", prostrated ourselves, gave him our donation and chatted for a short while.

Laddawan says she remembers the same Abbot as a very young monk more than 35 years ago, when she was only five or six years old; she often wore red, and he would call her over, "Daeng! Daeng!" — which means "Red" — and give her cakes and sweets.

Then two "dek-wat" or temple-boys took us to see the half-built new "sala."

After that we left the temple and crossed the road to see Laddawan's "hong taeo" — the first time I'd seen it. I felt a sudden pang of pity — it's so narrow for four people to live in, even though there are two storeys; but there was Sumalee's younger daughter Mook, placidly doing her homework...

Then we set off home.

By one of those curious twists of fate (or more accurately, the rotation of the earth) the sun had now moved further round to the west; so it was on our left as we drove northward. Jiap's front left-hand window is permanently jammed shut, so once again there I was, with the same old "greenhouse effect"...

However, there was still more heat to come...

Not understanding Thai when it's spoken between Thais, I

didn't grasp why we turned off the main road in the centre of Samrong, and down a small soi, until Laddawan explained that Jiap was just going to see a friend for a few minutes...

We stopped outside a pleasant modern wooden house in the countryside — where Jiap had spent the previous night at a New Year's party. After we'd hung around in the garden for a few minutes, Jiap picked up a large square galvanised-iron bin and, slightly to my consternation, put it in the boot of the car (with the bootflap tilted up above it at an alarming angle).

I was even more unnerved when the son of the house, Jiap's friend Sompong, got in the back of the car with Tukata — and Laddawan piled in front with Jiap and me!

Of course it's nice to be close to one's wife... But not to have her practically in one's lap in a steaming-hot "greenhouse"! We sat there sweating profusely while Jiap drove slowly along the soi...

(It's also nice to know, as of course I do know, that Jiap is a naturally helpful boy, always anxious to do a friend a good turn —but, boy, was it ever hot!)

I had a sinking feeling we were taking Sompong and his metal bin all the way home to our house (though I never remembered seeing that bin before; surely it wasn't ours?) — but it turned out that we were only taking the bin as far as Samrong market.

Even that short distance seemed an eternity, with the Sunday afternoon shoppers thronging the road to the busy market under the bridge.

Finally we arrived, and got rid of the bin. But Sompong now had to be taken home again. Another sweltering drive, with Laddawan and me, crammed like a pair of sweaty sardines — until, blissfully, we reached Sompong's house, dropped him off, and Laddawan was able to move into the back with Tukata again.

After that, the drive home was more or less plain sailing, if you'll pardon the mixed metaphor. That is, apart from being stuck immediately behind a stalled car on the incline going up Phra Khanong Bridge, and a bit later on our horn jamming, which meant business with a screwdriver...

We planned to go to the donation ceremony for the new "sala" at Wat Suan Soam the following Sunday. But we didn't go. Let me try to explain why...

My wife said there was no point in our going. When I asked why not, she said, "You know Thai people — we're always changing our minds!"

Asked what she meant, she said she was referring to herself. But I still wanted to know why.

So she patiently explained that she had originally thought the initiation ceremony for the new "sala" was to be held that Sunday; but then she realised that it couldn't possibly be, as the "sala" was only half-finished. That particular ceremony, the "yok chor fah" or raising of the new "sala's" gable, probably wouldn't take place for perhaps another year, depending on how much more money could be raised and how soon.

My wife had in fact confused it with the annual four-day temple fair, which is what took place at Wat Suan Soam the week after our visit. And in fact she went to this by herself on the following Wednesday.

This fair was combined, as every year and at every Thai Buddhist temple, with two religious ceremonies held for the express purpose of raising temple funds — and, of course, for making merit in doing so. One of these was the "Tod Pabpa" ceremony. Combined with this was the ceremony of "pit tong" or applying gold leaf to a venerated Buddha image in the temple.

I won't go into the details of that; it's too long. I'll just mention in passing that once again, for the thousandth time, I learnt something new about Thai religious customs through this conversation with my wife; something maybe she assumed I already knew — or more likely, something it never occurred to her to mention to me.

I'd always thought that devout members of the public applied gold leaf to Buddha images in any and every temple at any time, whenever they went to the temple; but that, apparently, is only true of particularly venerated images in equally famous temples — such as Luang Por Sothorn in Wat Sothorn at Chachoengsao. At smaller or less important temples, the applying of gold leaf only takes place once a year — because at other times there's no gold leaf on sale nearby.

I hope I've got that right...

Teaching film-making at "Chula"

Turning out an old cupboard one day, I was suddenly confronted with reminders of the past, as one usually is on such occasions. I found something which seemed interesting, so I decides to write about it.

The items in question were a whole pile of rather dusty exam papers (or rather, answers to exam papers) from the time when I taught film-making at the Faculty of Education at Chulalongkorn University. They covered a period from about 1968 to 1974, and they brought back memories of the amusing things that happened during what was in retrospect a very happy time — for me, at any rate, and I hope for my students too.

I should first explain that I haven't always been a writer working on the staff of a newspaper. Most of my career was spent in making films — documentary, educational and scientific. (During World War II I was making a very special kind of training films for the RAF, on a subject so top-secret that I wasn't even allowed to tell my parents about it. But now, after 40 years, I think it's safe to reveal the secret: it was called RADAR!)

After the war I had 21 fascinating years working for the Shell Film Unit, which took me to places as far apart as California, Portugal, Holland and Tunisia. Finally, having worked for some 30 years on professional 35mm film gauge, I found myself in Bangkok working on the humbler but much cheaper (and just as effective for teaching purposes) 8mm.

The films were of a special type called "film loops," "cassette films" or "cartridge films." They were in some ways the forerunner of today's videotape cassettes, but they were silent and only ran for a maximum of four minutes, after which they automatically started again without rewinding. This made them useful as classroom teaching aids: there was no language problem, and instant repetition helped the students to learn.

During those six years my job was to teach graduate students in "Chula's" Faculty of Education, as well as some undergraduates in the Faculty of Science, how to make these "film loops" from scratch. And although there was no language problem in using the end product, this was by no means true of my instruction in how to make them!

I'll never forget one pretty science undergraduate called Noppamas — partly because her name reminds me of the legendary 13th century Nang Noppamas who invented the first "krathong" of the type which are floated on rivers, klongs (and flooded streets) on Loy Krathong Day.

This latter-day Noppamas was one of a group of four girls whom I was teaching how to use the camera, tripod, lights, etc, and initiating into the mysteries of animation, slow-motion and time-lapse filming. At that time my knowledge of the Thai language was even worse than it is now — and that's not saying much!

Anyway I was speaking English (slowly, and as distinctly as I could) but it soon became apparent that Noppamas couldn't understand me. After a while she rather shyly asked me "Khor hy Ajarn pood passa Thai" ("Teacher, please speak Thai"). So I switched over to Thai — only to hear Noppamas say after a few moments, "Khor hy Ajarn pood passa Angkrit!" ("Teacher, please speak English!") This was naturally greeted by peals of laughter all round, and my ego took quite a tumble... (Khun Noppamas, if by any chance you read this, I hope you have forgiven me for being unable to explain things to you in either of our two languages).

The first thing my students had to learn was how to draw rough storyboards as working "blueprints" for the films they were going to make. During term-time I let each group of four students choose their own subjects for filming.

For the end-of-semester exams I had to set a written paper, and I always included a question which read: "Draw a storyboard for a film or film loop on one of the following topics: (a)...(b)...etc, or any other subject you like." It was these old exam storyboards which I found in the cupboard.

The special film techniques which I taught my students can be done just as easily on 8mm as on 35mm — animation, slow-motion, time-lapse (which speeds up movements too slow to be seen with the eye), huge close-ups using a simple magnifying-glass stuck on the end of the camera lens with scotch tape — a technique I learnt from a professor of physics in Israel — and even filming through a microscope.

The results of the students' skill and ingenuity were at times extremely beautiful to watch on the screen. A group of four undergraduate girl science students filmed the activities of a colony of red ants in the Science Faculty garden, and got some excellent big closeups of a single ant scurrying to and fro and filling the whole width of the screen.

Another group — girls again! — decided to film a bird (I think it was a duckling) hatching out from an egg. Of course one can't predict the exact moment when a happy event of this nature will take place; and as things turned out, the girls came bursting breathlessly into the classroom where I was giving a lecture, shouting in Thai, "Ajarn, quick! We need the camera — tripod —lights...! It's going to hatch right away!" Complete chaos reigned for a few minutes while they set everything up outside the classroom door — after which I went on with my lecture...

The 8mm gauge is the cheapest and simplest there is. Mostly we used high-quality cameras courtesy of UNESCO, the Colombo Plan and the Education Faculty's audio-visual Education Department whose graduate students I taught. But I also encouraged my students to bring their own movie cameras, or any they could borrow. As a result, we had a most weird assortment of cameras, some of them the like of which I'd never seen before.

On the whole these borrowed cameras worked quite adequately: but one day a girl student said, "Ajarn, this camera belongs to my aunt. She has kindly lent it to me. Do you think we can use it?"

I took a look at it and swallowed hard; it looked even less like anything I'd ever seen. "Have you got the instruction booklet?" I asked hopefully. "Oh, no, that was lost a long time ago," she replied. "This camera's rather old."

I looked at the instructions stamped on the inside of the camera door and at various places on the outside; they were in a strange script which yet somehow looked vaguely familiar. Suddenly realisation dawned on me — it was a Russian camera! "I'm sorry," I told her. "I can't read Russian, and I simply haven't the faintest idea how to use this camera." So she took it back to her aunt...

Some of my graduate students were already teachers or university lecturers, one of them with 10 years' teaching experience in Korat; they had come back to "Chula" to study for their Master of Education degree, majoring in audiovisual education.

One of my earliest such students was a charming and talented lady named Mrs Gobporn. She decided to do her entire Master's thesis on the subject I was teaching — the making and use of 8mm film loops.

She studied privately with me every day for a whole academic year. Since her other major subject in the Vocational Education Department of the Ministry of Education was Food and Nutrition, she embarked on the making of two film loops — "How to make pineapple jam" and "How to make tomato ketchup."

In the scene where the pineapple jam is boiled, a process which as far as I remember takes three hours, she decided to speed up the action on the screen by using the "time-lapse" technique — that is, filming one single frame every minute; the whole three hours would then be condensed into about eight seconds on the screen.

This turned out very successful (after a false start in which it was discovered that a vital ingredient had been left out); the reduction in volume as the jam gradually set was quite striking.

Inevitably when filming something of this kind, one has to do a few "retakes", and after Mrs Gobporn had finished her filming, I practically lived on her delicious pineapple jam for quite a long time!

Then there was Ajarn Ora, who taught English in one of Bangkok's universities. She decided to make a rather unusual film loop on "The Present Tenses," of which the English language has four — Present Simple, Present Continuous, Present Perfect and Present Perfect Continuous.

She designed simple but effective cartoon animation to illustrate sentences such as "The sun *rises* every day" (Present Simple) — the sun was a huge orange-red cut-out disc of paper which rose slowly from behind a rural Thai landscape with palm trees and a farmhouse; and "He can't go out because it *is rain-*

ing" (Present Continuous) — the rain outside the window was animated on sheets of acetate.

It took weeks of preparation and a whole arduous week to film (animation is very slow work, but the results when projected onto the silver screen flash before your eyes in just a few seconds).

After Ajarn Ora had finished her work, the film was sent away for processing. After 10 days, back it came: I was luckily alone when, with trembling fingers, I threaded it into the projector and switched on...

My heart sank into my boots and right through the soles — the first bit of animation was there, though badly "fogged"; after that — nothing, just clear, transparent film through the whole roll. Somehow, I had accidentally exposed the film to bright light, either before it was loaded into the camera or after it was taken out.

I broke the awful news to Ora next time she came. But all was well eventually; we refilmed the whole thing, and this time it came out beautifully. Later she used her film successfully as part of her English teaching.

The film subjects chosen by the students covered quite a wide range. Going through the old story-boards, I found "How to propagate papaya trees from seed," "The Thai Wedding Ceremony," "How to cook 'Krong Kraeng'," "How to make a ranad" (a classical Thai musical instrument), "How to make a simple electric motor," and "The silk screen process." Other subjects were way outside my own knowledge: "Wax-embedding of tissue followed by sectioning by microtome," and "How to make a slide by the Feulgen Squash method," whatever that is.

The films that I found the most fascinating were those showing the delicate, intricate, purely Thai arts and crafts — movements of the Thai Dance, How to make a "baisri", How to make a "krathong," and many more which I've long since forgotten.

I've already mentioned my very close friend and one-time student Sasithorn in this book. She's now a Ph.D., married to an Englishman, living in England and the proud mother of two young daughters. But when I first met her she was a first-year undergraduate in the Marine Science Department of "Chula's" Faculty of Science.

Entering my room after lunch one day, I found a young lady waiting for me. "Hallo, Ajarn Segaller," she said with that wonderful smile of hers, and continued in perfect English, "I'm Sasithorn. I'm your new student. I want to make a film about hydra."

"Oh," I answered rather lamely. "What is hydra?" "Oh, don't you know? It's a small marine creature about six millimetres long. I want to film its digestive process." I gulped, but a quick calculation showed me that we could indeed make this with the equipment we had.

Well, Sasithorn did film the hydra and its digestive tract, and a beautiful film it turned out to be, for hydra-lovers at any rate... And a wonderful friend and regular correspondent Sasithorn still is.

An all-male group of four graduate students once had me slightly scared when they announced the subject of the film they intended to make: The Care, Maintenance and Use of...the Revolver!

All went well with the Care and Maintenance part, which they filmed in the room placed at my disposal at "Chula". (The making of every film always took several weeks, because the students only had three hours a week allotted for this subject in their schedule).

Finally they finished, and I asked rather nervously, "Where are you going to film the use of the revolver?" I hoped they weren't going to suggest doing it in my room! They all had a good laugh at this, and asked me if I'd be free for an upcountry outing the following Saturday. I said yes, I would be.

Off we all went in someone's car. It was a typically Thai and thoroughly enjoyable day's outing. We went to Chon Buri, then turned left inland to Phanat Nikhom. We stopped on the way and called at the Nai Amphoe's house (I think he was the uncle of one of the students). Then we headed out into wild and lovely country. They knew the exact spot, a delightful open clearing dotted with trees and shrubs and with views into the distance.

On one of the trees they fixed the target. Then they set up the camera on the tripod, and the shooting began — in both senses of the word. BANG! BANG! BANG! went the revolver. "Whirr-rr..." went the camera. I was cowering behind a nearby rock; but

I needn't have worried — they were all expert marksmen, and every shot hit the target (and as we later saw on the screen, every film "shot" was in sharp focus, too!)

After the smoke had cleared and there was no more film left, we had a splendid picnic lunch, went to the kamnan's (tambon head's) house — another uncle, I think — and so eventually back home...

That was just one more delightful episode during my film teaching days at "Chula". But perhaps the group I remember as fondly as any were a mixed fivesome of young men and women who decided to film the process of mushroom cultivation.

They found a suitable farm near Pathum Thani just north of Bangkok; the farmer gave them permission to film, and they all set off one weekend (without me, this time; they were fully skilled in handling the camera and other film equipment). Afterwards they took the film directly to the processing shop in Bangkok, and when it was ready they brought it to me.

"How did it go? I asked them. "Well, Ajarn," they answered with what seemed like a mixture of embarrassment and suppressed amusement, "Just put the film in the projector and run it." I did so.

There on the screen I saw the action (including an excellent speeded-up "time-lapse" shot of a mushroom growing and swelling like a balloon being blown up) — but there was something faintly odd about the farm-workers spreading out the straw and so on.

Suddenly I said to one of the girls, "Why, Tuanchai, isn't that you?" This question was greeted with a loud burst of laughter. I looked some more. "And — why, Opas, that's you !" "Yes, Ajarn — it's all of us!" they said. "When we got there, none of the farm-workers was willing to be filmed. They were shy, we think. So we all put on their clothes and they showed us what to do — and we took turns filming each other!"

Anyway, after it had been edited, that turned out a very successful film too...

Happy days.

Some Thai ways at home

Here are a few assorted trivia — things that have happened at home and elsewhere.

I was once giving an English lesson to a Thai lady at my home. After we'd finished, she said goodbye and went outside onto the verandah.

"Why, where are my shoes?" she asked. I hadn't the faintest idea, so I called my wife. With unerring instinct, like Sherlock Holmes, she went straight to the heart of the mystery immediately.

"I think it may be one of the dogs," she said, and set off on a tour round the outside of the house. I knew exactly which of our six dogs she meant: The male member of our pair of twin puppies, black-and-white, adorable, but highly mischievous and utterly untrustworthy.

Sure enough, my wife found one of the shoes at the back of the house. I started to apologise profusely and offered to buy my student a new pair. "Never mind!" said she goodnaturedly. "They were only old shoes anyway, and I have another pair in the car." She got in and drove off.

It was just as well they were old shoes, because after she'd gone my wife found the other shoe, or what was left of it, in some obscure spot right at the bottom of our large garden... It now looked more like the remains of a half-eaten pork chop.

From time to time we have an interesting break in the routine of work at Allied Newspapers in the form of a school visit. Such visits usually consist of a small number of boys and girls in the M. 3 to M. 5 range, that is from roughly 16 to 20 years old, and one or more teachers, who are given a short guided- tour-cum-talk on how a newspaper is put together.

I got roped into helping out with one of these visits. It was a school with what is surely one of the longest school names in the world: Rachaprachasamasai (pause for breath) Ratchadapisek School. And it was almost certainly the biggest guided tour we've ever held — there were some 350 students altogether.

The four or five of us who were "guides" started off with the best of intentions. "OK, you take this group and start off first, and I'll follow with my lot in a few minutes," we said to one another.

Alas, our well-intentioned if somewhat hurriedly improvised plans didn't come off quite as smoothly and efficiently as we wished... The rather complex geography of our premises, with every room connected to every other room via a maze of passages, plus the intense curiosity and interest of our young charges in everything they saw, soon turned our "guided tour" into a relatively unguided one. It was like trying to control a swarm of bees in Hampton Court Maze or Lumpini Park. Notebooks, notebooks... Everything we told them and showed them was feverishly jotted down by each student. I must say it was all a lot of fun, if also a little tiring. The students seemed to be everywhere — except, usually, where we wanted them to be.

"Show them the library," our Managing Editor had suggested, and this I tried hard but in vain to do.

Before long many of the students had become scattered into small groups of close buddies, and whenever one of these groups swept past me I implored them, "wouldn't you like to see our library?" But they were always in hot pursuit of something else — our latest computer technology, or the pasting-up process, or whatever. I never did get to show anyone the library....

Finally they all went, and I sank gratefully into a chair. But not for long. "Hang on," said a colleague, "there's another busload coming..."

Any dream about fire is well-known among Thai people as being a portent of trouble.

Some years ago in the middle of the hot season, my step-son Jiap dreamt our garden fence was on fire. A few days later, he went down with typhoid...

And in October one year during terrible floods, Jiap had a similar dream — but this time he dreamt his hands were on fire! In retrospect, this was very symbolic, because two days later it was his hands that actually caused the trouble.

To be precise, his hands were on the steering-wheel of his old Fiat car. He was driving down Soi Kluay Nam Thai, taking his aunt Sumalee and his cousin Mook back to their home in Samrong and trying to avoid the deep flooding in the Phra Khanong area.

It was night-time, and the rain was pelting down, making visibility very poor. That was probably why Jiap didn't see the newly-erected dyke made of sandbags which stretched across the road, and which earlier in the day hadn't been there at all. Anyway, he drove smack into the sandbags, skidded, and collided gently with a small bridge.

No one was hurt, and after four months the car was repaired and back on the road again...

They say bad luck always comes in threes. (At least, we British say it; I don't think the Thais say it, but never mind).

One December Jiap decided to have a small end-of-the-year party in our garden, to which he invited "just a very few" of his close pals, male and female — about 30 or 40 of them.

The original plan was that he would ask each guest to contribute 50 baht towards the costs — for such things as food, soft drinks, balloons and so on. (Most of the latter seemed to go bang! while they were being blown up beforehand, shattering the normal peace of my Sunday afternoon).

Two or three nights before the party, Jiap again had a dream about fire. This time he dreamt that the new concrete wall along the northern boundary of our garden was on fire.

However, in this most recent dream Jiap found he was able to put out the fire — which according to Thai belief meant he would be able to overcome the trouble. Just to be on the safe side, he decided to ward off the impending trouble in a very simple way — by NOT asking any of his party guests to contribute any money; which meant that he was out of pocket to the tune of about 1,500 baht...

So much for dreams. But other weird things seem to happen at home these days. Things go twang, bump and crash — not in the night, but in broad daylight.

My wife really thought a ghost was around when she heard

her son's guitar playing softly to itself in an empty room... But her fears vanished when she found that one of our two tiny puppies had sneaked into the room and onto the bed.... And had walked across the guitar lying there.

But while I was writing this, there was a loud crash and a tinkle of glass. Our little maid from the Northeast was on her knees cleaning the living-room floor at the time, and my wife and I were sitting outside on the verandah.

It proved to be a pane of frosted glass high up above the living-room window, in which there was now a gaping hole. A few small pieces of glass were found on the floor inside, but the largest piece was in the driveway OUTSIDE... We never did sort out that particularly mystery, but my own theory is that it was a minor earth tremor in Outer Mongolia....

Now here's a Thai joke which involves a play on ENGLISH words.

A Thai doctor educated in the United States came back to Thailand and went to practise herbal medicine in a rural area upcountry. Thai herbal medicine often consists of little pellets, which must usually be taken together with some other substance such as honey.

A country fellow went to see this doctor for some ailment or other, and was duly given some pellets as a cure; but he forgot to ask the doctor what substance they should be taken with, and apparently the doctor also forgot to tell him.

Later he went back to ask the doctor what he should take with the pellets. The doctor, however, was now busy with another patient and shouted "Keep quiet!" Having been educated in the States, the doctor naturally shouted this in English; but he did it in the Thai fashion, leaving off the final consonants of both words, so that it sounded like "Kee kwai!" Now as any Thai will tell you, this sounds exactly the same as the Thai for "buffalo dung" — and this was what the unfortunate man thought the doctor meant. He went away scratching his head, muttering to himself, "Well, if 'khun mor' (the doctor) says so, I suppose I'll have to try it; but I must say it's not very pleasant!"

***

This section was written around 1980, since when the author has moved house twice. However, like most of the material in this book, it has been left unchanged.

Wat Pomaen — Thailand's biggest Chinese Buddhist temple

Tucked away in a part of Bangkok seldom visited by foreigners is a magnificent Buddhist temple that looks more like a Chinese imperial palace.

And indeed it is Chinese. Its name is Wat Pomaen, and it lies in a side road, Soi Sawang Arom, about half a mile away from Sathupradit Road, which leads down to the wide bend in the river south of the city. (You can find Sathupradit Road marked on most maps of Bangkok). As you drive down Sathupradit Road, you can see the curved roof and pinnacles of the temple's main chapel jutting up above the treetops to your left, just before you turn into the rather bumpy soi.

Wat Pomaen (its name means "Temple of the Heavenly Botree") is Thailand's biggest and most lavishly decorated Chinese temple, and is recognised as one of the finest in Southeast Asia. Although comparatively new, it has an interesting history interwoven with that of the Chinese people in Thailand as a whole, and with the even older history of the evolution of Buddhism itself.

The Buddhist Doctrine early on became divided into two major branches — the Theravada, or Doctrine of the Elders, practised in India, Sri Lanka, Burma, Thailand, Laos and Kampuchea, and the Mahayana, which developed in China, Tibet, Japan, Mongolia, Korea and Vietnam. This distinction is important in connection with the customs observed at Wat Pomaen, which being Chinese is a Mahayana temple.

Friendship between the Thai and the Chinese peoples dates back seven hundred years or more to the time of King Ramkhamhaeng the Great of Sukhothai, who sent an embassy to the Chinese court. From then on, Chinese people became more and more integrated into Thai society, and many of them reached the ranks of the nobility. King Taksin of Thon Buri, who rallied the Thai nation after the fall of Ayutthaya in 1767, was himself of Chinese parentage; and it was in his reign that the first known Chinese Mahayana Buddhist monks came to Thailand.

After this the friendship between the two peoples became even stronger through a more intimate sharing of their religion; and during King Chulalongkorn's reign the first Chinese Buddhist temple was built in Thailand.

In 1925 a young Chinese named Po Cheng came to Thailand from his native Kwangtung (Canton) province, attracted by this country's reputation as a land where Buddhism flourished. He was ordained in a cave at the famous Wat Phra Puttabaht or Temple of the Buddha's Footprint in Saraburi Province and stayed there for about five years, devoting much time to meditation. Later he built many new Chinese temples in Thailand and restored all the old ones in various parts of the country. Eventually he became head of Chinese Mahayana Buddhism in Thailand — the seventh in line to hold that position.

However, owing to the constant coming and going of devout Buddhists to make merit in Bangkok's crowded Chinese temples, Phra Po Cheng found them too restless and noisy for meditation. So he decided to build a new temple in quieter surroundings. Thus the idea of Wat Pomaen was born, some 35 years ago.

The 12-rai plot of land near Sathupradit Road was acquired and construction began. It was to take 10 years and cost more than 27 million baht. Materials were specially imported, some of them from Italy and Czechoslovakia.

Wat Pomaen was officially opened by His Majesty the King in June 1970. His Majesty hoisted up the "cho-fah" or topmost pinnacle of the roof of the main chapel, which was crowned by a gilt "chat" or many-tiered state umbrella, fixed on top of a miniature Tibetan pagoda.

That Tibetan touch is typical of the architecture of the main chapel. Although predominantly Chinese, there are Thai and Tibetan overtones which blend smoothly into the whole. The chapel towers above the rest of the temple, built around the polished marble courtyard in a symmetrical square pattern. The whole temple is as spotless and sparkling as when it was first built.

The large, intricate main gate through which one enters the temple is crowned with gracefully curving tiered roofs, like the main chapel itself. Inside the chapel, the main Buddha statue wears a robe covering both shoulders, unlike the Thai Buddha statues in which the robe covers only one shoulder. This symbolises China's colder climate, as do the saffron trousers worn by Wat Pomaen's monks beneath their robes — the normal wear for Buddhist monks in China. Beautiful mosaic murals on either side of the Buddha statue show scenes of 500 monks clad in this fashion, complete with trousers, gathering alms and listening to a discourse from the Lord Buddha.

The interior of the main chapel is indeed full of beautiful things — hundreds of small Buddha statues set in rows in the high, vaulted ceiling, in memory of the donors who helped to finance the temple's construction; delicate black-and-gilt panels on the insides of the main doors depicting different ways of showing mercy.

The splendour of the chapel is reflected in the halls and guestrooms ranged along the galleries surrounding it; all of them are well worth a visit.

All the temple's 50-odd monks and 10 to 20 novices are Chinese. They follow the Mahayana custom of eating a strictly vegetarian diet, unlike Thai monks who eat meat. Another difference is the lack of a morning alms-round such as is the custom at most Thai temples; at Wat Pomaen, all food is brought to the temple by layfolk.

Apart from these few differences, the daily programme of the monks is much the same as that in any Thai temple. The monks get up at 3.30 a.m., and morning chanting from 4 to 5 a.m. is followed by a meditation period. Breakfast is at 6.30, personal chores from 7.30 to 8.30, then religious instruction until lunch, the last meal of the day, at 11. The afternoon is taken up with other personal chores such as robe-washing, cell cleaning and so on. Evening chanting is from 4 to 5 p.m., and more religious study from 7.30 to 9.30.

Visitors are welcome at Wat Pomaen, and the helpful monks will be glad to show you around. Take a Thai friend with you if you can (unless your spoken Thai is good!). But even if you can't, why not visit this friendly temple anyway, and see the great beauty wrought by Phra Po Cheng and Bangkok's Chinese Buddhist community, out of veneration for the Lord Buddha and his Teaching.

A Thai miscellany

Whenever my wife says something to me in Thai which I can't understand, the chances are ten to one I must immediately (a) ask her to repeat it; (b) ask her to try and explain it in her rather limited English; and — in all probability — (c) rush for the nearest piece of paper and quickly jot it down.

It usually turns out illegible, as this seems to happen when I'm in the middle of shaving or just about to leave for the office. These precious scraps of paper are kept in a file on which is scrawled "Thai Ways — future articles." What is written on them has more often than not already found its way into print...

But going through the file recently, I came across no less than 22 more such pieces of paper, including the back of an old greeting card. The information comes not only from my wife, but also from friends and acquaintances. It's very varied and bitty — but all the pieces of paper have one thing in common: they are all very, indubitably, Thai.

So I'm going to give you these, for what they are worth. I'll try to bring some sort of order into them, but doubt very much whether I'll succeed.

First comes a torn-off slip of paper no more than an inch wide. I know, from something written on the other side, that it's been languishing inside the file for at least four years. It says tersely: "Library for all cremation books at Wat Bovorn ." Perhaps you can understand that, but in case not, I'd rather explain. Readers who have been to a Thai cremation ceremony will probably know that everyone who attends such ceremonies is given a souvenir book. The subject of the book is always something the deceased person was particularly interested in; perhaps cookery, or gardening, or in the case of a very devout person, the Buddhist scriptures.

Well, someone (I don't think it was my wife) once told me that a copy of every such cremation souvenir book is deposited and kept at a library at Wat Bowornnives, the Royal Temple on Phra Sumane Road. I can't even swear to the accuracy of this statement as I've never been to see for myself. But anyway, that's what the scrap of paper said...

The next bit of paper, probably just as old judging from its yellowed appearance, is about "Sahn Phra-Phum," which the dictionary gives as "the shrine of the household god" — that is, spirit houses, the tiny miniature temples on pillars within the grounds of many Thai houses, hotels, office buildings and so on. A little story on this scrap of paper was told to me by a Thai friend. She said that when she was seven years old she had hepatitis, and just at that time her parents were moving house. So they had to put a new spirit house in the compound of their new home, to make sure she would get better, which she did. (Not all houses have spirit houses in the compound, especially nowadays in Bangkok where among some people the belief is dying out).

Next come two Thai expressions written on the back of the aforementioned greeting-card: "Daed rom, lom dtok." "Daed" is sunshine, "rom" is an umbrella but literally means "shade"; "lom" is wind, and "dtok" is to fall. "Sunshine, shade, wind falls." So it means "the weather is cloudy and windy."

The next little note simply says "nam jai." The dictionary translates this as "sympathy, kindness or clemency," but something tells me that this expression carries overtones of Thai which are probably a bit too subtle to translate. However, not long ago I saw an example of what I think was true Thai "nam jai."

I was in a taxi waiting at the "mouth" of Soi Thonglor for the lights to turn green so we could proceed into Sukhumvit Road. ("Bpakh soi," "the mouth of the soi," is the Thai way of saying the entrance to a soi). A truck laden with fruit took the corner from Sukhumvit into Thonglor so fast that a whole basketful of rather pricy mangoes were scattered on the ground and rolled all over the road. The driver stopped the truck, got out and started laboriously picking them up one by one — in what was really a very dangerous spot, for that's a pretty busy corner with a lot of traffic. But every single car, truck and bus driver who passed, immediately sized up the situation and slowed down, taking the greatest care to avoid not only the man, but all his valuable mangoes too...

Now for two pieces of paper dealing with husband-and-wife relationships.

First, the bad news. There is a term used if someone eats from a dish which is inside another dish, or from two spoons held together one inside the other (why on earth would anyone do that, I wonder), or if someone is smoking a cigarette which is burning along one side only. In such instances Thais say of that person, "par[illegible]va..." ("Your wife," if it's a man) or "samee..." ("Your husband, if it's a woman) "...ja nork jai" ("...will be unfaithful and leave you for someone else.")

Now for the good news. At least, I'll do my best to explain it. I've written "Thais believe.." and later on the same bit of paper, "Chinese v. important." Anyway the message goes on, "...believe that the stars of a wife and husband can help each other. Four years of 'Thaht Thong' — if either the wife or husband is born in one of the four 'That Thong' years, he or she can help the spouse. Will tell me later.."

This refers to the years of the 12-year cycle. Each year has its own "element" or "Thaht", and if the "element" of one's birth-year is gold ("thong"), that's good, both for oneself and for one's spouse too. Therefore an unmarried man or girl in one of those years is said to be very popular with members of the opposite sex as a potential husband or wife. (If you really want to know whether you were born in one of those "gold element" years, it isn't too difficult to find out from someone who knows the names and sequence of the years in the 12 year cycle).

Here's what it says on another piece of paper: "Although I've lived in this country for over 15 years, I still occasionally put my cultural foot in it. The other day an office colleague asked me, since I was going to a nearby shop to buy a wedding card, to get her a 'get-well' card for a friend of hers. "In Thai or English?" I asked, and she said it didn't matter. At the shop I asked if they had "get-well" cards in Thai, and was told they had. I chose one and painfully read out in the Thai verses without fully taking in their meaning.

When I gave it to my colleague at the office she glanced at the verses and said "oh -oh! This is for an elderly person, and my friend is younger than me!" I'd missed the significance of the poetic Thai word "karawa" in the verse, meaning "to pay one's respects", which is only used by a younger to an older person!

Now here are two little anecdotes about monkeys told to me by a friend from the South of Thailand.

The first one is about the method used to capture a "ling gang" ("the pigtail monkey," says the dictionary, adding in its usual erudite manner, *"Macca nemestrina."* Biologists please note). These are the species of monkeys which are trained to climb trees and pick coconuts for their human masters — although nowadays this is only done in Pattani province and on Koh Samui.

These monkeys are quite greedy. So those who want to catch and train them will drill a small hole in a coconut just large enough for the monkey to get its paw through. The coconut is filled with rice to lure the monkey. The would-be catchers scatter a lot of these baited coconuts around a particular area and wait.

Soon a monkey comes along, puts its hand into the hole, grabs the rice inside — and then can't get its fist out again because it is now larger than the hole. My friend says monkeys have been found transfixed in this way by four coconuts — one attached to each hand and one to each foot as well. But he tells me the monkeys caught in this way don't suffer any pain because the edges of the hobs are rounded so as not to chafe the skin. The captured monkeys are well-trained and well looked after.

The other tail (sorry, tale) told me by my southern friend concerns seaside monkeys in general. Monkeys at the seaside are clever enough to recognise the holes in which sand crabs have buried themselves. Being natural gourmets, they find these crabs very tasty, and have adopted a method of catching them which is ingenious in the extreme, if you'll pardon the pun.

They just sit on their, ahem, on the sand with their tails dangling in the crab-holes; The buried crab, observing this strange object, attaches itself to the monkey's tail; whereupon the monkey withdraws its tail smartly from the hole complete with crab, and voila! One Crab Thermidor for M'sieu!

Occasionally, however, says my friend, a larger-than-usual crab clamps its sharp pincers round the monkey's tail, causing the latter to let out a loud yell of pain. Even monkeys, it seems, can't win 'em all.

Let's see — here are two pieces of paper dealing with days of the week. Never cut a topknot on a Tuesday or a Saturday, says one bit of paper, because these days are "hard days," and Thais say it won't be just the topknot that's cut off, but the child's whole head!

The second bit of paper's a bit confusing. It says "Tuesday's a strong day, and a good one — learning, etc. Monks bathe or sprinkle people with holy water on Tuesdays and Thursdays to get rid of bad luck. Thursday's a good day for planting, because Jupiter is connected with plants. Dton-mai metta mahaniyom (trees, loving-kindness, great popularity). Check again."

Well, I did try to check again with my wife, but all I could find out was that Mondays, Thursdays and Fridays are associated with personal charm. This has something to do with the variety of "wahn" plant called "saneh jan khao", "white charm of the moon."

Let me just add a bit more about Thursday. Being Jupiter's Day, this is indeed connected with learning. The Thai name for Thursday is "wan pareuhat" or Jupiter's Day, "Pareuhat" also being the name of the planet Jupiter. It is actually spelt "Pareuha bodi" in Thai characters, but the "bodi" is silent. However, the spelling indicates its Sanskrit origin, for the Sanskrit name for Jupiter is "Vrihaspati" — not too unlike "Jupiter" itself in fact. I suspect the two forms of the name may have a common Indo-European origin.

Anyway, to get back to Thursday's connection with learning. This is why the "wai kru" ceremony of students paying respect to their teachers is always held throughout Thailand on a Thursday. The date may vary from school to school, university to university — but a Thursday it must be.

And on another piece of paper it says "When one performs the "Wai kru" ceremony one is not only paying respect to an individual 'kru' but to the knowledge and to the earlier teachers who discovered and handed down that knowledge to the present teacher one is 'waiing' — just like the Buddhist Doctrine itself."

Now for three little pieces of trivia from my wife, on three more scraps of paper. She says that in the old days Thai country folk refused to have their photograph taken, because they were afraid they themselves would disappear inside the camera

— or else it would shorten their life. So they always ran away as fast as they could whenever anyone pointed a camera in their direction.

The second note reminds me that she talked, rather vaguely, about the first ice ever seen in Thailand (imported from Singapore. This was long before her time, of course, and she heard about it from her grandmother). It's nothing, really — except that the first ice caused a considerable sensation here in this tropical country where snow and ice were unknown except from photographs and the earliest movies.

The third bit of paper is simply a note that my wife was riding in a car in Phra Khanong one day and spotted a sign which she thought said "rap tam por" ("fathers repaired")! What it actually said was "rap tam dtor" — "water-pipes repaired." Soon after that, she started wearing glasses...

Under the heading "untranslatable words" on another scrap of paper is the solitary entry "sorm kang." Let's see what the dictionary says about that. "SORM KANG: To ask a question in such a way as to impute some guilt to the hearer, as 'How often do you beat your wife?'; to say something which presumes guilt on the part of the hearer, as 'I know you did not enjoy telling lies'." Yes — "sorm kang" is untranslatable, alright!

Another piece of paper says "long khaek" — community farming in old times, and today upcountry." The dictionary agrees; it says "to gather one's neighbours to help at harvest.."

Being an astrologer, my wife says that if someone looks fit and well (or "looks bright," as she expresses it in Thai), that person will have good luck. As a result, many of her relatives and friends have formed the habit, whenever they come to visit her, of asking, "Do I look well today?"

On the same subject (or to be more correct, on exactly the opposite subject), she has told me a Thai expression, "gai napahk." The dictionary gives this as "to put the hand across the forehead while lying down in deep contemplation or anxiety; to regret." My wife adds that there's also a mock variation of this expression, "ao dteen gai napahk," meaning "to feel very depressed indeed" — and I shouldn't wonder either, for it means literally "to put one's foot across the forehead!"

On another bit of paper is written a Thai proverb, "kai dee yang gap teh nam, teh ta" — "to sell well like throwing into the water, throwing into the harbour.” Or in its more usual English form, “selling like hot cakes”!

Another saying is “jeep bpahk jeep kor.” “Jeeb” means “to pucker the lips,” “bpahk” means “mouth” and “kor” means “throat.” So this expression means “to talk prunes and prisms,” which is rather old-fashioned English these days. According to the Oxford Dictionary, it means “a mincing way of speaking; see Dickens’ “Little Dorrit’.” Well — by all means see it, if you’ve got a copy; I’ll take Oxford’s word for it...

I’ve written often about the sacred white cord called “sai sin” which is used in most religious ceremonies to keep out evil spirits and protect everyone and everything inside it. Someone (I can’t remember who it was) has added one more piece of information about this, which I didn’t know before: When holding a “tam boon” or merit-making ceremony for a dead person, that part of the “sai sin” which passes round the “pahn” or pedestal on which rests the bowl containing the holy water, is formed into the letters spelling the dead person’s name. (I hope I’ve got that right.)

Now here is something a student of mine told me several years ago.

In the Thai alphabet there are two vowels which represent the short sound “-ai” as in the English words “by” or “my”. One of these letters is very common; it’s called “mai-malai” and looks like this: ไ The other is called “mai-muan” and looks like this: ใ (“Muan” means to coil or curl, like the top of the letter.) It only occurs in 20 words in the entire Thai language, and every young schoolchild has to learn what those words are.

They are taught to do this by learning a long, picturesque but meaningless sentence which includes all the 20 words. Translated, it goes as follows: “*An elder person finds new cloth, gives it to the daughter-in-law to use to put round her neck, she’s interested in wrapping it up in a parcel, she keeps it private and doesn’t show it to anyone; she wants to get into a sailing-boat to see clear water, fish and crabs; anything in the cupboard isn’t under the bed; mad, dumb, carrying lotus fibre, can’t see clearly, comes near.*”

This is followed by the instruction, which the children must also learn: “*Learn by heart, don’t wander away, remember all the 20 'muans' well."*

Fancy having to learn that lot. It makes "*A is for Apple, so rosy and red ...*" seem child's play. But as I said, every Thai schoolchild has to learn it so as to be able to spell correctly.

On the same sheet is written the memory-guide for the eight "middle-class" Thai consonants, which is translated as: "*The chicken pecks the children, the children die on the edge of the klongjar.*" (One of the eight, "dor chada," is missing because my student couldn't remember the correct word in the sentence.)

To end with, here are some scribblings on the last piece of paper, about food.

It starts off with the word "grayasaht" and the note says that this consists of seven kinds. The dictionary says "rice, bean, sesame and sugar cooked into a sticky paste, usually eaten during the 'saht' festival;" and it gives "saht" as "a festival at the end of autumn." My scribbled note also says these sweetmeats are given to monks on the full-moon day of the 10th lunar month.

The information on the sheet was written down in a car stuck in a traffic jam, so it's a bit disjointed, I'm afraid. It goes on to say that "kanoon" is a jackfruit, and the word "noon" pronounced in the same way as in "kanoon" means "to support" or "to encourage. "So jackfruit trees are often grown at the back of the house to "back up" or support not only the house itself but also its occupants.

"Foi tong," that popular golden-coloured sweetmeat, is said to bring good luck on account of its colour, while "kanom jeen" and "bamee," varieties of noodles, are believed — especially by Chinese — to bring long life, because they themselves are long!